CHILDREN IN GENOCIDE

THE INTERNATIONAL PSYCHOANALYSIS LIBRARY

General Editor: Leticia Glocer Fiorini

CHILDREN IN GENOCIDE
Extreme traumatization and affect regulation

Suzanne Kaplan

Foreword by
Arnold H. Modell

The International Psychoanalysis Library

**International
Psychoanalytical
Association**

LONDON

The International Psychoanalytical Association gratefully acknowledges the USC Shoah Foundation Institute for Visual History and Education, University of Southern California, for allowing us to use the testimonies as detailed in Appendix B.

First published in 2008 by
The International Psychoanalytical Association
Broomhills
Woodside Lane
London N12 8UD
United Kingdom

British Library Cataloguing in Publication Data

A C.I.P. for this book is available from the British Library

ISBN: 978-1-905888-15-3

10 9 8 7 6 5 4 3 2 1

Produced for the IPA by Communication Crafts

Printed in Great Britain

www.ipa.org.uk

This work is dedicated to my grandparents Blommy and Salomon
who fled from Norway
and to Sammy
who survived Auschwitz and could tell about
those who never came back

CONTENTS

THE INTERNATIONAL PSYCHOANALYSIS LIBRARY

IPA Publications Committee

The International Psychoanalysis Library, published under the aegis of the International Psychoanalytical Association, is the product of the editorial policy of the IPA Publications Committee: to serve the interests of the membership and increase the awareness of the relevance of the discipline in related professional and academic circles, and to do so through a continuity of publications so that the benefits of psychoanalytic research can be shared across a wide audience.

The focus of the Library is on the scientific developments of today throughout the IPA, with an emphasis within the discipline on clinical, technical, and theoretical advances; empirical, conceptual, and historical research projects; the outcome of investigations conducted by IPA committees and working parties; selected material arising from conferences and meetings; and investigations at the interface with social and cultural expressions.

Special thanks are due to the author, Suzanne Kaplan, for her remarkable work in bringing this volume together.

Leticia Glocer Fiorini
Series Editor

ACKNOWLEDGEMENTS

This book deals with affects and memories from extreme traumatization of Jewish survivors, who were children themselves during the Holocaust, and teenagers who survived the genocide in Rwanda in 1994. I present a theory that can serve as an analytic tool and may provide a foundation for an increased understanding of young people who have been affected by extreme traumatizing processes. My work as a child and youth psychoanalyst made me especially interested in the situation for these children.

I wish to thank first and foremost all of the people who have been interviewed and who have allowed me to partake in their life histories. The University of Southern California Shoah Foundation Institute for Visual History and Education is greatly to be thanked for opening its archives of videorecorded interviews to me and thus making this work possible, with special thanks to Kim Simon. I am also very grateful to Ervin Staub and Laurie Anne Pearlman, who welcomed me to their team in Rwanda; they were offering a programme to augment and enhance the healing and reconciliation efforts underway in Rwanda. Alfred Jahn, a child surgeon in Kigali, invited me to meet a group of teenagers who had survived the genocide, and he supported me in my proposal of interviewing them, which was of enormous value. I wish to express my deep gratitude to Siv Boalt Boëthius, Harald Runblom, Dori Laub, and Thomas Åström, who have encouraged me in my research process. Angela Hanke has given me valuable viewpoints in transforming my research into a book. Her special commitment has meant a lot to me. My son Jonas Goldmann has helped me with videotaping, transcribing, and with archive and computer issues, which has been a great satisfaction. My warm gratitude also goes to Pamela Boston and Josephine Kankundiye for the translation into English, and for the deep engagement that they have shown for the subject and the content. I also want to thank The Programme for Holocaust and Genocide Studies, Uppsala University, and the Bertil Wennborg Foundation, for their support. And thank you, Cesare Sacerdoti, IPA publications director, for your engagement, which has been most important, and Arnold Modell for the foreword. I am also very grateful to Pippa Hodges and Klara King for their skilful assistance in preparing the manuscript for publication.

"Why don't you do research?" my husband Tomas Böhm had asked. Thanks to his support, I decided to follow a growing idea about making a closer examination of what it is like for child survivors to go on living with recurring memories of the persecutions. All of my family have shown immense patience and have endured my abrupt answers on the phone and my quick glances when we have met.

Stockholm, February 2008

ABOUT THE AUTHOR

Suzanne Kaplan is a psychologist, psychoanalyst, and training analyst in the Swedish Psychoanalytical Society. She lives in Stockholm and works there with children and adults. She has a PhD in education and is an affiliated researcher at The Programme for Holocaust and Genocide Studies, Uppsala University. She is a researcher in the field of extreme traumatization and has twice (2001 and 2007) received the Hayman Prize for Published Work Pertaining to Traumatised Children and Adults.

She is the author of several papers as well as two books: *Barn under Förintelsen—då och nu* [Children in the Holocaust—then and now] and (with T. Böhm) *Hämnd—och att avstå från att ge igen* [Revenge—and refraining from retaliation].

FOREWORD

Arnold H. Modell

A distinguished anthropologist once said: "humanity is a species that can live only in terms of meaning it itself must invent". We who are witness to the horrors of the Holocaust and other genocides such as in Rwanda can only attempt to make meaning of this horrendous history. The enormous outpouring of books related to the Holocaust attests to the endeavour to understand that which is beyond all understanding. Human beings, when deprived of their humanity, teach us how the human soul, the self, can be preserved when threatened with extinction. If there is anything positive to be gained from all of this horror, it is that small measure of understanding.

Suzanne Kaplan, by immersing herself in the horrendous experiences of the survivors of the Holocaust and genocide in Rwanda, showed that listening—which must have been extremely painful—is in itself an act of courage. The atrocities committed in Rwanda,

Arnold Modell is currently practising psychoanalysis in a suburb of Boston. He is a Clinical Professor of Psychiatry, Harvard Medical School, and a training and supervising analyst at the Boston Psychoanalytic Institute. He is the author of: *Object Love and Reality*; *Psychoanalysis in a New Context*; *Other Times, Other Realities*; *The Private Self*; and *Imagination and the Meaningful Brain*.

solely for one's ethnicity, resemble the atrocities committed by the Nazis. Despite this emotional cost, she was able to enter into the narrative of these survivors yet retain her clear-sightedness and conceptual clarity. Bearing witness is a gift.

For me, what was most striking in the accounts of those who were children when they became victims of the Holocaust is the fact that the memory of their traumatic experience was retained in exquisite, almost novelistic detail. Massive denial or repression was not in evidence. What is of significance is that these individuals were not only survivors, but as adults were able to establish relatively normal lives. In contrast is the report of Dori Laub (2005), who interviewed individuals who managed to stay alive during the Holocaust but were subsequently hospitalized in Europe and later hospitalized in Israel and diagnosed as psychotic. Many of these patients were silent and did not speak to anyone. What is of great significance is the fact that these victims did not remember their experience. Laub reports that there is an underlying common thread to all of them, and that is that the memories of their experiences have been massively erased. It is if they have forgotten everything that had happened to them, as if the experience of massive trauma never took place. It was, Laub reports, as if the memory was registered and kept frozen in a different part of the brain that had no access to consciousness.

The striking difference between these two groups is that those survivors who managed to reach Sweden, whom Kaplan interviewed and coordinated under the auspices of the USC Shoah Foundation Institute, retained a complex and nuanced narrative of their experience. Not only did they remember their suffering during the Holocaust, but a least one interviewee used memory to recall a sense of self that existed prior to the Holocaust. He described how "a rock of salvation for me" was his ability to recall within his mind over and over again the happy memory of his family celebrating Passover before the Shoah. (The evidence of a survivor's ability to retain a complex, contextually accurate memory of his or her traumatic experience can be seen in the interviews with Emilia that are recorded in the Appendix.)

Those survivors who became psychotic lost the narrative of their trauma, while those survivors who established relatively normal lives retained a narrative of their traumatized self. From this we can conclude that the retrieval of the memory of feelings is essential for the survival of the self. The self is maintained through narrative affective memory. For reasons that are unclear, those survivors who ended up as psychotic patients in Israel did not retain the capacity to preserve their narrative memory of their horrendous trauma.

One may argue that those survivors who became psychotic lost narrative memory because of some cognitive process related to their psychosis. I suspect, however, that it was the other way around—that they became psychotic because they lost their narrative memory. Although they were diagnosed as schizophrenic, Laub questions that diagnosis and reports no specific symptoms such as hallucinations that are characteristic of that illness. A non-specific "functional" psychosis would fit my hypothesis.

This is not to imply that those survivors who found safety in Sweden escaped damage to their sense of self. In reading these interviews, one has to remind oneself that one is not listening to the voices of children, but to the voices of adults recalling their childhood. It is as if the I who experienced the trauma is not differentiated in age from the I recalling the memory of the trauma. Normally when one thinks of oneself as a child, the adult self and the childhood self are clearly differentiated. Our sense of self is commonly an integrated though an uneven procession of former selves, which we recognize as the same as well as distinct. The massive trauma of the Holocaust has clearly interfered with this process. There has been a collapse in the time dimension of the self. Kaplan has observed this phenomenon throughout all of these narratives. One survivor said: "I can't have a child because I'm a child myself." Many survivors seem to be age-disoriented and therefore cannot judge their own age and also the age of their relatives. From this we can infer that massive trauma disrupts the sense of continuity of the self from which our experience of time is derived. There is much about this process that remains unknown, but I suspect that these histories are witness to a failure of what Freud described as *Nachträglichkeit*, the failure to recontextualize or re-categorize memory, in which metaphor plays a salient part (Modell, 2003). It may be that, normally, the process of recontextualizing memory provides a sense of the continuity of the self and contributes to our experience of the expansion of time.

Kaplan introduces two organizing conceptual principles: *perforating* and *space creating*. The concept *perforating* is consistent with Freud's theory of trauma, which was later elaborated by Anzieu's conception of the skin ego (Anzieu, 1985). Both Anzieu and Freud focus upon the effect of trauma on the ego or the self. In *Beyond the Pleasure*

Principle, Freud thought of the self as a protective envelope, shield, or membrane. Freud wrote: "protection against stimuli is an almost more important function for the living organism than the reception of stimuli" (Freud, 1920g, p. 27). He also said: "we described as traumatic any excitations from outside which are powerful enough to break through the protective shield. This seems to me that the concept of trauma necessarily implies a connection of this kind with the *breach* in an otherwise efficacious barrier against stimuli" (italics added). Anzieu extended Freud's theory of trauma by focusing on the skin as an example of the envelope of the self.

Kaplan's interviews provide countless painful descriptions of the envelope of the child's self being repeatedly penetrated by the perpetrators. The penetration of stimuli through the skin is particularly relevant in Holocaust survivors. Mothers commonly protect children and induce a sense of safety through holding and touching, all of which contributes to a feeling of warmth. These survivors suffered enormously as children from the cold and the continual invasion of body lice. Furthermore, the bodily self, the skin ego, was invaded and violated by the perpetrators, who removed their clothing and jewellery. The skin ego is not only a protective barrier, but is also an affirmation of self-hood through the selective expression of bodily adornment. Children's jewellery, in addition, is also a concrete reminder, a talisman, of a tie to one's family. Therefore, the removal of clothing and jewellery is a further step towards dehumanization.

Penetration of the self, in resilient children, may be compensated for by attempts at restoration of the self. Psychological survival may depend upon another process that Kaplan describes as *space creating*: an attempt by the victim to restore a sense of self, and a sense of self that relates to others. From Kaplan's theory I would understand space creating to consist of two different processes. The first is to create a boundary around the self that allows one to think and to fantasize, which in turn reaffirms one's own existence. The other function is to reaffirm the self through making contact with members of the group. Kaplan notes the children's preoccupation with the facial expression of the adults. Bonds are established through eye contact, but scanning the face of others can also be used as an early warning signal. In both instances, eye contact reinforces a social bond.

The other's recognition of the self is necessary for self-affirmation. Kaplan reports that one survivor heard her neighbours say: "'I wonder what she is thinking about.' *I remember that my reaction was,*

'*What do they mean, thinking, I'm not thinking anything.* What do you do when you think? What does that mean?' Then it suddenly occurred to me that 'maybe that's what I am doing after all, when I sit here not saying anything but still talking to myself in my own head, maybe that's what thinking is'." This survivor felt affirmed by the other's recognition that she was a thinking human being. Thinking is what selves do. If one thinks, one still exists.

Kaplan recognizes that feeling is a form of knowing, and that trauma profoundly disrupts this cognitive process. The relation between feeling, memory, and knowing is extremely complex. I believe that metaphor is the currency of the emotional mind. We use memory to categorize experience, and in turn the affect categories that we establish in our minds are organized in accordance with metaphoric similarities and differences (Modell, 2003). In health, our past experiences are re-categorized, which Freud described as *Nachträglichkeit.* In trauma, this metaphoric process, which accepts the simultaneity of sameness and difference, is degraded. Recognizing the simultaneity of sameness and difference is implicit when one, as an adult, remembers oneself as a child. This capacity appears to be lost in many of the survivors. This loss, in Holocaust survivors, of the capacity to think metaphorically was previously observed by Grubrich-Simitis (1984). I believe that this cognitive failure has contributed to the lack of continuity in the sense of self that Kaplan reports as age distortion.

I look upon *Children in Genocide* as a gift to the reader that represents an outstanding act of courage on the part of its author, Suzanne Kaplan.

CHILDREN IN GENOCIDE

Introduction

Two women who had been children during the Holocaust were interviewed by me and told me about their lives. Their life histories evoked a great number of thoughts and questions and came to be the starting point for an extended research project on other Jewish survivors who had been *children themselves* during the persecutions and, later, for a subsequent study on teenagers who survived the Rwanda genocide in 1994.

How could children understand what it was they went through? We others—are our minds capable of comprehending the Holocaust and the Rwanda genocide? I have chosen to partake in the survivors' oral life histories, which, from my point of view, offer a possibility of coming close to what the genocide entailed. For this purpose I have maintained a close proximity to the data, and thus I have followed the content of the interviewees' life histories in detail, both regarding *what* they said and *how* they recounted their memories. I have also asked myself: how can I write a text that can, to the greatest extent possible, convey a fraction of the feeling of what it meant to be a child during a genocide, a text embodying the life histories in which I have taken part and at the same time giving that which is elusive—a level of abstraction, a paradox if you like, so that the reader will be able to rise above the flood of information and reflect about and understand what is being recounted? At the same time questions recur as to how I can do the interviewees "justice" and get to the heart of what they wanted to put across when they chose to tell their histories and how I can write about and "systematize" the experiences of the interviewees without committing an act of intrusion with my assumptions about their life conditions.

One of the interviews that I conducted—the interview with Emilia—is presented in its entirety (in the Appendix). This gives readers an opportunity to familiarize themselves with an entire interview at any time they wish while they are reading the main text.

During the past decade, researchers have emphasized aspects of resilience and conditions leading to health, salutogenesis (Helmreich, 1992; Suedfeld, 1996). I agree that it is important to note the resources and promising prospects of survivors, but we must not ignore the burden of memories that they bear, regardless whether or not they are consciously aware of them. We need to be receptive towards these difficulties. My impression is that to a great extent the child survivors can deal with their external life circumstances successfully, but their inner lives seem periodically to be tyrannized by the "meaninglessness" of the trauma in their life histories. Perhaps the difficulty of coping with this difference between outer and inner might fuel the debate about resilience.

Starting points

My starting points are my work as a psychoanalyst in a clinical setting with children and adults, my experiences as a coordinator and interviewer with the international documentation project, Shoah Foundation Institute for Visual History and Education, and my research on psychic trauma based at Stockholm University and in conjunction with the Programme for Holocaust and Genocidal Studies at Uppsala University. My Jewish background has most probably had significance as a personal point of reference. I was born and grew up in Sweden; however, my relatives in Norway suffered under Nazism. In the beginning of the 1980s I, together with colleagues, started discussion groups for children of survivors of the Holocaust and broadened my knowledge of the significance of what is carried over from one generation to the next (Böhm & Kaplan, 1985).

My interest in research concerning children who were persecuted during the Holocaust began when I conducted extensive interviews with two women. They were both born in 1931 and were both eight years old when their native countries were occupied. Despite having grown up under different life conditions and having had different experiences of persecution under Nazism, the two women described themselves in a similar way. Among other things, the consequences of massive trauma seem to have been a central factor in their attitude towards having children of their own. They actively abstained from giving birth. One of them said, "*because I was a child myself*". This statement has formed the basis for posing an important question, which has remained of great significance throughout the entire research process. What was the significance of a child's own age and conception of age during and after the war when it came to the possibility of maintaining the feeling of having inner links to significant persons, and how might these inner links serve as a lifeline to allow the creation of links to the next generation? This question guided my interest in studying more life histories recounted by women and men who had survived the Holocaust as children with regard to this aspect.

Generational collapse

Gradually other aspects that could prove to be significant for the interviewees were added. What I had earlier seen as a break in reproduction manifested itself later during the work with the extended study as being an important aspect of the generational collapse that genocides seem to entail—a process to which most of the clues in the life histories seemed to be linked. This process is built up from two concepts and the dynamics between these. I designate these as *perforating*—generations have been destroyed, dissolved when the psychic shield has been perforated by sensory perceptions—and *space creating*: the inner psychic processes through which the persecuted created their own space for fantasizing and acting in spite of conditions being absolutely minimal.

The design of the book

The book is divided into four parts, in which the text is built up with the evolving concepts as a basis in order to illustrate in a comprehensive way the psychological phenomena that emerged in the interviews.

Part I. *Interviewing child survivors:* The first contacts with the interviewees are described. Psychoanalytic viewpoints about children in war are presented. The theme "child survivors and child-bearing" is presented through a pilot study.

Part II. What *is being communicated?* I introduce here a conceptual model for analysing the contents of the interviews, which is followed by a presentation of what is told in the life histories about different phases of persecution under Nazism. The last chapter in this part is an introduction of the genocide in Rwanda 1994.

Part III. How *are memories being recalled?* Here I return to and highlight the interview situation and discuss how memories were recounted. I focus on two men who, each on his own, recounted memories of the "same event". They hid themselves together in the ghetto in order to escape a deportation of a large group of children. Here aspects are discussed concerning memory and narrative.

Part IV. *From conceptual models to a theory:* I have categorized contents and affects. Ideas obtained from the interviews have led me to the development of conceptual models that have been integrated into a theory about trauma-related affects. This theory is named the "affect propeller", a model that may serve as an analytic tool for the affect regulating of extremely traumatized individuals. Two new concepts are introduced related to how the life history is told. These concern associative patterns that alternate in dominance. *Trauma linking* is an inner psychological consequence of the outer events that the perforating of sensory organs has entailed, and *generational linking* is the consequence of successful space creating, which includes that the survivors have their attention directed towards significant persons and things in the past and in the present.

My goal is that a study like this one should result in a presentation through which people can learn from genocides and through which the dialogue between people who have been afflicted and those who have not been afflicted by ethnic persecution is facilitated. One often says that it is difficult—even impossible—to put yourself into the vulnerability of people during genocide. But we need to be present, to listen, and, as far as possible, to try to create a picture of the traces from the trauma of the specific individual. At the same time, I want to emphasize the importance of not stopping at listening to different human fates, which are themselves unique, but also to rise above what we may hear and feel when encountering the interviewee, to create a possibility for one's own thought space, in order to refine our own concepts and approaches.

I have learned about children and extreme traumatization, about genocidal processes, and about living with memories that "won't let go". This has been of enormous value for my psychological understanding and for my general perspective on life. For me, this research has meant staying on a constantly heightened but optimal level of anxiety that has functioned as the impetus in the work. It has expressed itself as "evenly suspended attention" and a continual refinement of the concepts that I have chosen to use.

I

INTERVIEWING CHILD SURVIVORS

1

First contacts

Point of departure

The point of departure in the research presented in this book is the analysis of 40 videotaped interviews with child survivors from the Holocaust conducted by me and by other interviewers, and 12 video-taped interviews with child survivors in Rwanda conducted by me, as well as 17 audio- and videotaped follow-up interviews. My choice of research area is grounded in the fact that research concerning the situation of people who were afflicted and who *were children themselves* during the Holocaust (Dwork, 1991) and during the Rwanda geno-cide in 1994 is very limited. Cross-scientific international research contacts with genocide scholars have strengthened my interest in un-derstanding more of psychic trauma and the dynamics of violence.

Shoah Foundation Institute for Visual History and Education (Shoah Foundation)

Inspired by his experience making *Schindler's List,* Steven Spielberg established the Survivors of the Shoah Visual History Foundation in 1994 to gather video testimonies from survivors and other witnesses of the Holocaust. In January 2006, the Shoah Foundation became part of the College of Letters, Arts & Sciences at the University of Southern California in Los Angeles, where the testimonies in the Visual History Archive will be preserved in perpetuity (http://college .usc.edu/vhi/history.php). Having collected more than 51,000 testimonies in 57 countries and in 32 languages, the Foundation's new and equally urgent mission is to overcome prejudice, intolerance, and bigotry—and the suffering they cause—through the educational use of the Foundation's visual history testimonies.

In 1996 the interview work in Sweden began. I was an interviewer and was given the assignment to be the coordinator of the Shoah Foundation's project work in Sweden from 1996 to 1998. I coordinated 300/330 interviews, 40 of these with child survivors born between 1929 and 1939.

First contact with the interviewee

After I had read the application forms in which the people to be interviewed expressed their interest in the project, I contacted them by telephone (300 people). The conversation was a mutual exchange of thoughts and questions concerning being interviewed and the interview procedure. The past was brought to the fore, and it was already clear from the reactions of the interviewees during this telephone call that the suffering they had endured during the Holocaust was a constant and active part of their memory, active in a part of the self. A number of them wrote letters to me. Emilia lives on the west coast, and she chose to travel to Stockholm to be interviewed. She wrote a letter to me before she came. This letter concerned a memory about a girl, and she referred to it during the interview in the following way:

> ". . . that little girl . . . the one I wrote [about] in the letter stood in the street outside the police station where, where I lived . . . she was little, stood there surrounded by Polish women, her hair was bleached with hydrogen peroxide. A bad bleach job. She was terrified. She was *just standing* there, making the sign of the cross, saying the Lord's Prayer from beginning to end, over and over and over again. The women who were standing around her were waiting for the police. She had already been discovered. They

were asking, 'Where do you live? Where is your mother?' . . . '*My mother lives in the closet.*' . . . They said things about her right in front of her. And I, I didn't dare come closer, because then they would have taken me. And *I have this on my conscience* [her voice changes] . . . I should have gone up to her, I should have put my arms around her, died together with her so that she would not be alone and afraid. This is the way I think. I think how it felt for her. She was a little girl. Alone. And no one to comfort her.

. . . I just walked away. I disappeared. You don't feel right when you do something like that. *I will never forget that girl.* I knew that I could not do anything, but I still felt guilty [sigh, silence]. I hope that it went fast. That is all you can do, hope. You have to accept."[1]

The descriptions of events that Emilia and other survivors gave on the telephone and in letters were repeated and developed during the interview that followed. It was clear that a recalling process began in the minds of the survivors from the very moment they filled out the application.

The interview takes place: Anna

When the photographer and I rang Anna's doorbell, there was a delay before she opened. Anna thought that it was *the next* day that we were to come to carry out the videorecorded main interview. Still, she says that it is fine for us to come in and make the interview as planned. We set up everything for the videofilming in her living room, and the conversation can begin.

Anna has already told me on the telephone that her husband passed away several months earlier. Now she is alone, and she feels very lonely. Perhaps she would have to move. Anna shows me her husband's study. Now it is empty. She shows me a folder filled with letters and drawings from schoolchildren who thanked Anna for coming to their school to talk to them about what she had gone through during the Holocaust. Anna also tells how her mailbox was once stuffed with neo-Nazi propaganda. That was after she had spoken on a radio programme. Before the photographer and I leave Anna after the interview, she wants to treat us to something to eat.

We sit in her kitchen. She takes out a large sponge cake—a "Babka", a "real Babka", she says, one like her mother made in the Jewish culture of the Baltic. Anna also wants me to take the rest of the cake home to my family.

Anna "forgot" that we were coming. An anxiety signal can have caused a warding off of the psychic intrusion that an interview with recollection of memories might entail. At the same time she invited us to stay after the interview and have some cake, which she had baked herself. She also gave me a piece of cake to take home to my family. The anxiety signal that made a link to the past is now replaced by a positive link to her mother and to me and to that which I represent as a *container for her life history*. Anna has taken me into her confidence. The feeling that the interviewer can have at first of being an intruder is changed to an experience of being a "receptacle" for painful memories.

The Rwanda study

Children living in the streets—"street children"—is a consequence of the unimaginable traumas and poverty that a huge number of African children experience. And the lives in the streets means additional traumatic experiences for children in Rwanda, who are continuously exposed to insecurity, poverty, and violence (Dyregrov, Gupta, Gjestad, & Mukanoheli, 2000)

The first study trip to Rwanda and interviews with teenagers were carried out in January 2003. A second study trip with follow-up interviews was carried out in April 2004. I interviewed 10 teenage boys who had lived as street children during six years after the genocide and two girls who now took care of their siblings in "child-headed households", the parents and most of the siblings having been murdered. When I met the boys, they had been receiving help for some months with a place to live and support for their schooling from a German paediatrician, Dr Alfred Jahn, who worked at the hospital in Kigali and took care of street children as a private initiative, with support from ESPPER (Ensemble pour Soutenir les Projets et Programmes en Faveur des Enfants de la Rue). This facilitated the interview process. At first the boys did not want to be interviewed: why should they tell someone—and especially someone white, a European—about their experiences? The hope of someone listening to them had probably been erased long ago, in a much-too-long "waiting for the object" (for the mother to return). When I told the boys about myself and my aim, they acted as if a switch had been turned on. They became clearly serious and even suggested that they could be interviewed one by one, in order not to become influenced by each other (Kaplan & Eckstein, 2004). The boys spoke Kinyarwanda—the local language—when they told their life history in videotaped interviews. A teacher functioned as an interpreter. The boys' stories were then translated into English by a Rwandan.

My studies concerning the Holocaust and the genocide in Rwanda evolved into an interest to find over-reaching psychological phenomena connected with children in genocide and the experiences of extreme traumatization that I present here. All of the names of the interviewees in the text of the book have been disguised.

Empirically grounded theory

By using the grounded theory method (Glaser, 1978), I have conceptualized contents and affects—*what* was told in the interviews and *how* this was presented—and created theoretical models from the development of hypotheses well grounded in the data, which is presented in my doctoral dissertation (Kaplan, 2002a). The core processes turned out to be affect regulating as an essential aspect of the generational collapse. A theory about the survivors' affect regulating has been developed—the "affect propeller"—showing the trauma- and generational linking processes (destructive and constructive linkings, respectively) within each individual (Part IV in this book).

Winnicott's (1953) and Anzieu's (1985) studies have had special significance as sources of inspiration for my research work. Winnicott's theorizing about the life conditions of small babies, the significance of transition, and the development of creativity, among others, as basic phenomena for the feeling of a self have had great relevance for studies of children and trauma, as has his stress upon the importance of a "containing environment" (containing in the sense of supporting). His method has also been a model for me, both in psychoanalytic practice and in the research work to be presented here. His interest and awareness as a paediatrician concerning the mother–child relationship can be assumed to form the basis of the theories he has put forth. These were considered innovative, as were his reflections on encounters with deprived children during the war years. His methodology is well described by Ogden (2001 p. 301), who refers to Winnicott's own words (1945, p. 145): "I shall not first give a historical survey and show the development of my ideas from theories of others, because my mind does not work that way." Winnicott seems to have gathered material on a continuous basis: he would "gather this and that", and then he would relate what he had gathered to his clinical experience in order ultimately to arrive at comparisons with existing theory. He expresses this in an amusing way: ". . . to see where I stole what. Perhaps this is as good a method as any." Ogden (p. 302, with reference to Heaney, 1980) emphasizes the last-mentioned as a central theme in Winnicott's work: "to create a 'method', a way of being alive . . ." that has its parallel in the baby's early experiences. I have gone into this in so much detail in order to show parallels both to what I understand as a human being's "natural" way of functioning and to the method, grounded theory, which I have chosen to use in this research work.

2

Children's experiences of war in a psychoanalytic perspective

Anna Freud and Dorothy Burlingham (1943), who carried out an investigation on children's psychic reactions during war, were pioneers in calling attention to traumatic experiences from a psychoanalytic perspective. Their work continues to serve as essential reference material today. Following these forerunners, Moskovitz (1983), Kestenberg and Fogelman (1994), Kestenberg and Brenner (1986, 1996), and Valent (1994), among others, have taken central roles in this field of research. Extensive research work concerning the sequential traumatization to which children were subjected was performed by Keilson in the 1970s but was not given international attention until later (1992). His results point to the great significance that the way the children were taken care of *after* the war has had upon their psychic health.

Winnicott (1984) had experiences from working as consultant psychiatrist in an area of England that received evacuated children during the Second World War. He studied the effects of deprivation and gained an important understanding of those children who experience painful separations. He was of the opinion that in order to understand how children are affected by war, it is necessary to know what capacity children have to comprehend war with regard to variations between different age groups. The effects on very small children come "from that they must be separated from familiar sensory impressions and smells and perhaps from their mummy and that they lose contact with the daddy". They perhaps "become forced to feel how mother feels when she is terrified". When the children become a little older and are able to talk about the war, they perhaps use the adults' language, and the fantasies may be "filled with aeroplanes and bombs". Amongst children aged five–eleven years it is not unusual for the actual violence of war to be experienced as extremely nasty, at the same time as the aggressivity is often expressed in play and fantasies with romantic overtones, he says. I perceive as particularly important Winnicott's emphasis that there are "many who never leave this emotional developmental stage. . . ." They adapt, and war can become *very shocking for the adults who have become stuck in this stage* (my italics)—something that one can bear in mind when encountering children in latency with war experiences behind them as well as in the encounter with adults who have not received help at the time of the trauma to put what has happened into words.

For children about twelve years old and older, the situation becomes more complicated as puberty can have been delayed or experienced "as left out"—something that the interviewees spoke spontaneously about: "More difficult as I lost my teenage years—*you feel that all your life*", "I was never a child—became an adult all at once, never giggled—*now! I'm giggling.*" Winnicott's studies confirm that those with war experiences "preserve to some extent those qualities that belong to the so-called latency period, or return to these values after an imperceptible attempt to attain a more mature developmental level".

Anzieu (1985) is one of the authors who is concerned with psychic pain and whose theories have proved to constitute a meaningful comparative material in relation to my categorization of psychic phenomena in the life histories of the interviewees. He makes connections to Freud's fruitful metaphors of a wound, a puncture in the psychic shield, internal bleeding resulting from psychic trauma. Anzieu asserts that the skin is the most important of all the sensory organs. He alludes to the fact that the skin is a system that embodies several types of sensory organs (touch, pressure, pain, and warmth). Moreover, he points to the outer connections of the skin with other external sensory organs (hearing, seeing, smelling, and tasting) and with perceptions of movement and balance. In studying the psychological significance of the skin in conjunction with the question of thought processes, he has mainly explored matters concerning the transition from feeling to thought, from the skin (skin-ego) to the foundation of thought (thinking ego). He has been inspired by, among others, Freud (1923b), who writes about the ego as "ultimately stemming from bodily sensations, primarily from the surface of the body . . .". Much attention in clinical practice and in research has been paid to human "fantasies about psychic content", but Anzieu considers that this research should be broadened by "an investigating of fantasies about the psychic container function".

I see knowledge about human strategies as general knowledge about human existence that is valid both for those who survived and for those who died. Similar strategies can lead to different outcomes, depending on more or less lucky circumstances. By strategy I mean situations in which the strategic/creative process is something that first and foremost emerges on the spur of the moment, based on existential needs. My interest has been in capturing whatever the interviewees felt was most urgent to communicate. Children's psychological reactions to persecution as well as the consequences in adult life are relatively absent from theories found in the literature. This situation, together with my interest in understanding more about psychic pain and about the questions surrounding human containing functions—an area that has been insufficiently investigated according to Anzieu (1985)—has formed my personal point of departure for this study. By "containing capacity" I mean the adults' possibilities of providing the child with a sufficiently good environment. This, in turn, means that the adults can bear and take in the anxiety that the child expresses without letting these difficult and almost insurmountable feelings rebound back on the child. I also include the child's own containing capacity—that is, the internalized capacity for "being alone". Winnicott (1958) writes that the capacity for being alone is an extremely sophisticated phenomenon, with many contributory factors, and the basis for being alone is the feeling of being alone in the presence of someone. This type of situation can have a parallel in the interview situation between the interviewee and the interviewer, in which the interviewee is a "lone witness" and the interviewer has the capacity to listen attentively to what is being told, with the advantages that are inherent in being an "outsider", a separate person.

Scholarly research into the history and memory of the Holocaust has expanded exponentially in the last several decades, not least in the 1990s. By the Holocaust I mean the entire Nazi period from 1933 to 1945, since the final persecutions were built up by earlier preparations. The fall of the Berlin Wall and the gradual opening up both of former Soviet archives and of archives in countries occupied by the Soviet Union has resulted in a considerable deepening of our understanding of the region where most of the killing of Jews took place. With each passing year new aspects, nuances, and previously unexplored questions become the subject of inquiry. Studies specific to certain nations, regions, camps, and personalities continue to be published on a scale that makes it difficult for any single scholar to keep up with the results. Significant recent syntheses, such as those by Friedländer (1997) and Bauer (2001), give eloquent evidence of the advance in our cumulative knowledge and understanding of the history of the Holocaust. Dwork's work, *Children with a Star—Jewish Youth in Nazi Europe* (1991), has been a significant port of entry to my studies. Dwork points out that research on the situation of the children during the Holocaust is extremely limited compared to other research concerning this time period. To study the persecution of children presents a special challenge. Moreover, the documentation of the fate of the children is fragmentary: the Nazis saw the children as appendages of the mothers, not as individuals in their own right. At the same time—paradoxical as it may sound—neither the world at large nor the child survivors themselves seem to have viewed the problems of the children who survived as being as far-reaching as the adults' problems. For these reasons, the situation of the child survivors has only been given any greater degree of attention in more recent years.

Research into the memory of the event—that is, the consequences and impact of the genocide—have also appeared in the last 20 years with reference to Laub and Auerhahn (1993) and Langer (1991). Recently, Volkan (2004) has made a synthesis between psychoanalytic and social psychological factors related to racism and xenophobia. He has demonstrated interesting processes that he calls "chosen trauma" and "transgenerational transmission of trauma". Varvin (2003) stresses the cross-scientific necessity of understanding complex phenomena such as terror and societal violence. Psychological aspects of reconciliation processes should also be looked into. Staub (1989) stresses that mass murder and genocide will go on as long as there is no international system that does not tolerate these acts and is engaged in earnest attempts at preventive work.

Sweden has belatedly and sparsely, but nonetheless noticeably, become part of the now decades-long international trend in exploring specific aspects of the Holocaust. The first important study was conducted by Steven Koblik in 1988. This research has been followed by, among others, Lomfors (1996) and Levine (1998), and by Bachner (1999) who has written about anti-Semitism in Swedish society. Current themes explored include the nature of human destructiveness (Böhm, 1993, 2006; Igra, 2001).

During the past decades the African continent has been ravaged by internal conflicts and insurgencies. The psychological situation that affect African children and youth has varying backgrounds and characteristics (post-war traumas and AIDS), which I have presented in a desk study (Kaplan, 2005b). Children in war-torn countries are often direct or indirect victims of violence and/or witnesses to various horrors associated with war. Children have been brutally taken from their homes to become child soldiers. More than 120,000 children under the age of eighteen are currently fighting in African conflicts. Green and Honwana (1999) stress the problems of using the PTSD concept in this context—especially the notion of *post* (past). In many areas it is a question of ongoing continuous traumas.

Research concerning psychological trauma treatment models developed for children in Africa is extremely limited. The main part of research is carried out in South Africa, where there is a more developed infrastructure and a larger number of academic researchers than in most other African countries. During the last decade, efforts have been made to try out possible models for reintegration of vulnerable children that has also taken the children's psychological state into account. Many of these reports demonstrate a concern to integrate *Western models* with *traditional healing models*. In the purification process of former child soldiers, people of the whole village gather. Clothes and things the child has carried as a soldier are burnt, and the child is literally washed so that the past is left behind and a new life can start (Hjern, 1997). Telling dreams plays an important role (Reynolds, 1996), as in psychodynamic Western methods. Body treatment is often a part of the healing method.

The focus in Part II of this book is upon psychological phenomena within a historical framework—the Nazi persecution of the Jews in 1933–45 and the Rwanda genocide of 1994—and their after-effects. It is outside the scope of this study to describe and discuss other minority groups who were persecuted or to go into the ideological and political background of the genocides described.

Interviewing about genocide

Several branches of knowledge have inspired me in the process of understanding the survivors' life histories. When it comes to the question of how people live with their past and try to create meaning in the present, there is, for example, a bridge connecting psychoanalytic theory, oral history research, pedagogy, narrative analysis, and neuroscience.

Interviewing about the Holocaust, Rwanda, and similar tragedies can be extremely painful, for both the interviewee and the interviewer as well as for the outside listener. When the interviewees describe images, smells, and sounds in connection with the destructiveness and killing that they have witnessed, memories are brought to the surface that no sane human being would wish upon anyone (Ringelheim, 1998). For the listener, the interviewer, there can be a resistance to asking someone to speak about these painful memories. Moreover, it can be very difficult to listen to traumatic life histories that cannot in any way be put into some category of experience that we ourselves have gone through. Authors often refer to the incomprehensible nature of events during the Holocaust. Indeed, is it really even possible to understand the unspeakable horrors that the victims had to endure or to understand the psychological processes behind the actions of the perpetrators? Some object that attempts to understand processes during the Holocaust are equivalent to rendering the incomprehensible "human" or "meaningful", which would ultimately lead to accepting it. Others argue, however, that it is our duty—as historians, psychologists, sociologists—to reflect and to make every effort to try to grasp what took place (Funkenstein, in Josselson & Lieblich, 1993).

What approach should be used, then, to pose questions to a person who seems to be isolating affects in order to open up a dialogue which engages both parties?

You cannot ask the question: "How did you feel when that happened?" People did not usually feel and think in situations of massive trauma. Children with direct channels to their own fantasy lives can have done so to some extent. Children probably could not grasp the magnitude of what they were going through: "I was scared of course [raises voice], he looked like a cannibal . . . we tried to play, children try to live *a normal life even in hell*, I am convinced of that."[1]

For the majority it seemed to be the first time that they found themselves in an interview situation in which they were asked to talk about their whole life from the beginning to the present day, in the absence, generally speaking, of any time limit. All of them have some memories that "never let go" (their grip on them) and which manifest themselves bodily in the form of a strong uneasiness or anxiety. Thus it seems first and foremost to be a matter of their being able to cope with approaching the past, of their being able to begin to think in terms of what has happened to them.

3

Child survivors and childbearing

"One should never build a new life on a cemetery—and Poland was our cemetery."

Janina, born in Poland

This chapter presents a pilot study based on the 40 videotaped interviews with child survivors from the Holocaust. I describe how memories from the Holocaust invade the present and affect one of the most sensitive phases of the life cycle—the period of reproduction. I give examples of how the Nazi deeds, which were intended to eliminate woman and children, to split families—that is, break down the continuity of generations—affected both those who were directly involved and those women and men who witnessed these deeds. The study was the starting point for my studies about children in genocide.

Chapter 3 is a revised version of S. Kaplan, "Child Survivors and Child-bearing—Memories from the Holocaust Invading the Present". *Scandinavian Psychoanalytic Review, 2* (2000). The article was also presented at the IPA Congress, Nice, 2001 (Hayman Prize, 2001).

The interviews that I conducted with two women—Emilia and Anna—form the basis for this chapter. They were both born in 1931 and were both eight years old when their native countries were occupied. Although they grew up in environments that were totally different in several respects and they had different experiences of persecution under Nazism, their descriptions of themselves as children before and during the war were in certain respects similar. The consequences of the traumatic stresses during the war seemed to be a crucial factor in their attitude towards having children. This led to my interest in studying all of the 40 interviews with child survivors from this aspect.

The interviewees come from nine countries and are now residing in Sweden. More than half of this group (13 girls and 10 boys) were prisoners in one or several concentration camps during the war, and fewer (12 girls and 3 boys) lived in ghettos and/or in hiding. A few (2 girls) came as refugees during the war. One third of the child survivors in this study lost both their parents in the Holocaust. More than a third lost their fathers. Many of them were separated from their mothers during the war years. One can ask how this background, with massive traumatic experiences, has influenced the rest of their lives. The mere thought of pregnancy may have caused some to refrain from parenthood. The fear of confronting painful memories may have deterred them.

Generativity

It turned out that the theme of *childbirth* was a strikingly and surprisingly recurring theme, both with those who do have children and with those who do not. As many as 9 of the 40 child survivors did not have biological children at the time of the interviews.

Among the other child survivors, more than half associated to pregnancy and/or to infants when telling about traumatic experiences in their life histories. My observation made me think about how internal conflicts about the child survivors' own childbearing might be related to repeated traumatization during the Holocaust, especially if the survivor had not reached adolescence before the outbreak of the war. The child survivors seem to live in a vacuum between, on the one hand, parents they have lost, and, on the other, a complicated relationship to childbearing. Is this a general problem

for child survivors from the Holocaust? How can we understand
these issues from psychoanalytic viewpoints? What are the possibilities of working through these issues psychologically?

The war has had repercussions for *generativity*, which, according
to Erikson (1982), includes *reproduction, productivity, and creativity*. As
regards pregnancy—the "creation of new people"—the generativity
function has stagnated or has been rendered passive for many in
the sample group and has become linked to a strong fear. Some
have chosen not to have children. On the other hand, a majority
have found a channel for success in the invention of new products
and other forms of creativity in their working lives. Some survivors
have been so traumatized, broken down, and fragmented that they
have not had the stamina or been able to testify about their past
during the Holocaust. Others, in spite of their feeling of resistance,
can tell their life histories. Because these narratives are intended
for future generations, their life histories—as well as their participa-
tion in things like this study—can be seen as an important aspect of
generativity.

Approaching pregnancy and parenthood

I focus on the interaction between, on the one hand, the self-image,
close relationships, and massive traumas in connection with persecution under Nazism and, on the other hand, reactions to pregnancy
and parenthood.

By *self-image* I mean the picture the survivors choose to paint of
themselves (in relation to others)—that is, the subjectively experienced conscious picture they have of themselves.

Massive traumas can in this context be described as events in the
survivors' life that are so intense that they cannot deal with them in
an optimal way. The psychic structure is broken down over a long
period. Freud (1920g, p. 31) and many of his followers illustrate the
trauma process with the concept of the protective shield, a barrier
between the outer world and the inner psychic life, which is perforated by a psychic overload. One can ask in this regard whether
the concept of time and time-related memory function are not also
damaged. It is as if the trauma did not happen a long time ago, but
takes place again every day.

Based on years of experience of interviews with survivors, researchers have clearly shown how a split in the self occurs as a result of the difficulties in dealing with massive traumas. Laub and Auerhahn (1993, p. 291) describe this phenomenon by showing how fragments "are recalled without the individual knowing that the 'I', or the subject who experienced the event is different from the one who recalls it"—"there is a collapse of the two at the moment of recall, with no reflective self present." The past and the present exist simultaneously within the experienced self, which coincides with my impressions in this study.

Pregnancy and thoughts of parenthood constitute both a development and a crisis period. Bibring (1961, p. 15) chooses to define this developmental process "in terms of the relationship of the woman to her sexual partner, to her 'self', and to the child as it is expressed in the level and distribution of object libido and narcissistic libido". This includes that the woman has a good-enough self-esteem from an erotic-bodily viewpoint.

Experience has shown that trauma can influence future family relations and create difficulties in intimacy (Laub & Auerhahn, 1993, p. 287). At the moment of—and after—learning of a pregnancy, conscious and unconscious fantasies linked to early experiences and identifications from childhood are activated in both women and men. The choice not to have children can in my view signify that the person has *perceived signals* of becoming more receptive to invading affects. This unconscious fear can, in addition to the conscious motive that "no child should have to suffer what I have suffered", cause them to decide not to have children. In addition, for child survivors there is also the fact that they have not "been children": they have been lacking parental care. A pregnancy may activate these unsatisfied needs, as well as repressed survivor's guilt. I would like to add that the established expression "invading memories" appears to be a contradiction, since memories are something that a person could think around and put behind them. What seems to be invading is the affect, the anxiety. My conclusion is that the concept should be *"invading affects"*.

In no case did the interviewer pose questions about pregnancy. Rather, this theme developed coincidentally from associations in the semi-structured interviews, but probably in connection with their invading affects. The time of giving birth is far in the past for the survivors. It is interesting that these events are treated by them in the interviews as if they were of *current interest in the present.*

I ask Anna at the end of her interview:

—"How have your experiences influenced your daily life, you personally?"

Anna says in a loud and very upset voice:

—"That I didn't want to have children. That I had two abortions because I was a child myself."[1]

This statement has formed the basis for posing an important question, which has remained of great significance throughout the entire research process. What was the significance of a child's own age and conception of age during and after the war when it came to the possibility of maintaining the feeling of having inner links to significant persons, and how might these inner links serve as a lifeline to allow the creation of links to the next generation?

When I approach the material from a psychoanalytic viewpoint, I am also influenced by other areas of knowledge that will colour my conclusions about childbearing—historical background, theories about autobiography/narrative, and memory research.

Several documents have shown that the Nazis' overriding objective was to destroy the biological foundation for future generations of Jews. Bruchfeld says:

> The very biological foundation of the Jewish people was to be "eradicated". For instance, to solve the problem of being able to use Jews as labour as long as possible without murdering them, ideas of mass sterilization were raised and Jewish (also Roma and others) men, women and children were experimented on to find ways to realize them. One method was to try assembly line X-raying. In Auschwitz and Ravensbrück Dr. Carl Clauberg experimented on fertile, mostly Jewish women by injecting chemical substances in the womb, which resulted in most of them becoming sterile. It was thought that such methods, if successful, could be used also in the "reduction" of non-Germanic populations, especially in Eastern Europe. The overriding intention was that the *biological* basis of Jewish existence should disappear entirely, one way or other. [Bruchfeld & Levine, 1999, with ref. to Graml, 1992]

In an interview in the documentary film *The Last Days* (Moll, 1998), the SS doctor Hans Münch says that women were sterilized in order to "diminish the race." "For all those who wanted to conduct experiments on humans this was a thankful workplace. Many experiments were done in Auschwitz to find ways to sterilize women, specifically Jewish women, in order to diminish the race without going through too much trouble."

* * *

Researchers in the field of Holocaust studies emphasize that there is a discontinuity in survivors' testimony when the life histories deal with massive traumas. This discontinuity is not in the manner of free associations with an underlying theme but, rather, a fragmentedness, as if there is a difficulty in the telling of the story.

Langer (1995) claims that oral testimony is not just a matter of describing experience, but *in its fragmented form it also conveys how the event itself destroys the possibility to integrate*. Therefore oral autobiographies can be said to be more accurate than an adapted written life history. In fragmenting the story there is both the inability to integrate, to create meaning, and probably also the defensive aspect of realizing the totality! Instead, the fragments do not stick together, because if they would, the pain would be felt even more. Laub and Auerhahn (1993, p. 288) describe "forms of knowing" on a scale from distance to integration of knowledge. Survivors at different distances between knowing and not knowing about trauma are "caught between the compulsion to complete the process of knowing and the inability or fear of doing so". Telling may be characterized by the failure to find meaning. Connected stories can, however, be an attempt to create meaning where there is none, as a step in the struggle for survival. Moreover, the survivor may be anxious to please the interviewer and may try to talk about what he or she thinks the interviewer wants to hear, that is, thereby making the interview meaningful. Langer (1991, p. xv) discusses how credible a reawakened memory is after many decades and thinks the terminology itself is at fault: "There is no need to revive what has never died."

The child survivors in this study were in the last phase of their active lives in their own new post-war families, which probably have functioned as a shield against invading affects. Now their children have left home, some live alone—they have reached an age when they want to tell. Usually one remembers one's youth better than what has happened recently (immediate past). The shock and personal reasons that existed to hide terrible experiences have disappeared, and the truthfulness of the stories may increase with age, which is stressed by the historian Bauer (2001). At the beginning of this investigation some interviewees said: "There are many boxes to open, but I haven't done so out of concern for the children", or "Some memories I will take with me to my grave, I have always thought so." During the interview they have then told it in an open, detailed way. Now the time to tell seems to be right.

Two autobiographies: Emilia and Anna

Background

Emilia was born in Poland in 1931. Her father was a physician. No profession is mentioned for her mother. Emilia was an only child. The family lived in a roomy apartment and had a nanny who meant a great deal to Emilia. The family lived in an area with a majority Jewish population, but they did not consider themselves religious. Emilia had never been inside a synagogue. Emilia was eight years old when Poland was occupied. During the war she was hidden by a Polish maid and was separated from her parents, whom she never saw again. They were most probably taken to the concentration camps. Emilia came from Poland to Sweden in 1980. She is a medical doctor, now retired. Emilia has been married. She has no children.

Anna was born in Lithuania in 1931. Her father was a dry-goods sales clerk. Her mother was a seamstress. Anna had three siblings. Their home was crowded, and they were poor. The family lived in the Jewish quarter near the synagogue, which Anna often visited. Her parents were traditional Jews and Zionists, and they spoke Yiddish at home. Anna was eight years old when Lithuania was occupied. During the war she was moved to the ghetto and camps in Estonia. Then she was taken to the Stutthof concentration camp and finally, together with 500 children, on to Auschwitz, where she was probably the only child in the group who survived when the children were shoved into the gas chambers/crematoria.

Several years after the war ended, Anna saw her mother and her sister again. They were all in poor health. Her father and her two brothers had been murdered. Anna came to Sweden in 1964. She has worked as an archivist, but was on sick leave for long periods and retired early. Anna is a widow and has no children.

I will show how these two women chose to present themselves, their memory images from the Holocaust, and the consequences in their adult lives, using my own interviews as source material. My interviews were extensive, and selected quotations do not do the survivors justice. My selection represents *my interpretation* of what I believe can contribute to a better understanding of their invading affects, specifically with regard to reproduction. I have chosen to present the quotations as true to their spoken language as possible. At the same time minor adjustments have been made in order that their messages will come forth as clearly as possible.

Family life before the occupation

Emilia's and Anna's stories about family life before the occupation give us a sense of how they perceived themselves as children and how they saw their role in the family.

Emilia describes herself as a child:

"Well, my first memories are perhaps from the time when I was three–four years old. . . ."

—"What do you see before you?"

"That I am sitting in a baby buggy and I am crying because *I want something and cannot have it*. I don't know who was with me. *I wasn't a nice child!*"

—"What do you mean by that?"

"*I was stubborn.*"[2]

Emilia often visited her father at his surgery.

"When my father was attending child patients, *I seemed to have a calming influence on them*. I went to them and said, You don't have to be afraid. It won't hurt, etc. Then we talked a little in there."[3]

The first conscious memory is when she wants something she cannot get. Emilia also conveys that she trusts her own abilities. She sees herself as even capable of helping others.

I ask her to continue to describe her relationship to her father:

"He talked with me a lot. We very often took long walks. *He treated me like a conversation partner, like an adult, not like a child.* I could ask him about different things, about religion, about politics, about ideas, and he treated me well, with dignity and tolerance, and *I think that was what helped me to survive. And later! To deal with everything afterwards.*"[4]

Emilia had only one vague memory of her mother.

"Remember nearly nothing at all. She didn't take care of me because there was a nanny who took care of me. *I don't remember that we talked with each other. I didn't know her. I remember nearly nothing about her.*"

—"Do you remember how she looked?"

"Yes, but *I don't know if I remember it because I have only one photo of her* and that I remember, but not her face. *Only Pappa has stuck.*"[5]

Emilia reflects on how her memory of her mother is constructed. We do not know why her memory of her mother is more vague.

Anna tells of her relationship with her father:

"When he came home he would say to my mother: 'Pack die kleine päcklach. I'm going to take the children for a walk.' And he went with us and took long hikes, or . . . he very much liked to go rowing, ice skating, and swimming. He could throw us into the water. We lived just next to a lake [my word] and we are going to swim, *he taught us that and I had great use of it during the war—great use.* My father was very keen that we children should do sports."[6]

Anna talks about her mother:

"My mother was very pedantic, that much I can say. *She unfortunately didn't have so much time . . .*"

—"Can you describe your role in the family?"

"As a little girl, we learned . . . because we were poor we learned that my mother always demanded of us children that we should, for example, . . . that we should wash the floor, that we should prepare the potatoes . . . *we were not spoiled* . . . In spite of the fact that we were poor, we were dressed very elegantly. Mamma sewed clothes for us children which everyone admired."[7]

Extremely traumatic moments

Beginnings of anti-Semitism

Emilia's and Anna's hometowns were in Poland and the Baltics (Lithuania), respectively—precisely those areas where children had the least chance of survival (Bruchfeld & Levine, 1999). Children were immediately seriously affected when there was a rise in anti-Semitism and persecution of the Jews. They lost their basic social structures: school, network of friends and neighbours. At the same time, many children had only a vague understanding of their Jewish background (Dwork, 1991).

Emilia is five–six years old. She is playing in the park, and the children are teasing her:

> "*I didn't know I was a Jew*, I must have been very little, I played somewhere in the park and the children called after me Jew, Jew—*then I thought it was like a strange being.*
> I went home and said that the children say: 'You are a Jew.' And they said, 'Yes, you are.'"[8]

Anna, who has a strong Jewish identity, tells of when she started to feel affected:

> "Yes, for example when I came out of the synagogue, the children would stand there and scream 'Judas, Jewish pigs.'"[9]

Separation

A directive was issued by Head of SS Security R. Heydrich on 27 September 1939 on how the Jews were to be gathered together in order to control them more easily and then transport them to other destinations. The Nazis started to organize the ghettos in 1940 (Gutman, 1990, p. 1156).

Emilia describes her family's situation just after her eleventh birthday. Luvisa, the maid, first hid her parents and then Emilia.

> "And I was supposed to go with them, but I had an ear infection so Luvisa said, 'No, she can stay here because she is sick.' So she was with me. At night, when it was dark, she went with water and with food so that no one would see. And I wrote small notes to them. *I remember that it was after my birthday.* I turned eleven, and then we were together. *It was normal.* One day Luvisa said, Quick, under the cupboard! and she pushed me. She was forced to push me in because there wasn't room, so the cupboard was almost standing on me. She said, '*Put your hand over your mouth and don't breathe for a while.*' And then the Germans came and some Polish neighbours. And they looked for me. *A girl was missing,* and I remember that I lay there and tried not to breathe and *I could see their boots* and I thought that when you look at a bird or an animal it doesn't move, but if you turn your head it flies away. So I should not look so that they don't feel my gaze. So I closed my eyes. And then they looked everywhere and in the cupboard before they left. And then Luvisa said, You can come out. They are gone. You can't stay here because they are after you. You must run away, but we will wait until it gets dark. *You mustn't draw attention to yourself, so you must act normal.* When it got dark, we went to the railway station and rode far, far, I don't remember how long. *I just thought I couldn't understand, I didn't think it could be happening.* I thought, 'Not them, it is not possible.' At the same time I had to keep tight, *not show anything.* So we came to, I thought: what is happening now, what should I do, now *I am alone.* I have nowhere to go. But Luvisa was there. And she didn't say much, she just took care of me."[10]

Emilia has just lost her parents, and at the same moment she has to change identity and pretend that she was not born to her parents.

Anna tells about how they came to their house and screamed at her father:

> "They came in and screamed, 'Aber forfluchte Jude, how much did you pay for that cross?' [a medal the father had received]. He has no time to say that he was awarded it in the war. My father was blond, with blue eyes. *He didn't look Jewish, but they shot my father*

directly and my brother. And my mother became mentally ill at once. She didn't react. She was like apathetic. She was not aggressive, *she was apathetic, and she didn't want to drink or eat. We even had to make her go to the toilet and . . ."*[11]

Anna's father was murdered, and her mother had a breakdown. At that moment Anna also lost her mother as a caring parent. Anna must now take care of herself.

Getting by without parents or another adult

The maid Luvisa chose to live with Emilia in an area where German families lived. No one would expect to find a Jewish girl there, she thought. The risks and the demands on them both, however, were extreme.

Emilia tells about a meeting where she was out playing with German and Polish children in a housing area and a strange man turns up.

"We were four girls. She [a playmate] started to laugh. 'Do you know what he said?! He said that you were a Jew and that he wanted your address. Of course he got your address.' *And then I felt that, now it's over. And I felt all my blood disappear, but I couldn't show it. So I sat on the street and started to fiddle with my shoes to control my expression.*[12]

Luvisa was out all day, and Emilia alone had to receive the man when he came to the flat. With great effort Emilia succeeded in tricking the man into thinking she was Luvisa's daughter. She played a role and showed him a photograph that she had found in a drawer and said that it was a picture of her father. This required courage and ingenuity and above all a calm state of mind."

Anna gives many examples during the interview of how she was exposed to physical violence. At the same time she was helped in the concentration camp by what she had seen her father do at home [inner father-image].

"The next day they wanted people to do work in the forest. And I ran to be the first. And he said, Aber du kleine . . . nicht arbeiten. And I remembered my father, how he was, you know, we had no heat, it was primitive, so my father sawed up the wood himself.

He always looked at the saw to see whether the blade was straight and he did like this [stretches out her arm and shows]. And I was so smart. There were many saws, and I went out and took a big, long one and showed how I checked if it was sharp enough, and he stared at me. 'How do you know that?' I said that I just knew . . . So he let me come into that group."[13]

Memories are closely connected with what, and under what circumstances, one has learned as a child (Pally, 1997, p. 1223). Identification with her father and the respect that Anna felt for him as well as the memory of the self-confidence he instilled in her helped her in threatening situations, when she risked being taken out of the group because she was a child.

Witnessing suicide and infanticide

Emilia tells about a family living above them who were terrified. Their fourteen-year-old daughter committed suicide.

"The girl, she didn't dare leave the flat. She was called Lena. *Then I heard when the Germans* came to arrest them. I stood in the big room and I saw something big and dark behind the window and a scream, it was that girl who jumped. Her foot got caught on the balcony and then down on the street. We heard screaming, and she was still alive, and we children were locked in the bathroom again. *Then I asked what had happened* to Lena, and they said that she has gone to the hospital, she'll soon be well, *but I knew that it wasn't true.*"[14]

The adults did not tell the children what was happening. The adults were fully occupied with arranging everything so that they would all survive. They felt anxiety and worry of their own and probably thought they were protecting the children by not telling them. This is most probably a rationalization, as they could not cope with the children in the tense situation.

Anna tells about when they were pushed into cattle cars and of her contact with a woman whose infant was murdered.

". . . She had a pillow with her. Everyone was very surprised. She asked me if I wanted to stand next to her. She came into the car with that pillow and stood there, you couldn't sit down. We couldn't really all stand next to each other. *Everyone was shoving. It was horrible. You can't imagine.*

. . . And then when we got to Latvia, to Riga, the cars stopped and the big doors opened. Then Russians, Ukrainians started screaming, *I can't describe it . . . and* they ran into all the cars, Get out, get out, like wild men. And can you imagine, a little girl [= the pillow] woke up. She [K] had a daughter whom she was putting to sleep, and she woke up and started to cry. *Everyone was surprised.* A small child! And then a Ukrainian came and pushed and shoved and wanted to know where the crying was coming from, and he trampled that little baby with his boots *until she died.* And when we got to Estonia, *K took her life . . . She took her life.*"[15]

The extreme cruelty of these actions, which at times was incomprehensible, as when infants were trampled to death or, in other examples, shot to death through the backpacks their parents carried them in, may have affected child survivors, both men and women, in their identification with the needy child.

Dressing up psychically or physically as a step in the struggle for survival

Hiding one's identity is a conscious change of the self, a step in the struggle to survive or, rather, "fend off" death.

Emilia tells how she woke up every morning and convinced herself that she was a blond Ukrainian girl. She went to school with Polish children and had a Catholic confirmation, not to deviate from the other children in the neighbourhood.

"Yes, I have understood that I look very Jewish and the only thing I can do is not be Jewish. So I made up my mind. I am a blond Ukrainian. If I show the least sign of worry, it's over! One has to be happy, relaxed, and I tried to do this the whole time. Not show the least, even if I heard Jew! I could smile at them. All the time, I felt people's eyes on me, and I knew I had to be invisible. But that was impossible, so I was very visible."[16]

Anna tells of seeking work as a nine-year-old, pretending to be fifteen:

"Then came the great Action. And I, what did I want to say, in order to get a little bread you had to have Arbeits . . . My Mamma, she couldn't, she was mentally ill. My sister wasn't as active as I was. My sister, she sewed small pillows in her chest. And I have always liked to eat, and I had long, long hair and had red [cheeks] . . . I was a very well-cared-for girl. Well nourished. And then a pillow, so that I would look fatter. And Mamma's shoes, which didn't fit. I took them anyway, with high heels. And then I went to the Arbeitsamt. I wanted to work. They looked at me, how old are you? I'm fifteen years old."

—"How old were you then?"

"I was nine and a half years old. So I got the Arbeitsschein. I worked at the airport. Dug shelters for the Germans. Heavy work. Very, very cold. We usually, like that. Stood and warmed myself near a German. He hit me with his shovel, on the nose. Look here [shows me]. Bled. We worked 12–13 hours. Then they chased us to the ghetto, 8–10 kilometres. Back and forth. I cannot stand it any longer."[17]

Anna had to care for herself—quickly learn to act like an adult, dress up, and take risks. During the interview she showed me a scar on her nose that was connected with the event.

Living instead of another child

Taking the place of another child elicits difficult feelings that have to be borne later, even though you rationally know there was no other choice. To be the one of two playmates who survived and not the one who died influences aspects of the self-image, both because you were the one who survived and because all the children were actually supposed to die. This could be expressed as: "I am a person who actually should be dead." Krystal (1978, p. 91) writes that the survivor may experience himself as "flooded by emotion . . . that will go on to destroy him."

Emilia talks about her friend Ester:

". . . they first took her father . . . Two people hid her in their house, it was two elderly women, sisters. Then I don't know what it was, if they were afraid, because they wanted to get rid of her.

I was at Luvisa's. Luvisa came with her and couldn't find any room. Nowhere. *And I didn't dare ask too much. And it didn't work* . . . And Ester said that she would rather die. Luvisa got hold of some poison, and Luvisa went away with her. We said good-bye to each other, and . . . . and when she came back, Ester was dead. *If she had been the first to come to Luvisa, then she would be sitting here, alive, if she had been the first* [very disturbed]."

—"So that is what you think!"

"Yes, she had better chances, because she was blond, bright-eyed—she was attractive."[18]

Emilia, as well as Anna, stresses the importance of *non-Jewish looks.*

Emilia is very upset and continues:

"Because . . . it makes me sad, because, I knew, she knew, Luvisa knew. *And all three of us discussed it, and we agreed that it was the only thing to do.* It's true, this is how it was. Today this is criminal. It was the best . . . *she was growing, she started to have breasts,* and what would happen to her, so a quick death was better. And she chose it. And I thought it was best, and Luvisa also thought it was best. *There was no choice.*"[19]

When Emilia talks about her guilt feelings, suddenly the memory and thoughts about femininity invade her, that Ester started to have breasts. Her budding womanhood was murdered, a death that Emilia might have internalized.

Anna tells of how she was in a group of 500 children who were informed that they were to be taken to a sugar factory to work. They were taken from Stutthof directly to the gas chambers in Auschwitz. This was in October 1944, when Anna was twelve years of age. Anna is probably the only survivor from that group—although there are unconfirmed reports of the possible survival of another. Mass gassing in Auschwitz started at the end of 1941 (Gutman, 1990).

"And when we came to Auschwitz, we were met by the murderer Mengele. Elegant. Nazi leather coat. With white gloves. Grim. And he said nothing. Just like that. Nothing. And they chased us further to barracks, and we had to take off our clothes, so that we wouldn't notice or suspect anything. There was a man there, his name was Steiner. I heard that later. And he walked around saying: 'Kinder, mach nicht panik.' [Anna says a few sentences in Yiddish.] Don't panic, you are going to wash yourselves and get rid of the lice. And before that, before we had taken off our clothes, I was walking, the last one. And I just looked at their faces. What? Which? . . . I studied them.[20]

Those who had jewellery had to put it in a box. A mother said to her children: 'Kinder slink, slink!!' That they should swallow. I remember the mother, with four daughters. They were from Kovna. And this Steiner left . . . no German guard, none [quieter, and she says with difficulty]: I can't talk about this [silence] . . . I was walking, the last one, until we came to concrete barracks and the doors opened and they chased us all in, all the children. And I was the last, last. But those who went in first discovered that there was no water [very upset]. WE ALL KNEW THAT A CREMATORIUM EXISTED, THAT A GAS CHAMBER EXISTED. BUT NO ONE KNEW WHERE IT WAS! NONE OF US!"

Someone calls out for a girl named Steiner, and Anna saw a possibility to get away. Anna is very upset and is shouting when she says this:

"There were seconds, seconds. There was a German, like he would burst through the door, and he shouted: 'Wer ist Steiner, Steiner?' I stood there, the last, and shouted Me, me, me!, and he grabbed me by the neck and threw me out to the Jew [Steiner]. And that Jew, he stood close to this door in order to close it, and around him there were SS men, and I don't know if there were any Poles, I don't know. I don't remember, don't ask me. I don't remember. I only remember [she is sobbing], when I talk to you I remember [sobbing] I hear the screams of the children. [silence]

Steiner expected his daughter to come out.

'Ja, aber das ist doch nicht meine Tochter.' I was blond, so they thought I was a goy, not a Jew. And then I threw myself at this man. The man then pushed—'Let go.'

'Pappa, Pappa, erkennst mich nicht? Pappa!' And he realized that it was already too late, that even if his daughter is in there, because someone said that to him, I was saved. How I was saved, I don't know. Whatever privilege he had, I don't know either, and don't ask me, I only know that they grabbed me by the neck, gave me a camp uniform, and sent me to a barracks. That's how I was saved."

—"And you were the only child?"

"Yes, the only child. And their shouting—when I talk to you and look into your eyes, I see their eyes and hear their screams. At first I did not understand that I was at the door. When I came to Auschwitz, everyone talked about the gas chamber, about everything, then I understood where I had been."[21]

When Anna looks at me, she associates to the sound of the children's screams as she projects her own fear into my eyes. This is a partly fragmented story that can be said to reflect Anna's condition at the time of the trauma, full of fright. She says "we all knew there was a gas chamber, and later I understood where I had been". Whatever they heard before arriving at Auschwitz, it was not until afterwards that they understood where they had been.

Liberation and the post-war period

After liberation, both Emilia and Anna contracted tuberculosis. Years of hospital treatments after the war and repeated foster homes have contributed to complicating the rehabilitation. The greatest psychic/inner difficulties started after the war. The tension between then and now was greatest. Parents were dead. Life would never be the same.

They were afraid that their skeletal tuberculosis might be able to affect their own children. Moreover, they did not want their children to have to experience what they had gone through. "*And I never wanted to have children, Jewish children in Poland.* Never thought about moving from Poland, because I didn't know anyone else in the whole world. I had nowhere to go. I had to make my life in Poland. *Then I will never have children. No child needs to go through what I did. I don't regret it.*"[22] One of the women terminated two pregnancies. The abortions in themselves can have caused another layer of trauma.

Summary of the whole group investigated
in relation to childbearing

In spite of the big differences in socioeconomic background, Jewish identity, and experiences during the war, both Emilia and Anna have struggled with similar coping with outer stresses in connection with Nazi persecution—for example, to cut the ties to their parents, to "grow up" early, to change identity, which means pretending that one's own parents are not one's parents, to have or not to have Jewish looks. Moreover, both experienced destruction of their own bodies (and what this means psychologically). Both have been in situations where they were forced to make quick decisions that may have led to survivor guilt.

Both Emilia's and Anna's relationship with their fathers was characterized by *mutual respect*. They internalized a picture of a father who is secure, a father who knows how to do things. At the same time the idealization of the fathers may have worked as a protection against loneliness and facilitated healing of narcissistic wounds (Goldman, 1986).

My impression from this study is that a strong relationship to and identification with the father has been important for being able to deal on one's own with *the struggle to avoid death* and to cope as an adult. We know too little about the quality of their relationships with their mothers to draw any conclusions. We can only speculate about the influence of a weak relationship to a mother, together with the stresses to which they have been exposed as children, on resolving the conflicts with childbearing that appear. Both have refrained from having children. On the other hand, the recurring theme of a weak mother might be an expression of an unconscious reproach against the mother for not being able to protect the child from the war. Künstlicher (2000) stresses the importance of having to wait too long for the object. He means that time is experienced as unbearable, and the frustration becomes a pain that lasts forever. Perhaps during the waiting period there is an image of a bad mother, whom the individual does not feel that he or she needs. At the time of the interview there were, as mentioned, 9 interviewees who did not have children (6 women and 3 men). Many examples illustrate the complexity of the conflicts centring around giving birth.

Child survivors who have no children

Anna said, "

> " . . . my husband so much wanted to have children [exclaims crying]: What have I done. They have destroyed my whole life [repeats, very upset] I had anxiety. *Yes, If you are afraid and have anxiety then you cannot imagine it, I had no one.* My husband was a weak person, he did not say 'Anna don't do it [abortion]. We will help you.' No one could, and myself I could have been a little smarter, but. . . ."

Eva, who was six years old when Poland was occupied and later lived in hiding, tells that her mother was forced to hand over her infant, Eva's little sister, in order to move with Eva to a family where she could work and conceal their identity. But her mother was exposed to threats of rape. Eva tells of her own sexual debut at the age of 36 and her fear of becoming pregnant.

> "It was the first time I slept with a man. The war has left in me, like tracks, a terrible fear of having children, or of getting married. I have thought that I will never have a family, I will never again have to be separated from the people I love. I cannot bind myself, I cannot have a family . . . and we didn't know it, but he made me pregnant. And he wanted to marry me, but I didn't want to . . . then I was in the fourth month, and I went to a doctor because I had diarrhoea, and the doctor told me I was in the fourth month. And then I thought like this. I was really happy. I was terribly afraid . . . I kept this to myself until I was in about the fifth month, and then I told L and thought of marrying him, but when I was in the fifth month, I had a miscarriage. I have often thought that there must have been something wrong with the child. Sometimes I thought it was my fear that made me have a miscarriage. I know, of course, that you don't have a miscarriage because of fear. But every other night I was very happy and every other night I was very much afraid. And the two foster children I had then, . . . They took care of me then, after the miscarriage, otherwise I wouldn't have made it. I became their foster child. I became disjointed . . . *but for me, this unborn child is still my daughter, who is 26 years old. It was a child.* Think that Pappa didn't get to see his grandchildren."[23]

Eva was both very happy and terribly frightened. Her fear is about having to be separated from people whom she loves, which has nothing to do with today's reality but with experiences from traumatic separations as a child. She also thinks that it was her fear that caused her to have a miscarriage—as if her body reacted to the fantasies and the unconscious memories that were tormenting her. The affects are present at the moment when these memories are recovered in the interview. "For me, this unborn child is still my daughter." The past seems to persist.

Everything associated with being alive, like giving birth to a healthy child, also reminds her of death, since she has a "death due"—she "should have died", according to Langer. He has coined the word "redeath" and expresses his thoughts in the following way:

> I have suggested a new concept, redeath. It refers to the missed destiny of death that many survivors talk about in their testimonies, the feeling that their real fate in the camps was to have died there like most of the other people. Since the logic of their existence was to have died, they sometimes speak as if part of them did die, and in this sense their redeath is the opposite of what we more often speak of as a rebirth. In the camps, staying alive and fending off death were interchangeable, and this tension often surfaces again in their testimonies afterwards. [Langer, personal communication, 1999]

We have seen that Eva thought there must have been something wrong with the child she was expecting, and that Anna was afraid of transferring her skeletal tuberculosis to her unborn child. Bergman and Jucovy (1982, pp. 21–23) cite Klein, who conducted a study of 25 families in Israel between 1967 and 1969. Klein found that many women who survived and became pregnant have a pronounced fear of being transformed from good mothers into monsters who give birth to damaged children, which can be seen as an internalization of the persecutors' attitude towards them during the war. Moreover, they confirm recurring persecution dreams about being captured, together with their child in a concentration camp, and how imminent the expectation is that persecution will return.

Child survivors who have children

It is important to note that a number of the interviewees do have children of their own. Sam said, "I was 30 years old. As soon as we got married, we got right down to having children."[24] Several child survivors question the meaning of surviving and coming back, but they also stress the importance of having healthy and successful children and grandchildren that are the great joy of their lives. In spite of enormous stresses, they have succeeded in creating a good and satisfying life. They may want to repair the past through their children, and the children also reinforce their feeling of living on, surviving. They often named their children after deceased relatives. A good adult life does not, however, seem to influence their invading affects, which are active in another part of the self. An essential conclusion is that both the choice *not to have children* and the choice *to have children* are thus in this group of child survivors tainted by intrusive memory images.

Motherhood after the Holocaust

Gynaecologists who have been working in Sweden after the war have described the enormous losses that the survivors endured and the ambitions to help them. B. Kaplan says:

> Among the patients there were many who tried to create new families. Many had been subjected to experimental operations, often on a gynecological basis, and their ovaries had been injured. I got patients from all over the country. Unfortunately there was not much I could do. These people were physically and often psychically seriously wounded. [Johansson, 2000, p. 23]

Nomi, who was one year old when Poland was occupied and later miraculously survived Ravensbrück and Bergen-Belsen, says:

> "Then I was told that I should be happy that I have one child, should be happy, and *that I should forget to plan for more children.* But I didn't listen to that, I am happy because those three children mean a lot in my life. So I absolutely don't regret that. I am happy I didn't listen to him, the orthopaedist."[25]

Marysia, who was ten years old when Poland was occupied and lived in several ghettos during the war, tells of how the memories of the transport to Auschwitz came forth *during the birth of her first child,* thus indicating how memories are unexpectedly recovered.

> "There were many children who lost their parents after the action in the ghetto. *When I had children myself, I thought, I remember, that it was the most horrible thing that could happen . . .* and we were going to Auschwitz . . . I said to the nurses then, when I woke up after the anaesthetic, 'you cannot imagine what a joy it is to have a child here. . . .' *I don't think I realized what I meant, they must have thought I was delirious, but in fact I thought about this when I was having my first child.* "[26]

Alice, who was one year old when Poland was occupied and who lived in hiding in a shed for two years, tells that she had three miscarriages. After that, she expected twins. First she gave birth to a son who was dead, and half an hour later came her daughter, who today is her only child. Alice tells about *the day when she gave birth* to her daughter and about a conversation with her husband the same day.

> —"Your experiences [during the war], how have they formed you, do you think?"

> [quietly] "In a strong way. . . . Maybe I should tell you [cries]. When Sara was born, I was very happy that she, that I got a child, because when I was pregnant they told me that this will not be. . . . I will never give birth to a healthy child if I can go all the way through a pregnancy. But she was born. She was a healthy child from the beginning, and she is healthy. When she was born, when we came home from the hospital after ten days, *I wasn't well,* but she was. *So I said the same day to my husband, that he has to know, that in case there is another war like 1939–45 with anti-Semitism, I will kill her and then I'll commit suicide, because I didn't want her to go through the same thing.*"[27]

Langer (1998) writes about women who had children in Auschwitz and points out that: "In the chaotic scheme of values created for their victims by the Germans, a birth moment is a death moment, and the mother's ambition is to leave her life to join her murdered infant" (p. 51).

When I speak to Alice in a follow-up interview four years after the videotaped interview cited above, she is very happy and tells me, "I have become a grandmother . . . my daughter has given birth to twin girls. So now life is worth living again."[28]

Fatherhood after the Holocaust

In this study, men have also felt damaged in their parent function. One man without children of his own tells about his resistance to having children from having seen so many children being sent to death in brutal circumstances, as when they were being burnt alive. Bauer (2001) stresses that children who are burnt alive are perhaps "the most horrible scenes that are recorded". This is so far beyond the tragedies of everyday life "that we tend to say to ourselves that we can never fully understand them, because we cannot imagine ourselves experiencing them". Some men who themselves have children have talked about how their own role as fathers was most difficult when their children were the same age they were when their traumatization was most massive.

Jacob, who was ten years old when Romania was occupied and was taken to Auschwitz, still sees his Mamma behind the barbed wire. Still today he cannot even "think the thought of his parents being dead." He thinks of them "as alive". He tells of the resistance he felt when his wife became pregnant. He wished that she had had an abortion: "I kept on nagging about taking it away, but she didn't want to. *I didn't want him to come. I didn't want any descendants.* My son has no one and nothing, a very unhappy boy. I pity the second generation."[29]

The abruptly broken-off contact with their parents probably also influenced the child survivors' choices of life partners and *thoughts of having children.*

The second generation

Two survivors in my group of investigation lost their children when they committed suicide as young adults. The survivors connected these events with second-generation depression. I will not elaborate on the second generation because their situation is not the focus of my study. But I think their situation should be mentioned in this context.

In one of the families the son, an only child of Janina, took his own life. It is the greatest catastrophe. It has erased everything.[30] For this reason I have chosen to include her in the group of those child survivors who are not the biological parents of children (at the time of the interview). Her husband wrote a letter to me when he found out about my research.

> The biggest injustice for me and my wife . . . is that World War II didn't finish, it still kills people. Our only son, P, 37 years, married, having two small children, . . . committed suicide. He left two children, four and one years old, his young wife and us in a traumatic state. He had second-generation depression.

The family lived in Poland in the first post-war years. They searched for their relatives and remained there. They were not allowed to leave the country until 1968, when they moved to Sweden. Janina, who at the time of the interview was very ill with cancer and is now dead, wanted to say this while she was still able to: "One should never build a new life on a cemetery. And Poland was our cemetery."[31]

Psychoanalysts have for decades observed traumatic memories that in a non-specific way are transferred from one generation to the next. Faimberg (1988, p. 104) expresses this as "the tyrannical intrusion of a history". Several researchers (Fonagy, 1998; Levine, 1982; Ofer & Weitzman, 1998) describe how children of survivors adequately experience themselves as victims of persecution, since the anti-Semitic extermination ideology of Nazism also includes them by virtue of the fact that they were as yet unborn bearers of Jewish genes. This phenomenon can be connected with Schacter's ideas about a downward-moving spiral, and I envision this as being able to continue into the next generation.

> Depressed individuals are often plagued by the persistence of 'overgeneral' memories that represent the past in a nonspecific and highly negative manner. These persisting overgeneral memories can be amplified by and also contribute to depressed mood, leading to a downward spiral that may culminate in suicide [Schacter, 1999, with ref. to Williams, 1997, p. 40]

Discussion

The child survivors in the pilot study show a strong determination to survive, and they also tell about fortunate circumstances. A majority describe themselves as active, curious, inventive, stubborn, difficult children.[32] The losses of the child survivors are, however, extensive. Memory images invade everyday situations and also central events in life, as shown here, in connection with pregnancy. The themes of the vignettes aim at indicating meaningful connections to the force of invading affects.

From time to time survivors suffer from their memories. Schacter (1996) emphasizes the impact of "memories that keep coming back". Emotional traumatic memories can be "vividly, intrusively, and re-peatedly recollected" (p. 195). The feeling of being constantly con-trolled by memories in this context probably even contains aspects of introjection of the persecutors' attitude towards the survivor dur-ing the Holocaust. Does the survivor suffer from not being able to forget enough so that the past is encapsulated and cannot reach the surface? Schacter (1999) expresses this idea as: "failures to forget can sometimes be even more disabling than forgetting itself" (p. 38). Survivors want either to be able to work with their memories or, otherwise, to be able to forget them. Do survivors suffer from invading memory images that damage the protective psychic barrier to such an extent that memories cannot be worked through? Can they perhaps only learn to adapt to them?

My conclusion drawn from this study is the realization that trau-matic memories from the Holocaust may have affected one of the most sensitive points in the life cycle: reproduction. Psychic devel-opment may have become complicated, particularly because chil-dren were the target of persecution. It is impossible to tell whether problems with reproduction are greater among child survivors than among survivors who were teenagers or adults during the Holocaust. However, we can see that this was a problem for those interviewed in this child survivor group. They were forced to become adults pre-cociously and were never actually able to be children or teenagers with access to parental care that they could internalize and transfer to the next generation in an optimal way.

Not having been a child can make it more difficult to provide a safe environment for one's own children. It can arouse regressive needs that feel threatening because they cannot be satisfied by either a husband/wife or children. Thoughts of one's own children, of initiating a pregnancy, bring a regression in the service of the ego, an identification with the coming child who, for child survivors, can probably release signal anxiety that warns of the coming contact with invading affects. In this situation, a number of women and men have chosen to refrain from having children.

Thoughts of having children seem to create confusing links between different time dimensions. Fragmented life histories indicate a difficulty in experiencing the past as something one has left behind in order to then get on with life (lacking life continuity). Grubrich-Simitis (1984, p. 303) focuses on the living conditions in the death camps and their influence on the ability of the ego to use metaphors, as well as the related ability to structure time in the past, present, and future. She points out that this type of diminished ego function can give rise to a timeless concretization in psychic functioning.

Childbearing as the focus of the trauma

A challenge for psychoanalysts is to help the survivor to see these memory images as memories, not as phenomena in the present. With massive traumas in the life histories of the survivors, psychoanalysts may see this as an impossible task. The current discussion among psychoanalysts (e.g. at the Congress of the European Psychoanalytical Federation, held in Berlin in March 1999) shows that one way to achieve psychic change while working through traumas is to "*reintroduce the concept of time*". Even with such an ambition, the prospects for bringing about change can be poor, although some analysts tend to doubt that this pathology should be more difficult to treat than any other. I want to stress the amount of time needed for working with massive traumas and also how the theme of reproduction seems to be like a focal point with links to different traumatic experiences during genocide. The testimonies seem to be meaningful for the survivors as part of their working-through process, and they also teach us about the Holocaust as well as about consequences of current ethnic cleansing.

> And then I thought that I will be able to enjoy
> such small things that no one else can understand
> Appreciate them. Just the fact that the sun is shining, just
> that there is a flower over there, that is fragrant,

such small things as drinking coffee, sitting and
doing nothing. That I can enjoy. That is life,
and I don't think ordinary people see how
wonderful it is. Just to be able to live. Not be
hungry, not be cold, not be afraid. That is the best
you can get out of life. I have that.[33]

Emilia, born in Poland in 1931

II

WHAT IS BEING COMMUNICATED?

4

Analysing life histories about trauma

I have tried not to be too quick to start theorizing about my findings. This approach has interacted with the circumstance that the interview material as such has "taken a hold of me" to such an extent that it is only in the later stage of the research process that I have been able to discern over-reaching aspects. This means that during the course of the work I have let impressions from the life histories flow in and at the same time I have trusted the possibilities of *containing* what has been conveyed. My professional background has, in all probability, been of great help to my ability to "step in and step out" of the data and to continue the work along the lines set out, without any significant interruptions.

The life histories consist of memories that originate in various *sensory perceptions* from the childhood of the interviewees as well as their conceptions in the present of what they were made to endure during the genocide. For the sake of clarity, I will describe the *content in the memories* and the *recalling of the memories* in the interview situation in two separate parts of the book, even though they constitute two aspects of the same original experience. I will then bring these two aspects together in a theory.

In this chapter a model is presented that has as its starting point the *content* of the interviewees' life histories. The following chapter consists of seven sections, which are organized on the basis of the interviewees' experiences of *historical events*, *life conditions*, and *self-images* during and after the Holocaust.

Detailed narratives

The memories of the interviewees contain a wealth of detail that can be assumed to stem from the fact that they are childhood memories that are often concrete and that the events concern extreme traumatic moments where details are imprinted. The details have been very significant for me in my endeavour to obtain a picture of what the interviewees had experienced. Several authors emphasize the importance of bringing forth the details in texts. Krall (2000), herself a survivor of the Holocaust, stresses the importance for her writing of being able to study "frozen pictures" through details. My effort has also been to create and to develop concepts that are grounded in the interviewees' own statements.

An example of the use of the interviewees' own words—the so-called "in-vivo" concept—is "herding". This is a word that I have heard used in this form only in connection with the survivors' narratives. At the same time, "herding" expresses in a clear way, much better than any other word, what is going on. Normally one would herd animals or things together. Now they felt themselves as human beings subjected to "the first or the second herding".

Rosenberg (2000, p. 6) points out that it is necessary to "have an open mind to the greatest extent possible, in order not to miss that little detail that might turn the whole story upside down or raise it to a new dimension, or make it change its direction. . . ." In addition, a careful retelling of the details is something that I see as especially essential in this text as a complement to the formation of concepts that are more abstract.

The background for this chapter is the development of a conceptual model, a developing analytic tool, which I have then used as the basis for the analysis of the life histories. This has meant that I have tried to bring out as many ideas concerning phenomena as possible in order to arrive at a broad picture of the interviewees' memories pertaining to situations as children and their experiences as surviving adults. I have not stopped at the high-frequency responses, which, as I see it, would not give a complete elucidation of the interviewees' life histories since the study is not based on a random sample. Moreover, information can be lost with such an approach. At the same time, high-frequency responses have sometimes helped to turn my attention in a certain direction.

Generational collapse as a core process

The major concern of the survivors, the core process to which most of the clues in the life histories seemed to be linked, I have named the *generational collapse*. This process is buttressed by two core concepts, which I designate as *perforating* and *space creating*, and the dynamics between these. "Perforating" comprises the inconceivable cruelties to which the Nazis subjected the Jews and the Hutu extremists the Tutsies, respectively, in connection with their systematic persecution. All forms of outward actions carried out by the aggressors and described from the perspective of the persecuted belong into this category. "Space creating" is my term for the inner psychic processes through which the persecuted created their own space for thinking and acting in spite of conditions being minimal and which they described in the interviews.

"Perforating" as a collective concept

The facial expressions of adults and the atmosphere in the home changed radically. Through parents' "discussing"—or the opposite, "being silent"—the children understood that something was about to happen, but not what this was. Generations have been destroyed, dissolved, when the psychic shield has been perforated by sensory perceptions. The psychic membrane has figuratively and literally become "full of holes" by *invading the senses* (something—for example, a frightening voice—forces its way in and destroys), *tearing away* (something—such as family members, important objects, and routines—is taken away and leaves a vacuum) and *body marking* (both actual, such as being abused, and symbolic, such as having to mark one's clothes with a Star of David or with a "T" for "Tutsi" on the identity card). Sensory perceptions have made "imprints" in the personality.

"Space creating" as a collective concept

The children's preoccupation with the facial expressions of the
adults constituted, apart from spatial orientation, probably also a
way of examining the possibility of creating a space and *recapturing life* as it had been when it "was normal". *Space creating* refers
to a psychic room that an individual, as a child, creates according to his or her needs. This phenomenon can have a link to a
real space where, for instance, they could hide for a short while.
Despite absolutely minimal space in the living conditions that predominated during a genocide, glimpses of experiences from the
children's fantasizing in connection with the traumatic events are
recounted associatively in the life stories. These experiences were
probably a prerequisite for existing at all and constitute meaningful themes for human existence. To highlight these moments gives
us a sense of how the interviewees may have used mental strategies
in creating links to inner pictures of important persons and events
to fend off perforating and the fear of dying. Culture and religion
may support this process. By "strategy" I mean situations in which
the strategic/creative process is something that emerges first and
foremost on the spur of the moment, based on existential needs.
Thinking/fantasizing and *thinking/acting* are the phenomena that I
see as the base for space creating.

Linking objects and linking efforts

During the war the children seem to have held on to something or
to someone—the psychic support person who was available. I have
perceived these phenomena as central in the children's space creating, both from the wealth of details in the descriptions and from
the interviewees' endeavour to fantasize and their longing. The interviewees give, for example, recurring descriptions of the nature
of the sleeping places—stumps for pillows, planks to lie on, and
paper sheets—during the war and immediately after the liberation,
respectively. They also describe their parents' songs and meaningful
objects/things they succeeded in keeping with them psychologically
or physically. These linking objects and linking efforts do not need
to have a symbolic value, but they are still important because of the
need for something supporting the self, a survival value.

Table 4.1   Analytic tool for the contents of life histories about trauma
(Kaplan, 2002a)

Perforating	
Invading the senses	Visual impressions, sound experiences, absorbing of atmosphere, facial expression, smell and taste
Tearing away	Father is taken away, school is closed, home is torn away, friends turn their backs, family is split up, hair is shaved off/cut off
Body marking	Star of David on the clothes for the Jews, 'T' in identity card for Tutsi (i.e. marking on the skin), being abused

Space creating	
Thinking/fantasizing	Wishful thinking, playing, assigning meaning, maintaining culture, creating excitement
Thinking/taking action	Having one's own activities, resistance

Age distorting	
Depersonalizing/emotional stunting	Becoming apathetic
Taking responsibility/precocity	Taking care of parents

"Age distorting" as a collective concept

Age distorting contains aspects of both perforating and space creating and can be seen as an aspect of the self-image. "Distorting" is
used here in the sense of "reversal" or "twisting". Thoughts of having children seem to create confusing links between different time
dimensions. Fragmented life histories indicate a difficulty in experiencing the past as something one has left behind in order to then
get on with life—lacking life continuity. Subordinated categories are
depersonalization/emotional stunting and *taking responsibility/precocity.*

I perceive associative connections between *perforating, space creating,* and *age distorting* that have led to the model that functions as
an analytic tool for the contents of the interviews (see Table 4.1)
(Kaplan, 2002a).

5

Children in the Holocaust

In the following, I present the living conditions of children during the Holocaust as described in the interviews. This gives us an idea of the child's perspective on the persecutions through the memories of an adult. The conceptual model serves as an analytic tool. My hypotheses concerning underlying themes are formed upon both the interviewees' statements and my preconceptions.

The presentation starts out with headings and figures that can be related to the life conditions treated in the text. The intention is to facilitate the reading of the text and to give the reader, via the figures, a picture of the phenomena that are brought to light and of the accumulation of massive trauma. I consider the choice of headings, placing the experiences of the interviewees in a historical context, to be essential, considering the relationship between history based on personal experiences and history based on other sources. I cannot know how the interviewees experienced something at the time when it happened. What I find out is how they think now about what they experienced then. I find out what memories and ideas the interviewees have. This is both subjective and contains a core of historical facts, of events that they have partaken in. I therefore see it as essential to have aspects, experience, and historical facts side by side when I analyse the interviews.

Every section begins with aspects of *perforating*. The outer threat was of such a nature as to make it reasonable to assume that perforating constitutes, beyond all doubt, the starting point for the interactions described by the interviewees. I refer to the child survivors as "interviewees" or "the children" in this chapter, as I intend to capture the "child's perspective" in the adult's narrative. I refer to those who helped or saved the children as "helpers"—"helpers" are people other than parents. They were present as significant persons with whom the children could interact.

The historical situations/experienced life conditions that I use as my point of departure are as follows:

A. Anti-Semitism and racial laws;

B. Deportation;

C. The ghetto;

D. Hidden / fugitive / partisan;

E. Concentration camps and work camps;

F. Liberation;

G. Transport to Sweden, and the first encounter with the new country.

With the focus on generational collapse, I illustrate how life conditions experienced by the survivors and expressed through various phenomena in the interviews have taken form and have been accumulated in different historical periods. Metaphorically, this can be thought of as a *spiral* that represents the relation of the interviewee to massive traumatic experiences. The spiral can be seen as *more or less extended* depending on the interviewee's distance or nearness, respectively, to the trauma. In my view the spiral is a one-way process in which I do not see that there can be any positive turning points: instead, what is possible are "islands" of space for thinking or, to be more precise, temporary standstills in a negative spiral that went on gyrating downward until some point in time a number of years subsequent to the liberation. After this, the majority of the interviewees seem to have had experiences that brought positive turning points and made a satisfying life possible. A feeling was engendered of wanting to "go on with life", to "continue surviving"—to have an identity composed of several aspects, not only a survivor identity.

The categories of experiences are based on the statements of the interviewees but have been formulated by me from my vantage point outside the interactional fields that they have described. The categories are, therefore, as mentioned, constructions designed to capture movements that seem to take place associatively between the phenomena in the life histories. They are also intended to help the reader gain a feeling for what the interviewees have experienced. The literature references given in succeeding sections are connected to my way of working with the thoughts that occurred to me afterwards.

As stressed earlier, my selection of quotations represents my interpretation of what I believe can contribute to a better understanding of the interviewees' experiences. I have chosen to present the quotations as true to their spoken language as possible. The 40 interviewees had originally come from as many as nine different countries with different linguistic backgrounds. Most of them came to Sweden directly at the end of the war, but some came later.

However, the use of quotations can bring about some difficulties. Also, since in oral speech the interviewees do not express themselves in complete sentences with a beginning and an end, it has been up to me to determine where the quotation should begin and end. The intention has been to keep the text from becoming too lengthy while at the same time preserving the person's train of thought in the presentation.

A   Anti-Semitism and racial laws

". . . now the inconceivable could happen to us, whatever that might be."[1]

Experiences \ Outer threats	Anti-semitism/ Racial laws	Deporta-tion	Ghetto	Hidden/ Fugitive/ Partisan	Camps	Liberation	Encounter with Sweden/ Post-wartime
Perforating							
Space creating							
Age distorting							

Since the points of departure for my study are historical events that took on a decisive significance for the lives of the interviewees, I have made a summary based on Dwork's research work concerning conditions for Jewish children (1991, pp. 7–25). The normal structure of Jewish life had begun to be destroyed from the time of the German elections in 1933 and the appointment of Hitler as chancellor:

1. Confiscation and destruction of Jewish property was the first stage in the machinery of the Nazis' genocide.
2. The destruction of the Jews began with a legal definition. The Nazis defined Jewish in terms of the concept of race rather than of religion. According to Nazi ideology, Judaism was hereditary.
3. Poland was the first country to be occupied by Germany, followed by country after country. Similar laws were passed in the different

countries. Legal definitions were extensive. They reflected an idea of Jews as "the others", "the strange beings" who, because of their lineage, could never be a part of Aryan society.

4.   The first actions with immediate consequences were the many laws and decrees that were put into effect in order to remove Jews from positions of general influence and to render them destitute by seizing their livelihood and barring them from a number of positions in Christian companies.

5.   The Nuremberg laws came into effect in September 1935 and meant far-reaching anti-Semitic legislation.

6.   As long as it was a matter of economic deprivation, the children were not especially affected, according to Dwork (1991). Their families were intact.

7.   The life situation of childhood was shaken, however, by the restrictions surrounding normal social life. This occurred when the second wave of anti-Semitic legislation, which was designed to ensure the social segregation of the Jewish people, came into effect. The subculture of childhood life was deeply affected by these decrees and rules. The consequences were felt in the daily activities of the children. The first and the worst of all was the barring of Jewish children from state schools. Attending school was the absolute social norm for children, a fixed activity in their lives.

8.   The immediate reactions concerned being excluded, which brought a psychic shock. The children's reactions were centred around their Jewish identity. They were confronted for the first time with the concept of being Jewish: they were no longer members of society, they were outcasts.

9.   There were three steps in the social isolation process to which the children were subjected:
     ⯈ being barred from school;
     ⯈ being forbidden to participate in countless aspects of daily life, which also meant a separation from their Christian neighbours and friends;
     ⯈ being forced to use the star of David, in the centre of which was inscribed "Jew".

As noted, the interviewees came from nine different countries that were occupied by Germans at various points in time. The lengths of time during which the respective countries were directly affected by the war thus varied. At the same time, it seems that the outbreak of the war in 1939 affected Jews even in countries that were not as yet directly involved, such as, for example, Hungary. Anti-Semitism made itself felt among the local population, and the interviewees sensed something threatening in the air. The home, the neighbourhood, and the school assume central places in their memories. Parents, friends, grandmother, and nanny are among the persons of central importance. Furniture and rooms—especially windows—belong to the significant attributes, as do bicycles, ice-skates, and head-dresses.

Perforating

Perforating is the utmost foundation for *generational tearing apart*. I am therefore beginning this and the subsequent sections in this chapter by describing how I form the basis for my assumptions about this aspect of the process. Then I describe how perforating appears to have affected the interviewees' *space creating* activities and how the force in the *breaking-point*, the confrontation between perforating and the need for psychic space, space creating, seems to have led to age distorting. Perforating constitutes, as stated previously, a collective concept for invading of the senses, tearing away, and body marking. In the sections that follow it will be made evident how various kinds of perforating accumulated for the interviewees—that is, how the later invasions of the senses were added to those that occurred earlier.

Invading of the senses

Absorbing the atmosphere: looking into the faces of adults

There are significant phenomena that manifested themselves from the time that the interviewees faced the early signs of anti-Semitism and that continue to manifest themselves in similar ways in the everyday life of the interviewees today. These phenomena concern observations of adults and seem directly related to traumatization during the Holocaust. One such phenomenon is *"to look into and read what is in a face"*. During the early stages of anti-Semitism the children interpreted the atmosphere at home in this way. When they themselves started to be persecuted, they saw in *the faces of others* how they themselves believed that they were being seen.

It made a strong impression on the interviewees that people who were close to them started *to act different* as anti-Semitism increased and racial laws were implemented. Parents appeared upset, sometimes panicky. Some parents went into a state of depression and cried but did not put what was going on into words. "My father . . . *he cried and said absolutely nothing . . .*" As I see it, even before the occupation of their home country, the children came into *contact with the persecutors indirectly*, through their parents. Faces and windows generally seem to have constituted meaningful boundaries for outer realities and inner fantasy life. At the same time, opposite reactions also occurred in the form of *silence*, which the children interpreted as *absence of reactions*. They could observe that "mother said absolutely nothing, and father spoke not a single word, and grandmother just sat there".

This led to great distress, since the children themselves registered by way of voices on the news on the radio and the atmosphere among their friends, among others, that serious changes were in the making. It seems as though they *thought with their bodies*. "In my absolutely childish spirit, in the absence of every trace of real information, I remember that I felt such *a concrete danger for our lives—I was thinking in principle with the heart of a child* because the adults, they did not seem to have realized the magnitude of the danger as yet."[2]

Absorbing, compressing, of the atmosphere

The facial expressions of the adults and the atmosphere in the home can be said to have been *absorbed* by the children. The children may have read their parents' thoughts when they looked into their faces. The parents' distress can have been generated when they thought about what could happen to the children and about how they themselves would not be able to cope with the children's distress in the threatening situation that prevailed for all of them. Perhaps the children tried to re-create the relationship that they were used to by seeking eye contact with their parents in the hope that this contact would assure them that nothing dangerous was going to happen. The interviewees give a somewhat different picture from the one given by Dwork (1991) when she says that the children were not so aware of the changes before they themselves were directly affected.

As one survivor expressed it: "The atmosphere became more and more *compressed*, dense. You could feel something in the air quite simply." Another remembered, "We started to be afraid of our neighbours." What the interviewees describe as *compressed atmosphere* can be understood to mean that *the air around them closed in, the space for their existence shrank*. This feeling could coincide with and possibly be intensified by the way the parents denied what was going on. Another said: "We really lived under threat and at the same time in some sort of idyll, isn't that odd? The duality was there all the time!" Relatives could show up and "in the middle of everything, the atmosphere was very bright". The parents might even deny the meaning of the attacks that the children were subjected to and say, "That was a silly girl, so don't let it bother you", or sometimes they might even suggest that their own child must have "done something to provoke the fight". It happened that the children had to ask the parents to follow them to school so that they would see with their own eyes what was going on.

False sense of security in the Jewish network

The Jewish network seems to have been strong. Regardless of whether the family had a strong or a weak Jewish identity, they normally lived in "Jewish" neighbourhoods. Perhaps the families were lulled into a "false" sense of security in that they had each other. They shut out the world outside as a parallel action to being isolated as Jewish families by non-Jews. To sum up, the interviewees give descriptions that could indicate that as children they were more unreservedly receptive to a changed atmosphere at home and in their surroundings than were the adults.

Absorbing sounds: hearing what the adults are talking about

In addition to the facial expressions of adults, a perceived invasion of new sounds seems to have been the most obvious form of perforating in what was otherwise a relatively secure atmosphere in the home and which as children they felt themselves to be a part of. The invasion of new sounds made for clear auditory memories. Recurring discussions among the adults constitute permanent memories that a majority of the interviewees have in common. As children, they were sensitively alert to how the adults spoke, but most often they did not understand the content. They could not piece together the auditory fragments into something that could be understood but "just felt that something was threatening us and that it could get worse". Julia heard someone say, "Don't talk in front of the child."[3] Sometimes the parents disagreed about how to deal with the situation. Eva remembers how they "quarrelled at night, and I eavesdropped".[4] In such circumstances the children could feel fear at the same time as success in learning the truth.

From the *parents' perspective*, a picture can be conceived of as an extremely strained position between frightening news and troubled, sometimes difficult children. From the *children's perspective*, a change could be seen in the adults, and this made the children even more anxious. Oscar said: "Lots of men came to see father, and they closed the doors, and they talked and they whispered."[5] The children understood in part by "picking up . . . what the adults said." "I was very curious, and I often stayed near the adults and listened to what they said and so on, so I was rather well-informed somehow to be as little as I was",[6] said Leon: "We were at my grandmother's and grandfather's for dinner sitting *around a large table,* and we were all gathered there . . . and then they started to speak . . . I remember that, that they spoke of mass graves and of people that were shot down in mass graves, they spoke of slaked lime that was poured over people . . . And then I remember that someone said, 'Don't say that in front of the child.' But this is to be sure something that I remember very very strongly, yes, and that I, I understood that this was something horrible that could happen."[7]

That parents did not talk to children about what was going on seems to have been connected to several factors. The interviewees believe that the parents thought that they were protecting the children by not telling them. Part of the explanation is most probably that people did not inform children about things in the 1930s in the same way as we do today. "In those days, it was not like now, when parents talk to their children right and left; no, back then, people did not discuss serious matters in the presence of children."[8] Many of the persons interviewed also believe the adults' silence can have had to do with their own denial of the circumstances—a way of shielding themselves, which the interviewees experienced that they as children were not fooled by. Some parents refrained from informing the children about what they knew and of the possible plans that they were making out of fear that *the children would not be able to keep quiet in front of the neighbours* and thus jeopardize a planned route of escape, for example. It was also to be kept from the neighbours that a person "belonged to the Zionist movement". Sometimes the children were aware that plans were being made for them. "A terrible sense of fright naturally arose when the adults spoke to each other." The mothers just said that now, "we are going there and going there", "I had no idea what it all meant."[9] The parents most often replied, "that's just the way it is", without explanations.

Sometimes interviewees express relief over not having heard everything that their parents spoke about. It has later become known that some people thought the children should be sent to the countryside. If the interviewees had heard that, they would have become very distraught.

Invading sounds: "a whirlwind of hate on the radio"[10]

After the German occupation of their native country had begun, most the of interviewees mention, directly or indirectly, that their first memory of something traumatic was "the *voice on the radio* . . . perhaps the atmosphere among people, the panic that broke out in the house."[11] Julia recalls, "As a child I often told my mother not to knit her brow. She could be strict sometimes, no doubt, but I think those wrinkles had more to do with what she was hearing on the radio."[12] The news broadcasts on the radio also seem to have been experienced as a *sound invasion* in the home. When the interviewees brought these memories back to life, they repeated the sounds just as though they had heard them recently. "Hitler's speeches were broadcast on the radio and through loudspeakers. And I thought it was really horrid to hear his howling . . . He howled that *Sieg Heil* and the chorus . . . the chorus of evil in the background when the crowd echoed him. *And it was that sound, his voice in itself was terrifying enough without needing to understand what he said.*"[13] "We had a short-wave radio that we could hook up. And that voice, *that's not something you easily forget.* So, of course, we knew then that those thick clouds, they

were there and they were moving around all the time."[14] This particular child survivor formed *her own images of what she heard as a young
girl.* "The BBC's broadcasts *dingdingdingding . . . dingdingdingding . . .*
I was still not very old when it happened. It was first at the time when
everything so to say came to a crisis, *it* was the autumn of 1943, that
I woke up and felt more like an adult. You know, I was fourteen years old."[15]
Regarding the cases in which the interviewees imitate significant
sounds, it is my understanding that it usually seems to mean that
they are being transferred to the occasion of the trauma. They are
repeating the situation that they lived through, without any change
being made in the psychic reality. In certain cases this can mean that
the event took on meaning afterwards, based on experiences and
knowledge that the person gained later in life.

At the same time, the radio as well as the telephone also meant a
sense of security, a contact with "the outer world". "We were still able
to have a telephone, and *I still can feel my heart beating fast when I hear
those familiar tones, tatatatum* [on the radio]. The signature tones were
from Beethoven's Fifth Symphony, because it was at . . . it was absolutely the greatest strength and comfort."[16] On 20 September 1939,
it was decided that Jews were forbidden to have radios (Bruchfeld
& Levine, 1999). In certain areas—such as, for example, in certain
areas of Czechoslovakia—the possibilities of hearing the news were
generally bad. Soldiers who passed by, as well as the mailman and the
priest, the people who "moved around", gave some information. "We
heard, but *no one believed it, that was our tragedy.* We did not believe
that such things could happen. We expected things to get better."[17]

Invading sounds: aeroplane noise

Sounds invaded the children's auditory barriers from many different
directions. Edith says: "I remember that we woke up in the morning
to wave after wave of aeroplanes flying over the house, and we had
the radio on at the same time, and we were receiving various messages . . . there was general chaos."[18]

Other sounds

Jeers and name-calling constitute strong sound memories.[19] They
perforated, they tore apart a sense of identity and context. Isolation
increased. Other children shouted "louder and louder that we were

Jews" and ". . . those words of anti-Semitism coming from other children had a certain *lilting intonation*"[20] . . . "stinking Jewess".[21] Even
before Jewish children were prohibited from going to school, one
of the consequences of the persecution was that they did not dare
or want to go to school. "I hated going to school . . . I thought it
was so dreadful to go there. I felt the whole time that *I could not say
what it was.*"[22]

We can ask ourselves which phenomenon develops first, both
in the world of a baby and also during trauma. Winnicott puts the
emphasis on the visual signals from the mother's face and says that
it is from these that the child builds up the self, while Anzieu (1985)
gives evidence for *an even earlier mirroring of sound*—or of a skin of
hearing and sound—and its function for the psychic apparatus's
ability to take note and later to symbolize. The adults' acoustical in-
terventions can constitute the very beginning and perhaps a *prototype*
for future differentiational abilities.

Observing the world: looking out of the window

Looking at what was going on by the window, just as "looking into
faces", has been shown to be an especially significant phenomenon
around which the interviewees have directed their attention during
all of the historical periods.

Many remember the occupation of their native country, usually
through some detail that caught their attention and was associated
with the trauma: "Yes . . . I must have been about four years old or
something like that, I would think. And I remember very strongly . . .
the 9th of April 1940, because I remember that I stood together with
my mother and *looked out of the window* and the sky was completely
black with those huge German bombers with swastikas. I remember
it really clearly. *I stood there and held her hand, and she had a little black
hat on her head,* a pillbox hat, one of those with a ribbon, and a black
suit, and we were going to run out and pick up my sister at school.
I remember, I remember it very well that we stood there and *looked
out.*"[23]

The *earliest memory* of one of the interviewees is how she literally
was about to fall out, over to the other side, "I was looking out of the
window at a red car, and I leaned so far out that I almost fell out,
and my mother caught me just in time."[24] Looking out the window
could mean witnessing acts of violence outside the home and out-

side the school. "I saw it from the window when the police smashed milk bottles and eggs and everything imaginable . . . the Ukrainian women had *white kerchiefs on their heads*."[25] "I remember their *beautiful hats with cock feathers* . . . in the hat. It was the Hungarian police."[26] Headdresses, when they caught the child's interest, can have served as a distraction manoeuvre away from the horrible acts that she saw before her, something to "*rest the thoughts on. And I don't know if we understood the seriousness of it* . . . I had just had *my eleventh birthday.*"[27] At the window they were *alone* or *felt alone* in the presence of their parents. The children observed their parents' reactions at the window. To hear their parents crying intensified the feeling that the safety in their life was being sucked away, sucked out the window by the power of the brutalities that they saw just outside their home. Parents warned them not to get too close to the window in case it might break. At school, "all of the children *hung out the windows* and looked at the aeroplanes". In most cases safety still existed *inside the window and walls of the house*. To be alone inside an air raid shelter was, however, a very threatening situation. "I came home from school and no one was home. Then the air raid alarm went off, and I had to go down to the cellar, and the neighbours were not at home either, so I sat alone down there in the laundry room. *Sandbags were stacked in front of the windows,* and I was terribly, terribly afraid . . . that I wouldn't be able to get out of that place and that no one would know that I was there—that terrified me. And that feeling *stayed with me for many, many years* and *led to claustrophobia.*"[28]

Tearing away

The children's nanny is forced to leave

Significant persons, toys, and pets were brutally torn out of the children's lives. Sometimes a Christian nanny was living in the family, and she was not allowed to stay with a Jewish family in accordance with the racial laws. These nannies often served as "assistant mothers", and their sudden forced departure was experienced as a "great tragedy."[29] According to many of the interviewees, this was "the first truly great personal tragedy": "a very great personal loss" . . . that she was no longer present. One interviewee said that her nanny had "a great influence on all of our lives . . . she had lived with us long *before I was born*, so she was a part of my world and of my family."[30]

Henry said, "We had help at home, there was a 'jadzia'. That is a person who . . . *was present at my birth.* She was a Catholic, and *she regarded us as her own children*."[31] Sometimes the nanny seems to have taken the mother's place. "I idolized her",[32] said Emilia. "I think it was the greatest love that I have ever felt towards any woman that I have loved",[33] said Eva.

A reunion with a nanny after the war could be the *only link to the past*—the only person left alive and who had met the parents and could tell the child survivor about them. Sandor says: "And then we found her, and she took out a little, I think it was a mezuza, one of those little holy objects that she had been given by our parents when she converted to Judaism (which she kept a secret) . . . she showed that she often took it out and thought about them."[34] The nanny's actions and the stance she took illustrate the positive force in the network in which Sandor grew up, of which the nanny was also a part.

Friends turn their backs—are "torn away"—through their betrayals

Auditory memories consisting of jeers and name-calling have already been described. The time had come when non-Jewish friends and neighbours were no longer a part of everyday life. "This meant great danger when dusk began to fall as we left school in the afternoon . . . to go *ice-skating* together with other children, who were Christian, I didn't dare do that . . . I had to stop any activities that I did together with anyone other than Jews",[35] said Lisa. The children could no longer "go to parties when it was Christmas, because I was Jewish. I could never act in their plays because I was Jewish",[36] said Ella. Isolation increased rapidly. Only among Jews could a Jewish child feel safe. It is my understanding that the memory of going ice-skating is connected to a sense of security and the playful, fun times before the persecutions, *the freedom to move fast and freely!*

As a reflecting adult, the interviewee can say that "there was this feeling of being *outside, apart*". Changes in their friends' behaviour were shocking for the children: "It was impossible to understand what was being done to me, to put it simply."[37] Surprise was expressed over "what they meant by looking down" at the Jewish children who had recently been their friends.[38] The earlier self-image that the Jewish children had as belonging to the group had to be abandoned. The children soon became aware that their appearance could reveal that they were Jews—at least, that is how they experienced it: they felt they emanated something special. They drew this conclusion based on the changes in the *atmosphere between themselves and the other individuals*. Friends were torn away because they were changed: "Seven-year olds in the first grade told me that I was a dirty Jew, and a damned Jew, and that I should go to Palestine . . . they *threatened to throw me down all the stairs*."[39] Liv found "drawings in [her] desk at school, caricatures of Jews, with illustrations of fruits, perhaps meant to represent fruits from Palestine. There was a rhyme in Polish, something like—'apples up there, lemons down there—get out of here, Jew, and to your Palestine fare'." The word used for Jews in Polish was an especially dirty word that cannot be translated. Perforating of the psychic shield could be expressed in bodily metaphors, and Sandor says, "the world outside generally felt threatening, and I *felt anti-Semitism on my own body at a* rather *early stage.*[40] The noose was pulled tighter and tighter as the time for the German occupation drew nearer."[41] *Having to re-assess friendship was extremely painful, "one of the greatest betrayals"*: "At the same time, I had a good friend . . . We had been together for two years . . . and that was one of the greatest betrayals, coming from a Hungarian Christian boy who *has one hand on the one side of my shoulder and with the other hand he punches me,* in the face and since we have been friends for two years *and I have not had, he did not have any direct reason, I had not given him any reason to do it, to call me a Jewish swine.* When my mother goes with me to see his mother and to complain about this, she is called a Jewish whore and is told to get out of there. And so I become gradually aware and a feeling of anxiety rises in me, I see that we are free game for the Hungarians or Rumanians who live around us. This kind of a thing could happen to me at the age of twelve."[42]

The interviewees seem to have bodily memories, both of being touched (the friend had his "hand on the one side of my shoulder"), and of being struck—body marking (see also below).

School is closed

School was closed, while everything else was going on as usual. The closing of the school seems to have been the *determining event* for making the children aware that something very serious was going to happen. They themselves were *directly affected*, sent home from school. The terror in the parents' faces seems to have been absorbed in the children: "I believe that I didn't feel anything up to a certain point, but then it came to me very quickly and the great shock, that I know, that on that very day we were sent home from school and I know that father came home very upset and then, then I know that the feeling in the atmosphere was like that at home, that now, now, the time had come, now the inconceivable could happen, inconceivable for me, it could happen to us. I did not really understand what it was, but now, now was the time, now it could happen, the thing we were afraid of, whatever it was [laughs]. And that *I saw the horror* that it meant for my parents, I took that in, but . . . yes, there's not much more you can do as a child, is there . . . And after that, things also became so, for example, to go to school was more dangerous, and gradually there was no school at all, you know, but there was a little interval in-between."[43]

The interviewees told how astonished they had been that everything in society outside *seemed to be so normal,* "*people lived like we did before,* and I saw children who were walking out of school, and they had those sorts of backpacks on their backs . . . and I was in fact very envious that they could go to school."[44] At the same time the person being interviewed emphasizes that there was a "little interval in-between"—a little space to get themselves together before the real danger came.

Space for play shrinks

It was popular to go ice-skating, but the good skating rink near the school could not be used. In those days ice-skates had to be screwed tight to the shoes "then when you had skated maybe two steps, they fell off, and you had to screw them on again . . . there was not much ice either, so you skated on the small spots that you could find."[45]

Bicycles are torn away

Rules were put into effect forbidding Jews from using certain means of transportation. The most tangible for the children was that they were no longer allowed to ride bicycles! *To ride a bike* and *to ride bikes together recur as significant phenomena* in several of the historical phases covered in the life histories of the interviewees. Both to ride bikes and to go ice-skating, as was mentioned earlier, can be seen symbolically as ways to move fast, as *symbols of freedom.*

Before the war toys could be things that people made themselves. They might take a bicycle wheel, set it into motion with a stick, and then run. The older children read a lot as long as there were books available, but the bicycle seems to have been in a league of its own, Sofia says: "I read as many books as I could get my hands on." "It was a very limited existence, and my little brother, he loved to ride a bike, and I did too",[46] Marysia says. "I was given a bike that was red and blue and very nice-looking, and *it was the only time in my life that I bicycled. It was . . . two months in the summer of '39.* Why I am telling this is just because *later the Germans took our bikes.*"[47] And Marianne remembers "that we had to turn in my bike. My father went and turned in my . . . our bi . . . my bicycle . . . and then a radio . . . (it is as) cloudy images in my memory from the one day to the other. And I loved (to) bicycle"![48]

Shifting of the sense of danger

The sense of danger was shifted from the real threat to the children's own things, toys, and pets, which by actual fact belonged to the *children's everyday life* and to the essentials of their lives. Fanny tells about a memory: "I was maybe six years old, it was a short time after my birthday in May and I had been given a *ball* . . . I was very pleased with it . . . with this ball; (my) uncle and I went to the park near us and suddenly the gates were closed . . . soldiers had closed the gates, and they rounded people up at the gates, where they divided them into groups for work camps or for interrogation, everyone stood in line, and they were all very frightened about whether they would be detained or not, and I was also very scared about whether they would take me or not and whether they would take (my uncle), *I was afraid that they were going to take my ball, and this illustrates very well . . .*"[49]

Body marking

Fighting between children

The children most often began to feel anti-Semitism in their very flesh as a result of having their senses invaded and having things torn away. When the climate became harsher for Jews, the children often experienced perforating of their bodies. "I hated winter because then . . . there were lots of snowballs that they threw at me . . . they threw them at everyone, but especially at me."[50] The body was injured, "had never learned to hit back", got "jumped on" by children in the street. "We were not equipped for . . . street fights . . . none of us had been brought up to be able to fight."[51] There are those who point out that "it always came from the children . . . most of the time it's the children who are the cruellest"![52] As described earlier, a profound sense of betrayal arose when people who had been known as good friends now attacked the children and their families.

Body marking can be compared to Anzieu's (1985) description of the vulnerability of the skin. According to Anzieu, the skin is a system that embodies several types of sensory organs (such as touch, pressure, pain, warmth). It has outer connections with other external sensory organs (hearing, seeing, smelling, tasting) and with perceptions of movement and balance. The skin combines the dimensions of space and time. He also states that the skin is meaty and easily hurt; it divides and unites other types of senses, and it has a middle position, a transitional role.

Marking of "the skin":
being forced to wear the Star of David on clothes

The humiliations intensified. As a part of the racial laws, Jews were forced to wear the Star of David on their clothes. This was experienced by the interviewees as "leprosy" and a sudden degradation into a "non-human":[53] "We were of another sort, so to speak."[54] The routines concerning the star are remembered in detail: "It had to have the yellow colour of a lemon", "canary yellow, not just any old yellow", "angry yellow", and "it had to be exact to the millimetre". In certain places they first had "white bands on the left arm with a blue Jewish star" and at that time the law applied to everyone over twelve years of age. Later even the younger children had to wear a star. The yellow star had to be sewn on. Maria has an image "in my memory of my mother sewing the Jewish star on my winter coats and dresses. And she sewed theirs as well, and I can see the needle . . . and thread in front of me."[55] Clothes were perforated like hides that had to be branded. So far, however, there was still a space left for this girl at home near her mother, who was doing her sewing.

Space creating

The interview sequences presented here have shown experiences of traumatic events and utilization of attributes that became significant. When the children listened to the adults talking and interpreted the looks on the adults' faces, they felt distress. The signals from the faces resulted in the children's having a need to create space for themselves. Winnicott (1971 p. 23) describes a potential psychic area of experience *between* the inner psychic world and the outer reality, which exists "as a resting place for the individual . . . and which is occupied with keeping the inner and the outer reality apart and with seeing the relationship between them at the same time." The concept of "resting place" resembles the aspect that I designate as "space creating".

As mentioned earlier, Winnicott (1967) emphasizes visual signals and discusses a child's reactions when confronted with "rigidity" in a mother's defence and says that *children look around for other ways to attain something for themselves.* The interview sequences in the subsequent sections show how thoughts have been woven around occurrences and attributes whereupon they have *provided substance for acts of space creating.* These creative acts made it possible for the children to preserve a sense of their own existence and personal integrity.

As long as anti-Semitism was in the early stages, the space to move around in was, of course, considerably larger than it would come to be during later stages of the Holocaust, when phenomena connected to the occurrences and attributes mentioned went beyond being *significant activities*—games, traditions—and became *defence strategies.* A piece of jewellery that a girl had received from her grandmother and that she wore occasionally later became something that she held on to tightly and kept secret. Prayers that a boy read on Fridays became something that he said several times a day. The way of relating to attributes/activities most probably changed in accord with the *intensity of the outer threat.* In the most perilous stages of the Holocaust the jewellery was no longer accessible, and the child was forced into silence. In these circumstances it can be said that the possibility for the child to create space for herself, even a little space, was *virtually non-existent.* My purpose in focusing on space creating in spite of this is to accentuate the creative process, which could be kept alive, like a candle that could be kept burning with a very small flame. It could thus counteract a total breakdown and function instead as *an element* in the generational linking process. The children's occasional thoughts and actions can be seen as aspects of cultural actions that could, in later stages of life, be transformed into productive work and creative endeavours, serving as a link, a reconciliation of generational destruction for the few who survived.

Thinking/fantasizing

The interviewees state that as children they had few or no thoughts about what war could mean. They "had other things on their minds" or "I heard people saying that now the war is coming but I didn't think it had anything to do with me."[56] However, some of the interviewees explain very clearly how "it was just as horrible for me, even though I saw it through the eyes of a child".

Spatial orientation

The interviewees describe different degrees of closeness and distance, respectively, to their parents. As mentioned earlier, they seemed to have made careful note of the *new sounds* in their environment, but they also noted *how* they stood in relation to their parents, *what* the parents were doing, and *how* the parents reacted in traumatic situations. Unusually detailed descriptions of the childhood home and of "forms of housing" during the later stages of the war recur in many life histories, as do accounts of phenomena such as *"looking out of windows."* Those who were younger remember individual items and how large they were. It could be surmised that these items had some significance. Alice has an image of some furniture in her memory: "a large chest, large bookshelf, I remember the radio, a huge radio which later disappeared . . . had to be turned in. It was huge, and I loved to listen to it, I remember that. But it's just an image."[57] *Auditory memories, memories of spatial orientation,* and *visual memories* are persistent memories that seem to *function as building blocks* in the memory sequences. Many memories of moments in the company of parents are carefully depicted in terms of spatial orientation and give us an understanding of how they as *children regulated the distance to their mothers and fathers* in order to feel safe. Sandor tells of an incident in which his family was assaulted by an anti-Semitic youth. "And mother and father had dressed up in their fine Sabbath clothes and I went together . . . and father was farthest out, then came mother, and I was next, and I *held my mother's hand on that side* . . . I remember that I saw him coming, and when we passed each other, he went up to my father's side and thrust his shoulder full force against father's shoulder. He said, 'Have you put on your masquerade clothes, you dirty Jew?'"[58] Eva remembers that "a clear change took place, partly because we had to change wagons (which were pulled) and we had to sleep in different places. The bed was large, and *I got to share a bed with mother.*"[59] "They often, very often, spoke of the war, and it . . . I was not interested in listening, so I always went off with some of my little cousins. But it felt like something truly horrible was going to happen, and the last summer that was normal, so to say, the summer of 1939, I spent that summer in the countryside."[60]

The phenomena that the interviewees bring into focus are similar to Anzieu's description (1989) of how babies prepare the self to be structured on the basis of the third dimension of space (orientation and distance) and on the basis of time. The nature of the childhood home has usually been recounted with a great wealth of detail, which is probably a strong and symbolic indication of the links to the interviewees' roots and families. That they had a need to limit the space for "their own world" was a strong element in the interviewees' memories. The children would go off on their own to play.

Determining significance of attributes

As we have observed in the sequences described, bicycles and ice-skates were significant attributes. Dolls and babies, which can signify fantasies about the future and about growth, are present in a number of remembered images. Marysia said, "*I was going to be a mother and have many children.* . . . I had dolls, and I made things nice for my dolls . . . and when the cook was not in the kitchen, I would go and take things from the refrigerator, and I cut the meat into small pieces, into small pieces of meat to give my dolls."[61] In this story we can also discern a recurring theme in the different life histories— that is, stealing food for the family. Stealing food can also be seen as a transitional phenomenon in Winnicott's terminology—that is, also as a psychological link to the mother.

The Star of David, which was primarily associated with degradation and being an outcast, could, in certain cases, mean an affirmation of a child's age and existence. The most important thing for
some children seems to have been the demarcation of who was
younger and who was older than twelve. This seems to have meant
more to them than the actual reason for having to be marked. "Before you were twelve, you didn't need to have any band, so I was very
proud when I could go and buy a band for myself. That's why I still
have it, because it was so fresh and clean."

"Normalizing": a child's birth and birthday

The associations that were often made by the interviewees to their
own births and birthdays in the context of memories of trauma—
like, for example: "It was some days after my birthday"—are interpreted by me as space creating. This reflects the person's need to
assert her own existence, a reminder that she existed then and exists today.
The example mentioned can be seen as a way to counteract the generational tearing apart that resulted from the Holocaust. I return to
this matter in Part IV, on trauma linking and generational linking
processes. Interviewees' accounts of birthday celebrations prior to
the outbreak of the war can be linked to other recurring Holocaust
themes that seem to touch upon an endeavour to maintain a "normal life" even under the most unbearable of circumstances. Oscar
says: *"I remember my birthdays very well.* They were extremely festive
occasions, with lots of children, and *since my father obviously loved me
more than anything . . . on earth,* I remember one particular birthday,
that he had rented a barrel organ, and he dressed up as an Italian
organ-grinder, and came into our large living-room. And there he
stood in his costume, and I did not recognize my father. And there
were balloons, there was everything. The traditional food to have at
a birthday was in fact not birthday cake. We had pastries, but this
time there was also a wonderful sweet roll with thick, rich icing and
loads and loads of nuts. *Since I was little, I thought that all of this was
more or less gigantic.* There was one of those little twists that you see
in bakeries sometimes. It looked like that, and everyone had to eat
it, and in the middle was . . . a hole in the middle where there was
always *one candle more than the birthday years.* And then you always
had to blow out all of the candles, but that one candle was not lit.

It was . . . it was supposed to bring luck during the coming year and was kept to be lit the next year. I don't know if that was a common tradition, but that's what we did in any case."[62]

Oscar has a special memory of that birthday when he did not recognize his father. That could be a cover memory, a displacement, for his experiences of the distortion that he later came to see in his father as a result of time spent in concentration camps. This kind of phenomenon has been described by Jucovy (1992). On top of this, he remembers delicious bakery goods in detail, the kind of thing that he was deprived of later, as well as the tradition of having "one more candle than the birthday years" on the cake in order "to bring luck for the coming year". He later came to change his age, to add some years, in order to survive.

Maintaining culture and religion

The memory of being close to their fathers and of the talks they had, which can have been idealized to a certain extent in retrospect, seems to have been fundamental for many of the interviewees. "He talked to me quite a lot. We often took long walks together." For the majority of the interviewees, the time spent with the family around the dinner table constitutes a positive memory. Those who came from Jewish Orthodox environments remember the walk to the synagogue on the Sabbath, side by side with their parents. Jewish traditions in the home were something that some of them could "rest" their thoughts in during brief periods of time in the later phases of the Holocaust (see further below).

Some of the interviewees lived a secularized life. Even though 98% of their social life was with other Jews, they did not observe any of the traditions themselves. "We went along, but we did not participate in the rituals ourselves. It was simply a part of our social life." Many saw their parents as intellectuals who were striving to "take themselves out of a restricted Jewish life" and to become "world citizens" in a world where "everyone was equal" and people were interested in a number of religions and ideologies. However, Jewish traditions and the *family get-togethers* in connection with them meant *a sense of security in life* for the majority.

Thinking / taking action

Resisting: being a "difficult child"

A majority describe themselves as difficult, refusing to eat, active, curious, or wicked as children. Julia recalls: "I was a difficult and spoilt child."[63] Eva comments, "I was no doubt a pest when I was little."[64] A number of children nicked apples and did not do as they were told. This can be understood in several ways. It may have to do with *survivor guilt*, whereby the feelings around having survived are easier to "bear" if a person connects her life history with having been a difficult child. It can even be an *attempt* at an explanation, that a person could survive by being difficult.

If reality was actually the way that the interviewees remembered it, that they were in fact difficult, this could be understood as a *natural reaction*. This was a way to gain the attention—and thus *the space*—that they as children (unconsciously) felt that they deserved. Perhaps they "provoked a crisis" so that they could be reprimanded and thus "repaired" (Winnicott, 1956)—that is, this was a posture of resistance.

Maintaining contact with friends

Some of the Jewish children tried to maintain contact with non-Jewish friends. "I was very small and skinny, but I made it"[65] (and was accepted by the others). The importance of maintaining contact with friends could be that it was a way of *maintaining contact with life*, with that which was *the normal*.

Protests against "marking"

Attempts were made among Polish–Jewish youths to create space for themselves, to resist, for example by breaking free from being marked. Sometimes the star was pinned on with "needles or safety pins" and "then I remember that they were hunted down, *I saw that myself*. There were some who used poppers, so it was easy to take it off and put it back, but that was absolutely not allowed." "And there could be raids, and then they pulled it off fast so that they could not see that they were Jews, and *they hid it in their pocket* or something like that. Of course the Germans soon got wise to what was happening, so it was not so practical. Then they decided that we had to wear the Jewish star, a yellow Jewish star with a black text instead, on the left side right under the breast [sobs]."[66] "So we took off the Star of David and you could see it, the mark showed up, because the coat was dirty and the place marking where the star had been was light."[67] Such action was risky. In addition, it was not possible to get rid of the mark once it had been made. You could see a mark where a star had been placed.

"Tricking" the soldiers

The interviewees who came as refugee children from Denmark told about "a resistance of sorts", which they tried to carry out "in their childishness". The children "hated it" when they saw German soldiers marching in the streets of Copenhagen and "*bellowing out their songs*", so they would go the long way round in order to avoid the soldiers. "Sometimes we were so happy that they asked us directions, because then it was quite fun to give them *the opposite directions.* That was our way of resisting."[68] There was even an organized resistance among children in Denmark: "You had a five-penny coin, a two-penny coin and two one-penny coins made of copper. Those were the Danish coins. They had holes in them, so you could tie these four coins together with a red and a white ribbon and then you could walk around with them, you polished them very nicely and went around with them. There were those nine pennies in four coins, the 9th of April. And I mean this was a sort of symbol of resistance. All the children had these copper coins. In a similar way we went around a lot with small caps, almost like yarmulkas, on our heads. We knitted them or crocheted them, and they were, you see, in the colours of the Royal Air Force. Red inside and blue . . . No, red inside and blue and white outside. Those three colours that made every American . . . all the British aeroplanes were marked with Royal Air Force. We were as many as was at all possible. So that was . . . that was a primitive way to show resistance that the children used."[69]

Hiding one's identity

Relatives of the interviewees sometimes chose non-Jewish last names as a way of hiding their Jewish identity: "Yes, they were hoping for a better life with non-Jewish names.—Hmm . . .—Less discrimination and. . . ."[70] Children camouflaged their identity by taking off the yellow star. "I took it (the star) off and just walked around anyway. I didn't care, I slipped through, so I went to the square and tried to buy food, and . . . yes, I circulated rather a lot. I was little, my *hair was rather light, my brown eyes told a different tale*, but I slipped through."[71]

Age distorting

Age aspects have taken up considerable space in the interviewees' life histories and in the text of this book as well. I see this as a direct result of the fact that this study concerns *children* who have been persecuted and subjected to a war in a phase of the life cycle when development is at its most intensive. Age distorting can be seen as an immediate and affect-related response to the stresses to which the children were subjected. Other affect-related responses usually consisted of somatic symptoms. One woman remembers that she wet her pants. Others refused to eat. Another type of distorting has to do with feeling "like a freak", like an object of ridicule. Both age distorting, as stated earlier, and a person's own conception of his/ her appearance are aspects of the self-image. Age distorting includes aspects of both perforating and space creating. Children suddenly felt older because of the demands they faced and sometimes they dressed so as to look older in order to escape deportation. To *undergo depersonalization* or *emotional stunting oneself* or to see parents/other adults undergo these is an experience that I characterize as perforating. I regard taking responsibility/precocity as ways of creating space even if they are coupled to enormous fear.

Depersonalization/emotional stunting

Feeling alone

For children to be pointed out as being different by way of having their clothes marked with a Star of David and being barred from school, as described above, means that perforating takes place: the children are *broken away from their own generation*. Under the life conditions accounted for, this most probably brought with it a feeling of being small and "*alone*" rather than a depersonalization, a feeling that was accentuated in the stages that were still to come. Parents and children were not always together, and the children could be forced to cope on their own with the changed nature of their surroundings and with the arising threats, as has also been described.

Being fetched from school for safety reasons

Children could be fetched on bicycles as long as families were allowed to keep these. "I wondered why, because I thought I could go home by myself, and the answer I received was that it was for safety reasons."[72] At the same time, the bicycle again contributed to space creating, creating a shortcut via bicycling.

Taking responsibility / precocity

Age marking

Increased *taking of responsibility/precocity* can be understood as adjustments that resulted when children were met with what they experienced as an inadequate response from the adults. That the interviewees give *a firm indication of their own age* in connection with an event that they recount can have served as a *point of orientation*, a space, in order to remember. It also seems to have been meaningful for them to make note of their own age in order to emphasize their *existence* and adulthood. Moreover, in this way they seem to open a possibility for the notion that they could "*control the situation*" in connection with the trauma, despite their age. Many of them stress the importance of comparing what is expected of children of the same age today. However, it does seem that the children often saw the situation in terms of their being the ones who informed their parents about the direct dangers present in everyday life in the neighbourhood, at school, and among friends: "When the war broke out, it was my birthday that precise day, the first of September 1939, I turned ten. What could be asked of a child? Think if I compare Anna [her grandchild], who has had her tenth birthday, with me as a ten-year-old. Think what I had already been through. You can't compare it."[73]

To summarize, one of the fundamental purposes of my presentation is to show the great significance that the experiencing of their own age seems to have had for the interviewees in their perception of their place in the generational chain. A significant aspect of the experiencing of age is what I have interpreted as age distorting. Both depersonalization/emotional stunting and taking responsibility/precocity can be seen as a distorting of the life cycle on the individual level and as generational tearing apart on the interpersonal and structural levels.

B Deportation

"They tried to talk about it in a way that the children would not hear. But we heard anyway. We heard terrible things, and then we started to be really frightened."[1]

Outer threats / Experiences	Anti-semitism/ Racial laws	Deporta-tion	Ghetto	Hidden/ Fugitive/ Partisan	Camps	Liberation	Encounter with Sweden/ Post-wartime
Perforating							
Space creating							
Age distorting							

The deportations of millions of European Jews were "necessary" in order for the Holocaust to be carried out. An "Umschlagplatz" was a place that had been prepared for loading operations adjacent to a number of ghettos. It was often a relatively large, open place. Sometimes these were located near railway lines. [Bruchfeld & Levine, 1999]

The period of deportations brought with it the experience of being moved around or being under the constant threat of being moved. All the children were subjected to this experience. Aggressive actions against Jews took place in their own neighbourhoods and in the ghetto. Homes were subjected to intrusion. It became more and more common for people to be moved to places where they were "herded together". Thus confrontations with aggressors became more frequent. A short time would remain during which parents as well as helpers were close by for the children. Significant linking objects were windows, backpacks, pets, plaits, small objects, clothes, and shoes.

Perforating

Parents became more and more vulnerable. The children began to feel more and more *alone*. Sandor stresses anti-Semitism's "systematic and psychological *breaking down* of every form of resistance" and "all those *rapes of normal life*".[2] The ongoing splitting up of families in connection with aggressive actions and deportations and the consequent imposing of non-age-adequate behaviour upon the children form the basis of the intensification of that which I have termed the experience of *generational breakdown*. Sandor's experience was that "the whole persecution and anti-Semitism planted *fright in my very bones, in the core of my very being*."[3] He is also of the conviction that as a child his thoughts about what was taking place were more logical than were those of the adults. "*Children think with their feelings*, which give a more logical result than the preconceived notions of adults. That's why it's hard to fool children. They feel it when adults are false."[4]

Invading of the senses

When people are living under the life conditions studied here, it becomes more and more difficult to distinguish between invading the senses and tearing away. The parents' vulnerability and reactions towards the perpetrators' aggressions right in front of their children meant that even if they were still physically present, they were "torn away" from their children in their capacity of nurturing parents. Mirjam remembers that she felt a "*vague danger*". She says: "I could never really understand the consequences. . . . *I don't believe that I could put that together* (as a child). I just felt that there was something threatening that could get worse."[5] The children "could not stand" to hear the "crying" of their mothers. Noa recalls that his mother was "very troubled, and she cried and cried very violently in the [train] car. But I could not listen to such crying and such grief, the way she said that now everything was over. Myself, I could not cry. I tried to tell my mother that everything would no doubt be all right."[6] Sandor describes a "vague recollection of what was being said in the way of subject matter but a distinct memory of feeling strongly, 'Dear God, please don't let the war come.'"[7]

"Suddenly all the windows were opened"

Henny remembers that "suddenly all the windows were opened, and people were screaming, "The war has begun!"[8] Maya recalls, "Through the window we saw Russians marching . . . we were all just as afraid, and the parents were also afraid, they looked out their windows, all the people sat in their houses and looked out."[9] Sandor looked into the faces of the adults and seems to have absorbed the image of the body language of his family members as well as the aggressors' characteristics and brutality: "the sight of them with skulls placed everywhere, on their hats and whatnot".[10] At the same time, the children tried to live their own lives—they just tried to get away from the turbulence at home.

Panic

Intrusions into homes often took place at night. Homes were "raped". Bella remembers: "At five in the morning, they pounded on our doors. . . . Hungarian gendarmes. They ordered us to get up and pack, to be ready within a quarter of an hour, and to take food with us for three days. . . . Everyone was in *panic!*"[11] The "soldiers" broke the windows and struck family members, who went into a state of shock. The children were witnesses. Sandor gives an account of how he hid and what he saw—memories that will not let go: "My very first really frightening experience was when it was night sometime during the winter, when we all lay there and slept, the whole family. *Two half-drunk German soldiers break in,* smash the *window* and doors and break into the apartment. Of course *our apartment had supposedly been pointed out by some Hungarian Nazi or Arrow-Cross-er.* And a frightful *panic* breaks out. And what they do is that they begin to beat up . . . *beat up my uncle who had a beard.* Everyone of course was still in *nightgowns and pyjamas,* and they go on beating him up. I discover myself—I don't know how I got there—*I find myself hiding under a bed, and I hear dreadful screams and so forth.* And when they had beaten both my aunt and that uncle to their satisfaction, they left . . . and the memory image that I have *when I look out from under the bed, it was of my aunt standing there in the middle of the room in a big nightgown and urine running right down on the floor.* They were, I tell you, in a state of complete shock. This was the first memory I have of the physical violence, of the brutality that the Nazis were capable of."[12]

The image of father changes

The interviewees have consistently emphasized the great significance of their relationships with their fathers. It is the skills of the father and the sense of security that he gave that are remembered. Now for the first time they saw their fathers cry. It made a shocking impression on the children to see their fathers put down, have their beards pulled, be forced into obedience, beaten, and even murdered right in front of their eyes. Such things were in every way beyond their imagination, as was the sight of other adults carrying out these acts. Marysia recalls: "And so the Germans came one time and boxed my father's ears, and this was something that we children had never seen, and we could never believe that someone would box our father's ears."[13] The adults' faces "*looked swollen*". They had seen the aggressors' "*hateful looks, which seared themselves firmly*" in the memory, along with their unpredictability. At the same time, they witnessed their parents' courage.

Oscar gives the following account of the selections: "My father held me by the hand, and so we walked up to those buses. There stood Latvians with rifles, and SS men. I actually see that man in front of me, *his face.* When you are little, of course, everyone looks huge, but *he was huge,* and he had an SS uniform. He wore a black leather greatcoat and a hat with skulls on it . . . he was apparently the boss. He stood with a whip, *with his hand like this* [demonstrates], and [pause], he struck his boots. I guess he was the head of that extermination camp. And I don't know what happened. My father dragged me by the hand, and ran up to that man. . . . *I actually see this scene before me.* He raises his hand and so he says . . . [starts to cry], 'This is my son, he is all I have, let him live.' And then the SS man says, 'Yes, after all, he doesn't look Jewish. What time is it?—Oh, yes, it's one o'clock, so we'll stop this procedure for now. *Let him live.*'"[14]

The image of mother changes

In the chaos that broke out, the children made careful note of the changes in their mothers' behaviour. In some cases the initial strength and courage of the mother is emphasized. She was "creative" and "inventive". Marysia remembers, "mother took her jewellery . . . and she made small bags, which we wore around our necks, in case anything would happen to us."[15] Sandor remembers his mother from her work at her hairdressing salon as "a clever and very well-appreciated artist, you can say. She had extraordinarily good taste and was an aesthete of high calibre."[16] Ruben's mother "had employees who made and sold hats . . . which was unusual for a woman at that time."[17]

Lisa points out that her mother was "a very strong woman . . . because she never gave up, either".[18] Lisa feels that it is her mother's strength that has been passed on to her, which makes her feel today that no one can degrade her. However, the dominating picture given of mothers has been characterized by weakness—either a weakness in the memory, of not remembering a mother's face, or, alternatively, a weakness in the mother, of her having been made weak by the persecutions. This seems to have been extremely frightening.

Mother becomes "paralysed", "speechless", "totally at a loss", "blind"

A large number of the life histories include memories of the mothers as becoming paralysed by the shock that the raids on the home and the deportations brought with them. This gives an idea of the character of the stresses on the relationship between child and mother. The interviewees remember at the same time and with clarity how and where they stood in relation to their mother, and they tell about how much, if any, distance they felt from the threatening events that were going on. Marianne relates how she reacted as a thirteen-year-old: "And I remember it so well. We stood a little farther down, *and mother stood on a. . . . I don't know, a little farther up.* There was a hill or whatever it was. And *I started to cry when I got separated from my mother,* and then I cried so that *I could not breathe. And my face turned blue and black, and I was about to choke.* And then my mother caught sight of me, and I suppose she *became totally at a loss, so she completely erased her surroundings.* At the top of the hill stood a German, and a Hungarian Arrow-crosser. And also a. . . . And then my mother looked at me and then. . . . she quite simply walked trance-like between those two men and came down and got in line. Acquaintances hid her. She needed to be hidden for two reasons. Because of what was happening just now at that moment, but also because she was extremely beautiful, and the Germans and . . . the Hungarians tried to take liberties all the time, all the time, all the time. To escape this, she took a little pillow, and then she gave herself the figure of a pregnant woman, and that was what saved her. It was very funny the way many, many people came up to her after the war and asked her how that little child was getting along. There was no child. And . . . and that was the way my mother saved me—and I saved my mother . . . but it was totally incredible that it succeeded."[19]

Marianne came to be separated from her mother because her mother was paralysed by shock, "became totally at a loss and *erased her surroundings from her consciousness*". For a child to be *torn away from* the mother seems to have been experienced as a mortal danger. My way of interpreting this event can be compared with Anzieu's (1985) theory on the psychological significance of the skin. He has paid special attention to the significance of separation, which can be reflected in ideas about a separation as being a breakage in the two persons' common protective shield. Somehow Marianne, together with their fellow prisoners, made her mother look pregnant by using a pillow, which gave them *space for taking action*. At the same time, it was precisely through a "pregnancy" that the primal relationship between Marianne and her mother could be re-created. Using Anzieu's (1985) terminology symbolically, this could be expressed as a *re-creation of the common protective shie*ld.

Liv tells how she, as an eight-year-old, had to *show her mother the way*: "Now I was standing with my mother up high, high up, and we looked down at the courtyard. *My mother held my hand,* and the Germans were running around with their dogs on our landing. . . . And then there was *someone who whistled,* and they turned away. They had been summoned to go out, there was something else happening. So just on that particular occasion we were saved. *Why I am telling this is, is that my mother was suddenly unable to see. She became blind, probably as a result of the shock*. She got her sight back later, but at this time she said nothing. I had to lead her down the stairs. It was dreadful because I was not really sure how to get to our apartment from that place where we were standing. I have always had a very poor sense of direction, but somehow I managed. She said absolutely nothing. This lasted for several days."[20]

Liv remembers her closeness to her mother and how her mother was torn away as a nurturing parent when she became "blinded by the shock". Liv became the responsible person and led her mother, even though she did not know the way home. The roles were reversed. Liv created a space: "somehow I managed". Anzieu, who has done research concerning the container function, cites Bion (1962) who has contributed three important concepts concerning the baby's transition from non-thinking to thinking—*perceptions, affects,* and *memory traces*—and the mother's possibilities to *contain these* as they break into the dawning psyche. It is my conviction that these concepts have relevance as a comparison to my way of interpreting the above-mentioned interview sequences, in which a perforating trauma has obviously taken place during the interview when links were made to frightening sound experiences. Linking to trauma and to generations, respectively, is discussed in Part IV.

The recurring theme of a weak mother, as mentioned above, can be an expression of an unconscious revenge towards the mother for being incapable of protecting her child from the persecution. At the same time, the picture of the mother has faded for some of the interviewees because of the ensuing long-term separations, which made it impossible to maintain an inner representation of her. Winnicott (1967) explains that long periods of an absent response from the mother can mean that the child's own creative ability withers away. Children, as mentioned above, will then look around for other ways of getting something of themselves back from the surroundings. The housekeeper or the nanny filled a very important function. From the balcony Eva could see how the men were being attacked in the courtyard and "our housekeeper took hold of me like this, with my head against her stomach"[21] [so that I would not have to see]. Sofia gives the following account of her mother's helplessness: "*and my mother was completely paralysed,* so she could not do so much and my grandmother could not either. So it was this Vilma who helped us pack, and I did too. *I helped with the packing,* and I don't even know what we packed, either."[22]

Maya explains: "We saw how mother had cried so terribly much. She did not answer our questions, she answered nothing that we asked her. She was almost *mute,* and we were terribly afraid for her" [cries].[23] When Maya says that her mother was "mute" and not "silent", she expresses the quality of what it was that was frightening.

The stresses on the mothers as the remaining parent were without doubt tremendous—they were in mortal danger and at the same time they had to care for their children. It was likely to have been difficult to maintain an optimal distance, a "space for playing", between the mother and her children, a space that could have made for permanent positive memories. The picture that the interviewees give of the speech and body language of their mothers and fathers, respectively, can also reflect a general child perspective of the world—that is, the social constructions made by a child in which people are divided up into water-tight categories of bad and good.

The sounds become more prolonged

The children were prevented from seeing what was happening, and their observations of the world were drawn from the sounds of frightening voices. After several months, Marie says, she heard that the "adults were whispering: 'deportations, deportations', but they had said nothing to us! And I think that was stupid."[24] Emilia relates that she heard "screams from the street as they were beating up an elderly Jewish man who had a beard. At that point my cousin and I were locked in the bathroom so that we could not see, so that we could not hear. No one wanted to speak to us. That scene out on the street quite simply was not supposed to exist. They tried to protect us. *But we heard anyway.*"[25] The Jews were transported away in freight cars, "*and there were horrible scenes in the dark that you saw once your eyes were accustomed to the dark.*"[26] Many tell how they heard "the desperate screaming of children" both in the freight cars and from the hiding places where people at a distance could hear what was going on.

Removal and the splitting-up of families

There was a great danger that people would lose each other. Bella recalls, "one of the most difficult memories that I have from that night was the vast number of people . . . and *people lost each other.* They spent entire nights running around and shouting for each other in that vast crowd of people . . . they wailed and cried and screamed, it was dreadful."[27]

Seeing dead animals and people

Recurring visual memories of animals that had died give an idea of war experiences *from a child's perspective*. Emilia describes "a wave of refugees . . . bombs were falling, and there were many dead people and horses on the street. When we heard aeroplanes coming, we ran and *pressed ourselves to the ground.*"[28] Liv gives this account: "The absolutely worst thing was that during one of those raids, one of the attacks, air attacks on Warsaw, well, we were in the air-raid shelter and when we came back, we saw that a *grenade . . . a part of a grenade had come in through the window* in one of the rooms and hit a cage where my *canaries happened to be at that moment.* Normally we let them fly around freely, but this time we had locked them in because we were going to go down to the cellar. [The birds, just like the family, were closed in during the air attacks]. And they were dead, *and I no doubt have never gotten over this.* It was you see a dreadful shock, and *it was the first time that I saw death.*"[29]

It is also possible that the anxiety over the all-encompassing threat hanging over her own existence was shifted to the loss of her birds. She adds that "it became a more and more common sight to see people out there by dead animals (horses), cutting off pieces of meat. And well, after all, there's nothing really strange about that, it's just that it looked so unbelievable." Generally speaking, the child survivors have memories of the Nazis' robbing them of their own pets. In Berlin Jewish families were forbidden to keep their pets, and they guessed that the animals were killed, even if they did not want to believe it. From the time of the deportation of Jews from their home district, the sight of dead people became more and more common (McIntyre, 1997).

Tearing away

Having home and human dignity torn away

People were soon forced to break up the natural network around themselves and leave their homes. Their sense of human dignity was lowered, as Sandor says. He remembers that "they subjected a part of the population to a kind of rape by *tearing them away from their homes . . . .*they made me feel, this too with my heart of a child, that respect for us as human beings was equal to zero."[30] The adults were in disagreement as to whether they should flee or accept moving to the ghetto. Eva recalls that "they quarrelled late at night, and I eavesdropped".[31] Lena describes how "it was a Friday evening, and my sister and I saw that there were two *SS men standing in the doorway and pointing at us with their pistols.* They ordered us to get up and put our clothes on. And we were *terribly embarrassed,* and then, well, they went all around in the apartment."[32] Marysia says that "I stayed in the bathroom most of the time, you know, we were so dreadfully afraid."[33]

Having father torn away

Marie recounts [very moved] how she heard her *mother scream,* "It's not enough that *my husband has died* as a hero, no, you are going to send my children to their death as well."

She tells of her mother's despair and of how it was when she heard about her father's death for the first time: "My father is dead! He is dead! And then I fainted."[34] There are many associations connected with the memory of father and with missing father. It was common for the father to be suddenly taken away from the home. Emilia says that she "went into a panic when I heard that father had been mobilized. I knew that in a war people can kill, and then I became panic-stricken. And my mother, she did not say much."[35] Liv stood in a food queue with her father, and a German officer was on the look-out for Jews. She recalls that "I *was suddenly alone* in the line. My father had been taken to be interrogated . . . a terribly shattering experience for me, that they took my father."[36] Mirjam remembers how her father did not want to say good-bye, "but I ran up anyway and saw him from the balcony as he walked away . . . . I had a horrible premonition that he would never come back . . . *my personal sense of security was very much tied to my father.*"[37] Many have a permanent memory of the *loneliness* they felt as well as the responsibility they felt they would have to take (see age distorting, below). At the same time, the memory of father seems to have given them strength to survive, based perhaps on the father's symbolic protective function. Anna Freud and Dorothy Burlingham (1973) describe children's attitudes towards their dead fathers. They find a striking contrast in the behaviour of children in an orphanage in relation to their fathers when they came for a visit during the war years versus their complete inability to comprehend the death of their fathers when

that occurred. The children spoke about their fathers as though
they were alive. This can be compared with adults' persistent, non-
worked-through grief and sometimes their denial that their father is
in fact dead, as observed in this study. Slips of the tongue and wishful
thinking show an "expectation" that he will come back.

"The teddy-bear disappeared"

Beloved things disappeared. Julia tells that "I had a teddy bear, which
disappeared. It was a little symbolic . . . that I grieved over a teddy-
bear, there were other things to grieve about. . . . It disappeared when
we went into hiding . . . this was a very powerful experience."[38]

Being sent away

Children were sent away to "someone" in rural areas, where the parents thought that there would be less risk of being discovered. These
were very traumatic separations. The children were (sometimes)
falsely told that the parents were dead in order to make it possible
for everyone to be saved. A number of them express relief that they
were spared from being sent away.

Body marking

"Herding" and pressing together

The rounding-up actions against Jews entailed herding, crowding,
waiting, loss of freedom of movement, and all of these under threat.
These took place, for example, in sports arenas or in other large,
open fields. "*Herding*" is a concept that recurs in the language usage
of the interviewees. Sonja remembers how they were herded away.
"We were supposed to assemble in a large field that had very high
planks around it. Whoever did not go there would be shot if they
were found." She remembers herself in detail in that situation: "We
put on the best clothes we had. I remember so well what I had. I
had a long *velvet* dress, *beautiful patent leather shoes,* and white stock-
ings. And I had the Star of David on that blue velvet dress, and the
dress had a little white *collar* with blue polka dots on it, and it was
hand-sewn. Then I had a coat, some type of trench coat . . . In the

beginning we kept ourselves fairly optimistic. But then after a while there was a delay, and the Germans didn't come, and we stood there, and they *herded us together more and more. Children were trampled* and others were too, and there was less and less place to stand. And then it began to rain. It was *muddy.* . . . It must have been late summer, because I had *knee socks*."[39]

Sonja conveys the feeling of the soft velvet material, and of the collar that encompassed her, and the beautiful patent leather shoes. Putting on thick layers of clothing had a practical aspect to it: it was a way for people to take as much as possible with them. In addition to this, it can be said, with reference to Anzieu's view (1985), that clothes meant a strengthening of a person's *own protective shield.* According to Winnicott's terminology, the clothes may have come to function as transitional objects, *a link to the mother* and to the home that had been left behind. My interpretation of the clothes as having symbolic significance is heightened by the fact that Sonja *remembers them so distinctly.* Sonja says that it was raining, it was muddy, and there was less and less firm ground to stand on. The patent leather shoes seem to disappear in the mud, and it becomes harder and harder for her to maintain her foothold.

No windows: the air shield shrinks

Odour memories are pronounced when memories of being herded together or of being transported from the home are described. I call the atmosphere or "the bubble" that surrounds a human body the "*air shield.*" This air shield was dented by recurring experiences of *waiting* while being deprived of freedom of movement. There was also actual crowding and a limited space for movement, in which the oxygen was reduced to a minimum and whatever air remained stank. The "air shield" was perforated through crowding during the train transports in cattle cars. Jenny recalls that "there were *no windows,* only *cracks* in the walls" through which they could catch a glimpse of what was on the other side or through which they *could breathe.* "Everyone ran, we crowded in on each other and *trampled on each other* to keep from being struck [cries]. When we finally were inside the cattle cars, 70 to 80 people, this I know now, they were *locked from the outside* with a padlock. There was hardly enough space where we could sit."[40] The possibility of getting air was drastically reduced. Moreover, the *darkness made it hard to get oriented.* Children wet their pants. On the boat transports, people vomited, cried, and were forced to take care of their needs on the floor of the car or in the hats they had with them. Lena remembers a pregnant woman who needed to go to the bathroom and "all of us let her use the hats that we had".[41] It was as though something was *running out* of all the openings.

Space creating

Thinking / fantasizing

The living environment in the home has been memorized

The special orientation and the furniture arrangement in the child-hood home seem to have been significant. The home served as the secure structure in their existence to which the interviewees could return in their thoughts and creative activities. Photographs and paintings of their own that the interviewees have brought out to be videofilmed in connection with the interview show the significance of life's "frame", the structure that was destroyed and must be memorized in order to be possible to repair. This seems to be as essential aspect in combating generational tearing apart.

The family gathers together

Julia has a "strong, concrete memory image of the occupation", despite having been only six years old: "My mother had burned herself in the bathroom and everything was understandably in chaos . . . then later in the afternoon we were at my grandmother's and grand-father's and ate dinner at a *large table.*"[42] The family came together and talked. They seem to have arranged a space in which to think and to reflect.

Linking objects

The time was coming when they would have to leave their homes, and thus they had to decide on the few things that they would be allowed to take with them. For the girls this meant dolls and teddy-bears. Julia had a "big, beautiful doll that we dragged along with us . . . one of those celluloid dolls . . . and I also had a teddy-bear that later disappeared."[43] Elias, who was thirteen years old at the time, remembers "the gathering together of the things that we considered to be the most important. . . . I had a . . . little piece of jewellery or whatever you might call it. It was not real jewellery either, it was a calendar on a chain to be worn around the neck. It looked like a necklace. That was the only thing I took with me. I dragged that with me all the way to Auschwitz. But that is the only thing that I have a clear memory of having."[44] Henny tells about a "little gold ring that my grandmother gave all of her grandchildren, a little ring with a blue stone, when they had their tenth birthday. And that was the only thing I had from my home." She hid it in a piece of bread, which she abstained from eating, "just so that I could hold on to the memory of my grandmother. The bread turned to crumbs, and so they took the ring. That was the last link I had to my home."[45]

Pieces of jewellery could seem to function as transitional objects, according to Winnicott's terminology (1953). They can be said to symbolize the area for play between the child and the mother, the bonds to the mother (here through the grandmother), which the children carried with them into the unknown. What is significant does not need to be the object itself, but rather the actual using of the object. Elias does not remember exactly *what* the object was, but he remembers the *actual event* concerning it. The linking object can primarily have had a survival value for him. These linking objects with different degrees of symbolic value are taken from the outer reality, from the home, that is soon to be torn away. At the same time the objects have links to the child's inner psychic world.

The children create excitement for themselves

Children looked out through windows, holes, and cracks in the freight cars in order to be able to fix their gaze on something that existed outside, something that appeared secure out there. By doing so, it might also have been possible for them to fantasize themselves away from their horrifying reality: the reality of being closed in, of being in captivity. The size of their own bodies took on a significance for the possibility of obtaining a psychic grip on "something outside". A number of them were of the "right height to look out through the hole". Elias comments: "For us children it was exciting in some way: remember that we had never ridden on a train before."[46] Ester remembers that "Sometimes it seemed like an infinity. We didn't really know how long we, how long the journey would last. We just knew what we could see through the cracks. Sometimes we could see other, very high mountains and then I thought to myself, 'no, but can it be so? Now we are in Czechoslovakia, and we see the Tatra Mountains, which I have always dreamed of going to'. So there was a little of that sense of adventure, that now we are travelling out to new, foreign lands."[47]

Marysia remembers what she saw when the Germans arrived: "And they came with wonderful green trucks, and their boots were so well-polished. . . . They were young, handsome, well-groomed. There was such a contrast between them and the Polish army that I remember it to this day."[48]

Relation to aggressors

Wishful thinking could take expression in fantasies about having good rapport with the aggressors. Eva remembers how her mother and other Jewish women were put to work scrubbing the floor: "I remember that a German officer came up, after all, we did speak German, and the Germans spoke to me. *And the idea crossed my mind that they liked me.*" The officer poured out water with broken glass in it and ordered the women to start all over again. "Mother made a corner very clean and said that I should stand there and not move"[49]—and again the space shrank! Perhaps the feeling that there was some concern on the part of the aggressors was tied to the recurring unpredictability of their behaviour. In the deportation context, the aggressors were not able to "see the Jews as human beings". The Jews can, instead, have become targets for their projections, and they thus projected qualities onto the Jews that they did not want to admit possessing themselves. The projections seemed to "function as outlets and vents for the personality" (Böhm, 1993). Nevertheless, the findings of the present study appear to show that for a few seconds the aggressors could behave in a "human" way, as though they *had had enough.* They could suddenly "show mercy", and in exceptional cases Jews escaped with their lives.

Maintaining culture and religion

The possibilities of carrying on with cultural activities were drastically reduced. Liv tells that they managed to celebrate a Pessach (Jewish holy day) in the ghetto together with a boy and his parents.[50]

Thinking/taking action

Disobeying

Sometimes the children did things that were forbidden. As mentioned already, they might take off the Star of David at times and venture out on an errand. Marie was not allowed to open the window, "but I did it anyway, and we saw on the left side how a large mass of people were coming."[51]

Retreating into one's own shell

Through *fortifying their boundaries* towards the outer world, the children could create a space in which they could think and fantasize and maintain a feeling of their own existence. Sandor found himself hidden in a threatening and absurd situation: "The only thing I can try to do is *squeeze myself into a tight little knot* and sit on my bed and *be the little boy that I in actual fact really am*."[52] He speaks in the present tense, as though the situation is taking place at that actual moment. Emilia had the feeling that "the cupboard almost stood on me. She (the helper) told me to *cover my mouth and hold my breath* for a while. And then some Germans came in and some Polish neighbours. And they searched for me. *There was a girl missing*."[53] Emilia was not supposed to breathe, not let out any air, keep everything inside her air shield. All the holes had to be sealed up. Sonja "sealed up all the holes [in the air-raid shelter] . . . we were afraid of that mustard gas that we had heard about, and so we made mouth protectors."[54]

Hiding one's identity: being provided with false papers

The children were given a "new" identity. Henny tells about her confusion: "I had to wash, they got some new clothes for me . . . .without that star, of course. I had already received a birth certificate . . . false

of course, *I don't remember what my name was supposed to be or anything.*
Those were false papers."[55] Many of the survivors feel that their "false
identity" was a part of their personal identity, and they have kept
their "new" names to this very day.

Hiding one's identity:
taking another religion and having a non-Jewish appearance

Conversion to Christianity was carried out in a number of cases, as
a way of trying to achieve freedom to act. Lisa, whose mother was
not Jewish, explains that "my mother and my sister, who was four
years old at the time, were counted as Christians, and my father and
I were counted as Jews (because) if conversion takes place before
the age of nine, they are counted as Jews". Lisa could still *move about
freely* as "I resemble my mother rather much and *thus I did not look
like a Jew.*"[56]

Parents could differ in their opinions of converting and of an
appropriate school in their aim to hide their child. Bella went to
a Catholic school but was transferred to a Jewish school when her
mother saw her make the sign of the cross outside a Catholic church:
"I made the sign of the cross, and that made something flare up
inside my mother."[57]

Hiding one's identity:
creating links to friends and origin

Some families arranged to move in with a relative and escaped from
one town to another where they could feel safer before they, despite
these attempts to escape, were deported to a ghetto. The children
found their own ways of concealing their anxiety. Marysia describes
how "we always had some game or cards under the table so that if
the Germans came we could pretend that we were playing cards or
playing a game. . . . I felt much safer, however, when I went to my
friend's place, because there was a Polish name on the door, than I
felt at my own home."[58] Maya tells how "There were some of us the
same age, we got together, we sat somewhere in a corner, and told
different stories, and we were afraid of everyone and everything."[59]
Sonja comments that a helper used her *nickname* when addressing
her in order to hide her identity, a name that Sonja mentions fondly

in the interview: "Sonja, or 'S', . . . as she called me [laughs] in Polish [short pause]. She told me to pretend I did not recognize her." She should *pretend that she is not who she is, and at the same time she can rest in the thought of her nickname,* that she is who she is.

Creating links by writing notes

As mentioned already, Emilia wrote notes to her parents, who were in hiding. When German police came to Lena's home to deport her family, she managed to smuggle a note under the back door in the hope that her best friend would find it later. Her friend did, in fact, find it after Lena had been deported to Theresienstadt. "I tore off a corner of a newspaper to write on. I wrote, *"Dear Kamma* [swallows], *we have been taken away by the German police. Tell them at school."* Then I *rolled it up and managed to get it through the kitchen door* without its being discovered by the Germans. That was, after all, a rather dangerous thing to do, and it *was found later by my friend.*"[60]

"If you save one life, you save the whole world"[61]

This is a Jewish saying, which Henny quoted. There were women who *saved children* at the risk of their own lives. Sonja was going to ride on a streetcar (which was forbidden for Jews) together with a helper, a woman. She recalls, "I had that Jewish star on both my dress and my coat, and we started to rip it off, you know, velvet leaves a mark. So I had to hold my coat like this the whole way (demonstrates) in order to hide the shadow made by the Jewish star."[62]

A helper could have a "motherly instinct".[63] Jewish women also took risks and helped Jewish children to have something to focus their thoughts on when their parents were not present or did not have the strength to engage themselves in their children's special needs. "Lita was . . . she had a *motherly instinct.* She took care of all of us children who lived there. She played with us and taught us different things. She read books to us. [The police took her away and one day.] I saw her with other prisoners on the street. They were marching, so to say. *When I saw her, I didn't think . . . I just shouted "Lita",* and she looked at me and turned away. Then I understood that I should keep quiet. You can't just cry out like that. I will never forget her face.* She was a wonderful person."[64]

Bodily contact

During the transport in freight cars, it was essential "to have contact with each other, my sister, my mother and I and grandmother and grandfather sat very close together. And we were as children so very shocked and exhausted and the most important thing was to feel closeness, bodily, physical closeness to each other."

Age distorting

Depersonalization/emotional stunting

Losing foothold

The children "lost their foothold", and their own identity became less and less clear when they were separated from their parents or saw their parents being robbed of their dignity. Nomi experienced it as "I knew nothing about where I was or how I was. Everything was strange. I never really got to be a child, you know."[65]

Being closed in

The interviewees have told about persistent memory images of being confined in air-raid shelters and symptoms in the form of claustro-phobia and terrible nightmares. Sonja had "a slight phobia about sitting in a shelter. Many times I wanted to run out. I thought that I might as well run out and let whatever happened happen. It was important to be quiet. They told me not to make a sound, even if people trampled on me."[66]

Birthdays disappear

The children's experience of their own existence often appears to have been rooted in associations having to do with birthday cel-ebrations, their own or other family members' special days. Jacob remembers: "We were going to leave our home, and it was to take place in 1944 on the fourth, the exact day of my *mother's birthday*. It is with great sorrow that I . . . *this memory is so very strongly imprinted in my mind* that I will never forget what a *dreadful feeling it was to leave our home*."[67] Liv explains: "I remember the date because my birthday was the day after. In my childish way I remember it exactly for that reason. Everyone was ordered to line up, I think it was five and five, and wait for further orders . . . and it turned into a totally *nightmarish* day."[68]

In the cargo area on the boat transport to Germany en route to the concentration camp, the rabbi passes out hard bread. For the time being this can have been experienced as a spur-of-the-moment attempt at normalizing the situation. For Lena, whose birthday fell on this day, this space-creating attempt seems to have felt meaningless, whereas the memory and the consequences stand out clearly: "All of us received a piece of square hard bread. It was obvious that there were many who had taken it with them. But that day was my 14th birthday, and I got two pieces of hard bread. . . . I have never cared about my birthday after that."[69] When the families were forced to leave their homes, "that was when I lost my childhood, because that's when horrible things started to happen",[70] as Marie expresses it.

Taking responsibility/precocity

Taking over father's role

Many felt a great responsibility being openly placed on their shoulders despite their young years, while others perceived that they were given responsibility without anyone's explicitly saying so. Sandor felt instinctively that he should flee, "but I could not leave my mother helpless".[71] The mother was alone with many children and a little brother in a cast. Noa says, "I told my mother that we were going to make it through this. And I comforted her. I have become *so hardened.*"[72] This can be compared with statements concerning "retreating into one's shell" (see above) and statements for denial of the massive trauma to which the children were subjected. The children became thick-skinned in conjunction with having to serve as "care-givers" for their mothers. Noa further states in the interview: "I never cried in the camps, not once, the whole time." He also says that "there were many people in that train car who kept crying and *praying to God that the Germans would spare* them."

The fathers were forced to leave their families. Ester describes her parting from her father: "He knew, of course, that we would never see each other again. And *then he told me to take care of everyone, he said that to me, who was the youngest in the family.* He said to take care of them, to watch out for each other. *He said this to me, I had just had my fourteenth birthday.* And it was . . . . I felt the solemnity of the occasion when we said farewell to each other. Did I get that right, did he give me a huge task? *Then yes, I will take care of them.*"[73]

As we have seen in previous sections, Ester and other child survivors orient themselves in terms of their birthdays. She does so here when she thinks about the most painful events. Ester, as the youngest in the family, must suddenly function as the eldest, abandoning her chronological age. She experienced it as a "very heavy testament, that I would take care of them." She repeats their parting: "I saw him through the *window* . . . he got smaller and smaller as he blended into the crowd of people, and I saw his *backpack,* and he waved and stopped and waved, and then he disappeared. And he disappeared from my life . . . [sobs]."[74] Mothers tried to preserve the children's links to a hidden or imprisoned father as long as it was possible. One of the interviewees recounts, "Father had been taken away to prison, so he was in the cellar. Mother wanted father to see me a little. So that was why we took walks sometimes. My mother told me about this after the war. Of course, my father, I never saw him again."[75]

Sons had to become "the men of the house": "When my father was on the way with the prisoners from Bor, he wrote a card to me. A card wishing me a happy birthday. He wrote on the card 'Now you are the one who is the man in the house, and you must understand what that means' [cries]. That was the last sign of life from him."[76] Once again, a birthday is tied to a trauma.

Warning the neighbours

Children could be given the task of warning the neighbours. Emilia tells of such an instance: "Yes, they came with a list of names and addresses. . . . I know that I was very frightened . . . because I was sent to warn those people, and I know that I ran to the first [family], and the Germans were already there. So I ran to the other place, and I had time to say that they were on a list of people to be arrested, but I do not remember who they were. . . . I was thinking that it was not possible that they killed people, I thought that maybe they did something, prison or . . . *Such horrible things were unthinkable.*"[77]

The children experiencing their parents' vulnerability
and the mobilizing of their own capacity

Marianne describes the "*first herding together*", and her father's desperation. As a child she helped her father with his heavy coat, and
she later prevented his attempt at extended suicide. "The first herding together was when we were ordered to go out on the street, and
there we were told to form a line. A man cut off my plaits. We had
to keep our hands in the air the whole time . . . the whole way, and
I helped my father, because he had a heavy coat, a winter coat. Yes,
that's right, it must have been snowing and cold and chilling . . . and
we stayed there one day and one night. But we were taken home in
the night. What my father wanted to do that night was to put an end
to all of us, to gas us to death, but I discovered it and turned everything off. He used to make pear liqueur, and this time he gave us all
some, grandmother and grandfather and everyone who was there.
And I noticed that he had something in mind. He wanted us to drink
and even to get drunk. My cousin, who was three years younger than
me, got to drink. Then I discovered what was going on, and I turned
off the gas, and father did not succeed. So that's what happened,
that's what the first herding together meant for us."[78]

Changing the way of dressing

The children dressed so as to look older. Short skirts were made
long, and girls put kerchiefs on their heads.

Having plaits cut off

In Marianne's account above, she tells how she was forced to have
her plaits cut off. Ester recounts, "Not looking young could be a
decisive factor when selections took place. I turned fourteen, and it
was a little . . . yes, sad. *I had to leave my home then,* and *my mother cut
off my long plaits.* It became, it meant, also a certain degree of adulthood. I no longer had plaits or ribbons."[79]

Orienting oneself quickly and trying to make contact

When children are put through the inhuman conditions that occur
in connection with sudden, brutal intrusions into the home and violence towards family members, they cannot make sense out of these

actions in any way whatsoever. The events forced them to confront age distorting in adults, and this can have affected their own self-image. Some children, thanks to an outgoing personality or a fearless naïveté, could interact with the aggressors in such a way as to create some freedom of action for themselves. Anna explains: "I was a very crafty girl, and I was quick at getting oriented. Maybe that developed in me as a child."[80]

C   The ghetto

"I had to look older, and my grandmother had to look younger."[1]

Outer threats / Experiences	Anti-semitism/ Racial laws	Deporta-tion	Ghetto	Hidden/ Fugitive/ Partisan	Camps	Liberation	Encounter with Sweden/ Post-wartime
Perforating							
Space creating							
Age distorting							

Under the pretext that Jews were bearers of typhus, the Nazis separated them from the rest of the Polish population by shutting them into confined parts of cities, surrounded by walls and barbed wire (Baumann, 2003). The interviewees tell how they were herded together in different places, such as sports arenas, fields, and factory warehouse areas. Usually they were with their mothers and the other children in the family, and sometimes with their fathers. It was important to take along as many clothes as possible. Certain pieces of clothing and things, dolls, and teddy-bears proved to serve as essential linking objects. At the same time they remember the beloved and soft toy animals that they had to abandon. They were forced to choose in the chaos that had arisen.

Perforating

Invading of the senses

Cold

The winters were very cold. Marysia remembers that "the windows were broken. We had a mattress, otherwise you had to lie on the tile floor. It was cold, pardon the expression, damned cold. I just wanted to die. I could not stand it any longer."[2]

Eye to eye with the aggressors and with death

The children were subjected to direct threats in the streets of the ghetto. The faces of the aggressors are memory images that never loosen their grip. Liv recalls an instance in which the perpetrator "raised his pistol and aimed it at me . . . and I was completely sure that he would shoot me, and I just continued to the nearest entry door and went through it. For some reason he did not shoot. *That was probably the nearest I have ever come to death.*"[3] The deportations intensified. Henny describes how she was loaded onto a truck, and how her mother saw her, "*and then she started to scream.* And she screamed and screamed, and finally they started to hit her with a rifle butt . . . and this I remember . . . that the man in charge shouted: "Was für scheiss da!" So he told them to take me down, and I was united with my parents again. *He* [the aggressor] *granted me this life,* because it was, after all, as a matter of fact, his . . . decision."[4] The aggressor's actions were characterized by unpredictable abuse of power. We can only speculate about these moments of seemingly human behaviour.

German shepherd dogs are remembered with horror by everyone. Alice relates how "their head was at my eye level, and I was terrified of them because I had seen several times when the person leading the dog just said 'bierz ta!', and the dog thrust itself on someone, right on the neck, against the neck. And then the person who had been attacked never moved again."[5]

Not wanting to hear

Alice remembers the sound made by the boots, "that whip that they had when they walked along and struck it against their boots . . . that sound . . . . I cannot stand it."[6] The German language also breaks through in the memories of the soldiers' commands. Liv recalls how "German cars with loudspeakers drove by and gave instructions in Polish, in Yiddish, and in German about what we should do next."[7] This persistent sound does not seem to be possible to convert in the memory but instead exists only in its original form.

Not wanting to look

Liv speaks of the risk of "tripping over those who very soon lay dead and were often covered with only some strips of paper."[8] Ella notes how sickening it was to see dead bodies: "It is difficult to describe, because I tried to close my eyes." She also remembers her little cousin who was carried on a brother's shoulders and who asked to be warned in advance "every time we were going to pass by dead bodies, so she could close her eyes".[9]

Tearing away

No food

Liv tells how the availability of food in the ghettos was minimal: "There were hundreds and thousands of begging children who stood there and rattled a metal dish or asked to have . . . it wasn't a question of money, they just wanted a morsel of food."[10]

Staying away from other children

Children were requested by their mothers to run errands and at the same time to stay away from other children in order to avoid contagious diseases. In Liv's words: "They took great care to tell us not to try *not to have bodily contact with, not to rub against those* who. . . . This typhus fever, it was spread through lice and everyone had lice, and I mean everyone. . . . Well, *it was mostly children and those who begged on the streets and who lay dead on the streets.* Because it went so very fast. My mother told me that whatever I did, I should try *to avoid letting my clothes or my body touch* all those hundreds and thousands of begging children who stood there rattling their metal dishes or asked to have . . . it wasn't a question of money, they just wanted a morsel of food."[11]

Being forced to move

Liv tells how she often got lost, "in the midst of all those teeming crowds, the terrible chaos and the *crying* and everything, I suddenly got lost and started to run in desperation."[12] The children were separated from the adults both in the prevailing chaos and through the deportations of groups of children.

"Rumours started to circulate": two ghettos and two kinds of leadership

The children heard rumours from the people around them, and they heard the Germans' shouts from the places where people were being herded together in the ghettos. J. Bauman (2003), herself a child survivor and a writer, has made a study of "Moral Choices at the Time of the Gas Chambers" and she made a comparison between Adam Czerniakow, the leader of the Judenrat in the Warsaw Ghetto, and Chaim Rumkowski, the leader of the Judenrat in the Lòdz Ghetto, based upon their characters and their moral positions. "Judenrat were set up by Nazis . . . to see that the German orders were carried out with dispatch". The ghettos under their supervision were the two largest and most documented ghettos in Poland. Bauman poses the question, "Can we now, wise after the fact, pass a verdict on what Czerniakow and Rumkowski did? Can we pass a moral judgement? [The point is], can we who have never experienced what it was like to face the choices that those men faced, can we judge them?" How far can we stretch our imagination when we ask ourselves how we would act under similar circumstances? In short, Czerniakow did everything he could to get closer to "his people". For example, he made things better for the children by setting up play areas; ultimately he refused to obey orders, and he committed suicide. In contrast, Rumkowski became more and more disliked because he distanced himself from the inhabitants of the ghetto and could be seen to be "adopting immediately and with gusto the German *Führer Prinzip*". He made sure that Lòdz became a productive ghetto, and the Nazis saw no reason to interfere.

Marysia, who was twelve years old when she lived in Lòdz, remembers what Rumkowski looked like because she had met him with her father when he was Rumkowski's doctor. She mentions her birthday and her separation from her relatives in this context. "My father met Rumkowski, who had been his patient before the war. Then Rumkowski invited all the doctors who were going back to Lòdz to come to a cafe. I was twelve years old, and I remembered Rumkowski from before the war. [Now] he looked quite handsome, with his silvery hair, he was large and powerful. He always wore boots, but they were shiny boots, like the Germans had. He had a secretary with him. He had become, I don't know . . . a king all of a sudden."[13]

Marysia comments that "there was much more order in the Lòdz ghetto." She remembers how "Rumkowski said that he was very proud of his ghetto . . . he said that his ghetto worked like clockwork, that the children loved him. I can add that in that ghetto people worked and sent shoes to the front."[14]

Sending all the children away

In January of 1942 Rumkowski was ordered to select 20,000 Jews for "resettlement elsewhere". The ethnic cleansing was intensified, and Rumkowski decided to follow an "order of the devil": the children must be sent away. Rumkowski held a speech in which he said that he was going to see that the following order was carried out: "All children under ten, all adults over 65, and all unemployed" were going to be deported, "as a way of keeping the capable ones". "Fathers and mothers, give me your children!" (Bauman, 2003). Marysia thinks she can recall the precise occasion to which Bauman is referring. She speaks of her fear when she saw Rumkowski through the window on his way to the place where everyone would be rounded up: "I sat in the bathroom most of the time. I was so terribly frightened,[15] and I remember this because I saw it from our window when Rumkowski rode to the meeting-place where everyone would come to hear him speak about this. And when you are a mother yourself and you hear that mothers have to give up their children, you know it's absolutely dreadful."[16]

"The freight cars started rolling"

The ghetto was going to be liquidated, and Noa tells how they started to load the trains in the morning and how the "freight cars started rolling". After half an hour people started trying to get out: "They

ran or jumped . . . started to pry up . . . pried up the floor . . . edged
themselves down between the wheels and the track."[17]

Body marking

Being seized by the scruff of the neck

The children were seized brusquely by the scruff of the neck when
they were herded over to the side. Ruben, three–four years old, and
his mother were stopped as they tried to escape. He remembers
looking at his mother, "and then that man took hold of my chin
and twisted so hard he was about to bend my neck out of joint, and
he practically lifted me up. To me he looked like he was two metres
tall."[18] When Sam was twelve years old, "an SS guard came and
grabbed me by the nape of the neck and dragged me to a house and threw
me in there" (during the interview he places his hands on the nape
of his neck).[19] Liv remembers herself as "terribly little and awfully
skinny", and the aggressor became irritated with her and "chopped
at me with his hand on the back of my neck". He *marked her body*, "he
did like this (demonstrates) very forcefully, which caused *great pain
in my neck,* and I could hardly move",[20] she adds.

Space creating

Thinking/fantasizing

Convincing oneself that life is "normal"

Leon, who spent the first seven years of his life in the ghetto in
Shanghai, where the conditions were better than in Europe's ghettos, emphasizes that "we tried to organize our lives in as similar a
way as possible to what we were used to from home and to convince
ourselves that everything was fine". A "positive" aspect of living in
the prevailing chaos, with many people in a small area, was that
the children lived near parents and other relatives whose presence
increased a possible sense of security. Leon remembers how the refugees transformed the "slum" to a "living" and "vital" city. Many years
into his adulthood, Leon lived under the illusion that he had had a
"happy childhood"[21] in the ghetto. After going to psychotherapy, he
has realized that the situation was different.

A friendly face

Spinning their thoughts around a friendly face created an inner distance to the dreadful visual invasions. Recognizing a friendly woman who played with them is mentioned by a number of interviewees as leading to happy thoughts. In addition, Liv and Mirjam describe resemblances in looks to relatives who were near them in the ghetto: "I was almost an exact copy of my aunt." In this way they stressed their sense of belonging and probably the sense of security that came with it. Liv saw the "familiar face of Dr Korczak in the ghetto. He used to come to our home before the ghetto time when I refused to eat."[22] Janusz Korczak was a well-known and generally very appreciated paediatrician, writer and educator (1878–1942). He dedicated his entire life to children. Instead of letting himself be saved, he followed his group of children in the ghetto to an inevitable death. His life and work are currently the subject of ever-increasing interest (Korczak, Swedish edition, 2002).

Excitement

Children can create excitement even under frightful circumstances. Marysia remembers that she "had just turned twelve. Before you were twelve you didn't need to have any band, so I was *very proud* when I could go and buy a band for myself. That's why I still have it, because it was so fresh and clean [laughs]."[23] Leon mentions how the sirens went off at night: "I remember that I was afraid, but it was also exciting to be awakened and go down to the shelter. We didn't really think anything could happen to us."[24]

Thinking/taking action

Arranging a "corner of one's own"

Marysia had her private place in the bathroom. She recalls: "Then my aunts came, and that made us seven people who had to live in that room. When I was going to do my homework, I went to the adjoining bathroom, which belonged to the bedroom, and there, on a clothes basket, I did my homework. There were always crowds of people there. That's why I escaped to the bathroom."[25]

Games

It happened that people played football in the ghetto, "the Jewish prisoners with those firemen, the Poles who were guarding us. Both Poles and Germans guarded us."

Studies

Sam notes that it was forbidden to go to school, but there were "underground schools". He adds: "If you had a book, you often went around with it inside your trousers."[26] Liv tells about "fantastic people who taught us (in secret). There was one woman, she made things like mountains and rivers out of kitchen utensils to teach us . . . it was so exciting, wonderful! But then one day she was just gone."[27]

Memories of good voices

Sonja, who spent time at an orphanage, tells how she came to hear lots of stories, and "There were lots of songs, we always sang very much." Her favourite game was a game they called "the telephone of the deaf. You whispered a sentence in the ear of the person next to you, and then that person did the same, and so on the whole way until at the end, *when the last person had to repeat the sentence out loud, it could come out in the most ridiculous way*."[28] Perhaps this is also an act of symbolizing concerning the good that will come out when everything is over.

Taking care of hair

Emilia recalls being helped with her hair: "She combed my hair. She was wonderful. I had rather long hair in plaits. Thick plaits. I had lice. I had scabies."[29] The interviewees have many memories of combing someone else's long hair or of having their own hair combed. The hair seems to recur as a significant linking object.

Making shoes

To combat the starkly cold weather that prevailed, a number of the children and their relatives found creative solutions. Marysia tells how her mother "had an acquaintance of father's make shoes for me out of her purse, and this way I got a pair of moccasins. I was so proud of these shoes and didn't dare to use them."[30]

Various sources of help

There were cases where families managed with the help of their rescuers to escape from the ghetto and then go into hiding. The risks were great, however. The parents' professions, their contacts before the war, language skills, especially being able to speak German and Polish without an accent, could sometimes serve as advantages. Having the economic means to bribe a guard could sometimes facilitate an escape for a number of family members.

Age distorting

Depersonalization/emotional stunting

The birthday as a benchmark for trauma

Under the life conditions in the time before the ghetto, as described above, birthdays seem to have had significance as a normalizing, space-creating factor. However, it now became increasingly difficult to retain these important milestones for the children, and birthdays are connected more and more frequently with memories of massive trauma. Events that had previously served for *space creating now become primarily aspects of memories of perforating.* Marysia says of her 12th birthday: "It was without a doubt the dullest of all my birthdays. I remember that I got a couple of Vienna sausages as a present, and that was admittedly fantastic, but in any case I remember it as very, very dreary."[31] Liv says that she remembers the date because "my birthday was the day after. In my childish way I remember it exactly for that reason. Everyone was still there, they were ordered to line up, I think it was five and five, and wait for further orders. And then the Germans were going to take out the ones they wanted to send on . . . and it turned into a totally *nightmarish* day." However, the birthday itself would be celebrated. Liv continues: "In any case, when I had my birthday that time, when we were staying with a German woman, my parents decided that I would get an egg for my birthday. It was a big event in life. So they bought an egg from that sadistic woman, and made some koggelmot [egg toddy] out of it, whatever it's called, with sugar. And it was going to be very big, so we divided that egg up, all four of us, and I'll never forget it. It was such a fantastic meal. And I just keep thinking about how that was a birthday present for a little girl that we all had a part of, because it was no fun for me to eat it all by myself."[32]

Interrupted thinking

Sometimes the children got a chance to study with a teacher in the ghetto who might be an acquaintance. However, their own possibilities of taking in new knowledge were often severely limited. Marysia remembers that she did not go to her lessons: "I didn't have the strength . . . my head could not cope with such atrocities [closes her eyes and shakes her head]."[33]

Feeling pushed aside

Spatial orientation was made difficult in a drastic way because the children "lost their bearings" in the chaos that arose. If there were beds in the available apartments, they were often too small, or people lay "like sardines". Leon lay in a bed with slats on it and remembers how his feet "stuck out through the slats at the foot of the bed."[34] Sandor recalls that "the ground opened itself under my feet, I was totally horrified".[35] When the liquidation of the ghetto took place, Noa had to stay out of the way: "I had to hide, because officially I did not exist."[36]

Taking responsibility/precocity

Concealing age and ethnic identity

In the high-heeled shoes that she had borrowed, Anna looked older. Girls were sometimes given hairstyles like those of the German girls so that they would blend in. The German girls wore plaits just as the Jewish girls did, but, in addition, their hair was coiled into a special "curl" in the front.[37] Jakob remembers how he tried to compensate for his small stature: "I was so little, you know. . . . I stretched myself as tall as I could and said in German, 'ich kann arbeiten', I can also work. And after several minutes he said that we can stay, and he said something that we did not understand at the time. He said it in German: 'I grant you reprieve.'"[38] Marcus, who was six years old in the ghetto, tells (very emotionally) how he was hidden because of his young age in "a bucket, which they lowered into an earth closet" and how he was later given a new birth certificate. "They hid me in a bucket, which they lowered into an earth closet. I had to spend the day there, all the time until the evening, when they hid me in an attic. I don't really remember [how long I was there], but it was somewhere around a week to ten days, and during that time they made some new documents for me, which meant that they made me four years older. And in that way I suddenly became ten years old, and that meant that I could work. They also found me a job during that time. The interesting thing about this is that I actually have papers showing that I am four years older than I really am. *The playing time of life had so to say ended for me.*"[39]

The manoeuvre that Rumkowski carried out in Lòdz, as mentioned above, led to the removal of children and adults over 65 years of age. Marysia's family struggled to avoid being put into these categories. As she says, "I had to look older and my grandmother had to look younger."[40]

Children taking responsibility for adults

The children took risks in the ghetto to get their hands on a bit of food for themselves and a parent. Ester recounts: "I did not care if it was dangerous . . . perhaps I took chances like that, as an ordinary fourteen-year-old, . . . in a state of total unawareness. . . . I did not ask her for permission."[41] An extremely tense situation arose for those families who had to select one member for further transport. Janina thought that she could be the one who took responsibility for her family and signed up: "Every family had to abandon one member to be sent away [to Auschwitz] because the authorities did not think that there was enough work here. And I really thought so, that I can sacrifice myself."[42]

Those children, like Leon and Ruben, who did not have any sisters or brothers, most probably stayed closer to the adults. Leon "kept close to the adults and listened", "was like a miniature adult . . . was very curious." He has been stuck with this "being clever and good syndrome" for the rest of his life.[43] Julia was also "grown-up" for her age and "very much with the adults."[44]

Curtains dangling in empty windows

The inhabitants of the ghettos were deported to death camps and to concentration camps. A small minority escaped or went into hiding. The ghettos emptied. Sam recalls: "And then we were sent to a rounding-up place, an old synagogue on the other side of the ghetto. We walked there, mother and father and I and an SS man. It was a terrible wandering because the ghetto was completely empty. *We saw curtains dangling in the windows. There and everywhere* lay people who had been shot, and from time to time we saw someone we knew. This was not a pleasant walk."[45]

The following sections concern the life situation that was in store for them.

D   Hidden / fugitive / partisan

"So we were people who did not exist."[1]

Outer threats / Experiences	Anti-semitism/ Racial laws	Deporta-tion	Ghetto	Hidden/ Fugitive/ Partisan	Camps	Liberation	Encounter with Sweden/ Post-wartime
Perforating							
Space creating							
Age distorting							

In all historical periods, there have been cases of children going temporarily into hiding. The special focus of this section, however, is on situations in which children *were hidden by others*. In the majority of cases, the children were hidden by Polish women who may have been in contact with the child's family earlier in some context, in some instances as a nanny. On the one hand, many of the interviewees make statements such as "the Poles had a very hostile attitude towards Jews. If they had been friendlier, many Jews would have survived the war, because there were many hiding places."[2] On the other hand, the interviewees who were hidden by Poles testify to the great risks that they took for their own lives.

Some children escaped with their parents or, in exceptional cases, were active as partisans in the resistance movement, in spite of their young ages. The life conditions for the interviewees described in this section may have been very different. What they have in common is that they avoided being transported to concentration camps.

Perforating

Invading of the senses

Experiences of having things torn away,
having the body compressed

Alice's first memory is of being put in a chest drawer full of sheets by the woman who was hiding her. She remembers the horror that she experienced: "She said to me, 'You must keep quiet. *You must keep quiet.* I beg you, don't cry. I will come and get you in a little while.' *And so she covered me with sheets and almost closed the drawer.* This was a horrifying experience. I don't know what happened while she was away. I heard screams, I heard crying, and then I remember that she took . . . she took me away from there. She was crying, and her face was swollen. . . . Then I remember that my mother disappeared, and I asked, 'Where did my mother go?' That was the *last time I can remember anything having to do with feeling my mother's presence.* I recall earlier occasions, when we went for walks. But I don't remember my mother's face."

Later, people felt that they had to hide Alice in a shed because she could not be quiet enough. She remembers, "I kept calling for my mother." About the shed, she says, "the worst there was the *loneliness and the cold.*"[3]

Helena remembers the escape from Denmark to Sweden and spending the night in a little fishing cabin: "I remember that the *room was small*, I remember that in the evening. . . . I *saw a black cat.* My sister and I *shared a little bed with slats on it,* and I remember that it *stank of urine.* I remember that my father stood over us and cried."[4] Helena has memory images of that *cramped space.* She also remembers what kind of bed it was, a bed with slats, and what the air was like, reduced and penetrated by the odour of urine. The cramped space meant a closeness to her sister and to her father. She also remembers the man who saved them: "He was wearing a big Icelandic sweater [laughs] and had high rubber boots." The helper's Island sweater can have functioned as a safe and enclosing cover in which

Helena could rest her thoughts. She also describes the tortuous transport across the sound: "The weather was incredibly rough, with high waves, and I remember how we were *thrown back and forth all over the place* and vomited and vomited."[5]

Observing what is happening

At the time of the trauma, the children's own energy was concentrated mostly on hiding their identity and on feelings of loneliness and of being outsiders. As Teresa puts it: "The feeling of fear, that came, of course, afterwards, when they had gone or when everything was all over." What took place in front of the children's very eyes was most probably not possible to put into a comprehensible context at the time it happened. Only later have they understood what happened to them.

Maya was a partisan and lived in the forest. She remembers: "The hardest thing for me, that was the way we all had to take turns standing guard—sometimes we were two, but sometimes alone. And at night I was always scared. I did not let anyone see it, but when it was my turn, I was more or less terrified. I thought, 'My God, what will happen when I see a German, when they see me? How will I manage?' Then at other times I wondered how I would keep from falling asleep. And it was so cold, it was terrible, terrible."[6]

Tearing away

The helpers' fear

Maya tells of being hidden for a time with her little brother and of his difficulties keeping still in the hiding place: "He sat there, my little brother, and if someone came into the house, he wanted to know who it was—he was, after all, just six years old, and so he looked out. He had the hardest time of us all. It was hard for a child to keep still. Our helpers were very scared that someone would see him do something, and it was hard to keep him hidden behind there, where we were. And suddenly after some time they could not live with their fear any longer, and so they told us that we had to leave. We had to get out. It wasn't that they did not want to help us, but they were afraid."[7]

Terrible things could happen to the helpers. Maya heard later that "the first house where we stayed, the woman who helped us first, who took care of us, they burned her house down . . . the police tried to get rid of her and her family."

On the other hand, a number of the helpers could turn aggressive. Eva heard a helper say, "If you don't move immediately, I am going to report you to the Germans, because I know that you are Jews."

Being separated from parents

However, the most crucial aspect of being hidden was that it meant that the ties to the child's family and origin were completely cut off. The majority of the children who were hidden would never see their parents again. They were sometimes transported far away from their home environment and given the task of living their life in hiding and of avoiding being found out. Sometimes parents did not dare to trust their children. They did not think that their children could keep "secrets". Added to this, parents and children were sometimes forced by circumstances to hide in different places.

Body marking

Compressing the body

Invading of the children's senses now took place through their having to compress their bodies in their hiding places: "She was forced to press me in, because there wasn't enough space for me, so the cupboard was almost standing on top of me. She told me to hold my breath and not to breathe because they were searching for me."

Sometimes the children had to share a bed (in houses where they were being protected). "It was a double bed. We slept eight children in it. We slept head up feet down, feet up head down, and so on."

Space creating

Thinking/fantasizing

Thoughts about living quarters

The children paid special attention to the rooms and to the general layout of their hiding places: "There was only one room. Well, it really wasn't a room at all, it was a little space with planks around it. More like a little hut. No, it wasn't a room. It was something that was boarded up. It was fairly empty, but there was also some rubbish and junk there, things people would throw in, not garbage, but things you'd put in an attic."[8]

Looking out

Alice looked out through the knot-holes of the wooden boards that made up the shed in which she was hidden: "If I stood on tiptoe, I could come up to the hole, and I saw the sun and I saw the specks of dust floating in. I saw a little bit of the sky, too. I saw the birds, geese, I remember, when they flew in their formation. I knew that when they fly in that direction, it is going to get cold, but if they come from the other direction, it will be warm. I remember aeroplanes, and I remember the cows that I could see through that hole."[9] To keep the loneliness and the cold away, she hummed "all the songs imaginable", and she recited poems that she remembered from her early childhood.

Making themselves invisible

The children hid their faces as much as possible. Emilia elaborates: "I didn't know what was important and what was not important. . . . I felt safe in the church, because it was so dim in there. I could be on my knees and *hide my face* so that people could not stare at me. I did not attract attention in there. When I was outside, I could a woman whispering: 'She is a Jewish girl.' In the church I was almost invisible."[10]

Seeing the beautiful

Maya was going to escape over the sea in a boat, together with some other youths: "We were extremely scared, we just sat so still. I remember that night so well. It was actually so beautiful. It was pitch-black dark, but the water was so still."[11]

Thinking/taking action

Several dresses on top of each other

Many of the interviewees tell how they tried to take as much as possible with them when they were escaping or being deported. Liv got out of the ghetto with her mother, "so mother and I put on all of the clothes that we had, this was very poorly planned, we put several dresses on top of each other. Mother bribed the guard. I remember this scene so well, it is as if it happened recently. We were stopped by a young Pole, and I felt my legs give way under me."[12] Liv's mother went through agonies when he said that she had to give him her wedding ring, but she did and they could continue to their hiding place.

Sometimes relatives could serve as helpers by virtue of their attitude towards the life conditions around them and their contact with the children. Mirjam tells about her aunt, who was a "rock of strength for me, because she was able in some way to maintain a little distance to all of this. To be able to talk about other things, that was, I think, my salvation."[13]

Fixing shoes

Alice made an invention out of the only pair of shoes that she had, shoes that were actually too small, in order not to freeze too much: "I ripped up the toe part of those shoes with a nail so that I would have enough space for my foot."[14]

Maintaining a "normal contact"

As Emilia expresses it, "and I wrote little notes to my parents in their hiding place. I remember that it was after my birthday. I had just turned eleven, that was it. It was the 24th of July. And then we were together. *It was normal.*"[15]

Hiding their identity among non-Jewish children

In some cases the children exerted indirect resistance by hiding their identity and keeping in the company of non-Jewish children. This is simultaneously a "space-creating" and an "emotionally stunting" act. Emilia speaks of her actions in hiding her identity, "I built on that. I had two girlfriends. One girl my age who was Reichsdeutsch and the other was Volksdeutsch. I was very aware of what I was doing, even though I was so young. I reasoned like this: when we play together, no one can suspect that I am Jewish, because her father, the father of the girl who was Reichsdeutsch, he was in the SS, I believe. I remember his leather boots and his manner. I went wherever they went. Because I thought that it was safest to be with them."[16]

Participating as partisans

Maya was only twelve years old when she, as mentioned above, joined a partisan group hiding in the forest. She stayed with them for almost two years: "We met two boys, partisans with rifles. They took us to their group. They had earthen huts. They were Russians. So began our new life. My sister and I became partisans."[17]

Age distorting

Depersonalization / emotional stunting

Being closed in

Liv describes how they were in hiding, "just like Anne Frank, behind a bookshelf in a little closet. We were crowded, shut in, and undernourished." Liv "fainted", and they had to "sit quietly and keep from coughing or sneezing. It was better to suffocate than to let any sound come out. I have enough to say about this to last ten days."[18]

Making adjustments

Depersonalization in the cases of the hidden children is connected to *receiving or being forced to take on* "a new identity", which could mean that they gained some freedom of action, whereas they otherwise might have become incapacitated. However, this space in which to act was subordinated to maintaining the greatest possible self-aware-ness and careful behaviour in order not to be found out. In this sense it constituted a "shrinking" of their existence. The children were left on their own more and more. As hidden children, they were, as noted already, preoccupied with how others saw them, but also with how the other children behaved. They could hide themselves by re-sembling other children and by giving up their own identity.

Being the object of special treatment

Children hidden in a family were treated differently from the fami-ly's own children and the other children in the area. One woman remembers tearfully how the family's own daughter received a bicy-cle for Christmas, while she did not. Hidden children were also in constant fear that the adults would send them away out of fear.

Taking responsibility / precocity

New identity

Another aspect of the adjustments that the children had to make was that often they understood the seriousness of the situation in which they found themselves. Thus they precociously took responsibility for the new identity that they had been assigned as hidden children. Emilia was asked by a priest what name she wanted to have: "I said that I wanted a name that was similar to E. I was thinking that if someone called out to me, I wanted to recognize that it was me they meant. So I chose a name that resembled my real one."

Feeling grown up

Emilia remembers how her father happened to come home one day for a temporary visit: "I must have grown while he was away because I know that I thought that he had become smaller, very thin." She adds, "but I just know that I was like bursting with happiness to have him there."[19]

Being older than their parents

Julia comments that "it is so difficult to imagine that my father was so young. For me, I believe he somehow gets older in my head the whole time. Also, when you are little, you think your father is so grown up, and then suddenly you find yourself 23 years older than he ever got to be."[20]

Having false papers and being forced to lie

Members of the same family had to take on the names and dates of birth of dead people in order to hide their own identities, and thus "new" relationships were created. Eva explains that she was assigned to be her mother's niece, and that her mother was supposed to be dead. Julia was given another girl's name. She says: "I was conscious that I must not say any other name but my new one. However, I could not bring myself to stop addressing my mother as 'mother'."[21]

E   Concentration camps and work camps

"I always tried to keep a little to the background, so that no one would discover that I am a child."[1]

Experiences \ Outer threats	Anti-semitism/ Racial laws	Deporta-tion	Ghetto	Hidden/ Fugitive/ Partisan	Camps	Liberation	Encounter with Sweden/ Post-wartime
Perforating							
Space creating							
Age distorting							

The systematic murdering of European Jews and the genocide of gypsies were preceded by state-sanctioned murder of physically handicapped, mentally handicapped and "asocial" people. The operation was begun in 1939. In 1941 the mass shootings of the Jewish populations in the Baltic and in the occupied areas of the Soviet Union had become routine. Nazi Germany's invasion of the Soviet Union on June 22, 1941, Operation Barbarossa, marked the beginning of the systematic murdering of Jews. The mass gassings in the concentration camp at Auschwitz began in the end of 1941 and the same was true of other death camps and concentration camps. In 1942 a conference takes place in Wannsee to coordinate "the final solution of the Jewish question in Europe" [Bruchfeld & Levine, 1999]

The only task of the *death camps* was to put people to death by in-dustrial methods. In the combined death–*concentration* camps people were sent directly to their death or were selected for slave labour. Around every concentration camp there were work camps, which were, in turn, often placed beside large factories.

The prerequisites for a continued life were annihilated for the majority of those who were transported to concentration camps, as was witnessed by the survivors. The interviewees describe how the space for their own possibilities of surviving physically and psychically was reduced to a minimum. They were separated from their families, and they could only relate to their fellow prisoners to a very limited extent. Significant objects are metal bowls for the "soup ration" and perhaps a straw mattress.

Perforating

Tearing away

The splitting up of families

In the train transports children could end up in one car and the parents in another. Sofia tells how she was "crushed against a wall, so that I saw absolutely nothing. I only had one thing on my mind, to find my mother, my father, and my little brother." Upon arrival at Auschwitz she was made to witness how "they took my grandmother and threw her up on a truck. . . . I just saw it, how she flew up there." After a short time Sofia was reunited with her parents and her little brother: "We stood there holding hands, and then they ordered me to go to the left and the others to the right."[2] It was common that children were separated from their parents as part of the selection routine, since they would not survive then. However, in exceptional cases children were sent to "work" and thus got a chance to avoid death; in even more exceptional cases they could be together with a parent or a brother or sister, at least for a time.

Children were accepted only to a very limited extent. Children who said that *they were older* than they were and who were *relatively large in stature* could make it through the selection and were thereafter treated as adult prisoners. In later selections children could be taken out and entire groups of children obliterated. "They could just take out some of us when we had roll call." "They took the children away." Parts of the accounts of the interviewees who were in the camps and survived against all odds are given in the following sections.

Invading of the senses

"Russian roulette"

Oscar describes going into the shower room as comparable to Russian roulette: "I was almost sure that I was the youngest. I was twelve years old. In some strange way I got on the right side of them. We were stripped naked, herded into a shower. I don't know if people who have never experienced terror can really understand this. If you go into a shower room and think that you are going to start taking a shower [pause], it's about like Russian roulette, you can put eight bullets in a pistol . . . but you put in only one. If you try to imagine that this evening I am going to take a shower but if I turn on the wrong faucet, I am going to die in the shower. I wonder what feeling a person would have, and then turn on that faucet. But we had no choice."[3]

Looking into the adults' faces

Everyone was rounded up, and, as Oscar describes it, "taken to huge open areas, I remember it as though I see it today, for me it represents the *Sahara Desert*".[4] Time in the camp often consisted of "waiting." Many of the interviewees depict this in such terms as "being in a world of fog . . . we did not know what was going on. We just waited." Lena tells how the children "read" the faces of their fellow prisoners in order to *orient themselves* in the context of their present situation. Lena explains: "The SS came and checked us a couple of times and we children had as you understand nothing to do. It was hot in the daytime out there, so we got together and *looked at the adults and at the adults' faces*. They obviously expressed confusion and anxiety and horror. No one knew what was going to happen to us . . . *we only had to look at their faces*."[5] She adds that no one ever cried in the camp. The adults did not cry, and so the children did not cry either. It was taboo.[6] The children also tried to form an idea of how the aggressors looked at them. They tried to figure out if the aggressors could feel the vibrations a child gave with regard to age and fear.

The aggressors' appearance

The appearance of the aggressors seems to have imprinted itself as a permanent memory image in the minds of the child survivors, as have their assessments of who was cruel and who was "nice". Jenny, telling about her arrival at Auschwitz, says that after the disinfection routine had been carried out, a woman came and told them to follow her, "The Blockälteste [leader], she was Czech, and her name was Joli. I can't remember if she spoke to us in Hungarian or German." When Jenny asked about her sister, "she just made a crude remark and said that we were not allowed to talk, Ruhe!" They were taken to Children's Block 12, where there were other children and "even adults and pregnant women".

Joli was "short, plump and had curly hair. She was 25 years old. She did not hurt us. She shouted all the time, but she did not hurt us." Jenny thinks that she would have helped the children if that had been possible. She was being "worked to death". A kapo, a Polish woman, "had very fat legs, you could recognize her from a great distance". There was a German who "is fairly well-known, Gresi or Greta, a blond, very beautiful woman. There was a very nice doctor lady, who was Jewish herself, and she told us in Hungarian that we should try to avoid getting sick and absolutely make sure that we did not end up at Revier. She told us to keep clean." This "doctor lady, this auntie" told them that Revier was cleared out every second, every third day. Revier does not appear to have functioned as a hospital. "She had brown eyes and was a nice little auntie . . . auntie, well, she was maybe only 30 years old, so she was probably just an auntie in my eyes."[7] Nomi was "hideously frightened" of "those German women with those rubber truncheons in their hands".[8] Sofie speaks of "Mengele" and of "Ilse". Ilse was gorgeous, "such a cruel human being in such a beautiful body".[9]

Being forced to look

Sonja tried to *avoid looking*: "I could never keep all of those guards straight, I did not want to look at them, *I did not want to see their faces*."[10] Sam remembers how he was forced to watch the hangings, "and they went around and made sure that we didn't close our eyes or look away [his voice shakes]".[11]

The aggressors' unpredictability

The reasonable attempts made by the children, in accordance with their earlier experiences in life, to turn to the *adults*—in this case the aggressors—and to *appeal to them for warmth* appear to have been consistently and brutally knocked back. A girl asked the guard if he could close the door because the girls, who sat there naked, were cold, "and then he went over and opened the door even wider, so that we would freeze a little more".[12] Sandor asked, in German, "May I warm my hands so that I can work?" whereupon the guard shouted in German, "Was du verfluchter Schwein!" Sandor continues, "Then he got up and kicked me in the small of the leg, making two deep wounds which bled heavily. God or angels must have been protecting me because I don't understand how I kept from bleeding to death. It gradually healed, luckily I have flesh that heals very well."[13] During the interview Sandor pulls up his trouser leg a bit and shows me the white scars on his leg, which are a result and a constant reminder of the kicks. There is a great amazement about how those who behaved so brutally towards the children "could go home at night and hug their own children".

"The latrine grapevine"

The children were confronted with the *shrieking* voices of the guards, who at the same time—as in the example above—told them that they had to keep *quiet*. When they did get a chance to talk to each other, as in the latrine area, they would hear horrible things. Lilian tells how she heard in Ravensbrück about "experiments that were being carried out on human beings". That was the kind of thing they heard. She calls it the "latrine grapevine".[14]

Memory images of dead people

The children saw mountains of corpses. In the words of one of the interviewees, "I didn't know what it was the first time, it was so *white*, I thought it was a . . . so then I saw that it was actually human beings who were lying in all directions and their hands and legs were sticking out and their mouths were open and they were so emaciated, just skeletons . . . [cries] . . . and our thoughts were that, yes, one day we will be lying there ourselves because we could not see any end to it all."[15] Many of the interviewees emphasize their distinct memory of that special stench.

Tearing away

The threat to the attachment to the family

An early memory of a boy who was only three–four years of age when he was put in Ravensbrück can serve to illustrate the lack of food and the attachment to a parent. David recalls: "I slept with my mother on the top bunk, it was the third or the fourth bunk. I woke up in the middle of the night, and I remember that I said to my mother in Slovak, 'mother, schleba', mother, bread. I could not find her. 'Mother, where are you?' 'I am here', she said. I started to crawl towards where I thought she was, but I came to the edge of the bed. 'Here', she said from somewhere. So I crawled right out into the thin air and fell down three or four bunks. Suddenly it got light. Then I don't remember any more."[16]

The children would walk along the barbed wire fence to see if they could find their relatives. As one of them says, "I was, of course, so painfully lonely, even though my father was with me in the beginning. I missed my mother and my brother."

Nomi was just one year old when the war broke out. She tells about a woman she happened to be put together with in the concentration camp. Her mother had been taken away in one of the transports. She never saw her father again. She appears to have realized that the woman was getting worse. Then she died. Nomi explains more about their relationship. She was about six years old at the time: "People teased me because I did not have a mother and whatever. So I asked this woman if I could call her my mother. But she answered that I had a mother already, and you only have one mother in your life. She said that I had a mother and maybe she . . . . But she told me that I could call her 'tjotja', which is auntie in Polish. So I did that and on this particular day I called out, 'tjotja, tjotja' but she didn't move. I didn't know what was going on. The others lying in the room knew what had happened. She had died! I just clung to her and kissed her so they had to pull her away from me."[17] Nomi tells what happened from the perspective of a child, which illustrates the power of such traumatic memories. They can also think in such terms as, "if someone's eyes are closed, maybe she is sleeping."

Having the birthday torn away

Sandor recalls: "I had not turned thirteen yet. We must have arrived at Auschwitz some time in June, in the middle of June, because I know that I was thinking, 'Well, well, it's getting to be time for my birthday soon'."[18]

Having clothes, shoes, and other objects torn away

They took away Sofia's "little earrings"—the kind that children were always given at birth—and her glasses. They cut her hair off, "shaved it off".[19] Nomi had been given a metal ring, and she gave it up, she put it in a box where she saw all the others abandoning their possessions.

The loss of shoes was disastrous. Anna tells how she was "in the forest, and there was just snow everywhere, and I went there with only a blanket around me. I had no shoes, only 'schmattes' [rags] on my feet."

Body marking

Being marked by the aggressors' glances

The children's human dignity was torn away. From the very beginning of the time in the camp, the girls were made to feel a sense of shame. Bella explains: "We had to sit in a cold room with the door open. The guard sat there fully dressed with his rifle and guarded us. We women were completely naked. This was so extremely degrading. It wasn't just that it was cold, we were completely naked, we were young, we were ashamed. There was a completely different morality in those days; nakedness in front of a strange man was unheard of. We stood there naked and had to let the air dry us. The German soldiers were walking around there. It was unspeakably humiliating [she looks down]."[20]

Being assigned a number

The interviewees remember how they were stamped with numbers: "I was assigned a number that I will never forget, I memorized it, so I could recite it if I was awakened in the middle of the night." To make sure that the prisoners did not run away while marching, "we had to cut out a square on the back of our uniform, and then we got patches that were green and grey, and we had to sew these patches onto the back instead".[21] If the patches were ripped off, the back became bare, and the hole that remained could then function as a marking. To get rid of the whole upper part of the uniform was not possible in the "bitterly cold winter". They were without protection, "without skin".

Being herded

As one interviewee puts it: "In Ravensbrück we were *herded onward*. I remember that I had no socks, no cover for my head, even though all my hair was shaved off. I was given a pair of wooden shoes, a summer skirt, which probably belonged to someone else from whom they had taken things earlier. And they gave me a jacket that belonged to a summer suit. In this biting cold, that was all I had."[22]

Sustaining injuries to the skin

Sam's feet were frostbitten, and the itching sensations that resulted lasted for many years.[23] Henny tells what happened to her sister's hands: "We had a square crate with four handles, and we had to walk several kilometres with it. There it was filled with turnips. And I know that my sister's hands were frozen and she suffered frostbite from that night."[24]

Lice caused untold torment. They had to be sure not to scratch themselves too much. If they did, they would pierce their skin and "open sores could not heal properly".

Nina recalls that "the Sturmbanführer saw that I took my bowl, which was dirty, and fetched [more] soup, and he gave me a beating, and he did this to my nose, they say that it's a little crooked." Anna's nose was also injured. During the interview she shows me a scar on her nose that resulted from a Gestapo man's blow.

Having the body compressed

One of the interviewees remembers:, "They pressed my chest in. Yes, I could not get any air, I had so much trouble with this. But they had put that thing on my shoulders, and that's the way it went. I was not built to bear that frightful weight. So I fell down again and again, and they beat me again and again."[25]

Being broken down still further during the "death marches"

In the final phases of the war the prisoners were made to move yet another time: a forced evacuation. Under extremely severe conditions, they were forced on the so-called "death march", kilometer after kilometre to the west, in order to get away from the Soviet army.

Space creating

Thinking/fantasizing

Younger children had no way of grasping the magnitude of what was happening to them, which possibly in one sense helped to create small spaces for thought.

Finding interesting aspects

Elias comments on his arrival and how he had to be shaved: "I remember so well myself thinking that it was weirdly funny that they even shaved my chest, even though I was only thirteen years old. But apparently some hair had already started sticking out there."[26]

Longings

Sandor remembers talking about "our homes and food and if we would ever get out of this, this captivity, and if we would ever see our families again. Those were our subjects, those and only those. Every normal frame of reference was gone. All that counted was surviving for the day."[27] Jenny elaborates on the same subject: "*We always talked about the future and the past.* What else under such circumstances? We were hungry . . . we talked about the food we would prepare when we came home . . . what was on everyone's mind was, where is my mother, what is my father doing, my brothers and sisters?. . . . In general, everyone shared the same fate. No one had a mother or father there any more. We told each other how our fathers had been taken away. They were all about my age, we were in the same grade. We talked about school, and so on."[28] Even if many became passive, they could still retain a feeling of "a self". "Being able to maintain the integrity of an individual by sustaining his core self was instrumental to survival, and that is different from simple passivity" (Balas, 2000).

The children had brief moments when they could look out through windows, holes, and cracks, they could look over the fence to the other side in order to be able to fix their gaze on something that *existed outside*, something that *appeared secure out there*. By doing so it might also have been possible for them to dream themselves away from their horrifying reality, the reality of being closed in, of being in captivity. Henny observes: "I saw a woman hanging up her wash on a clothesline. But everything was electrified, so I couldn't get out of there. And I remember that I promised myself that *if I survive this war,* I am going to hang up my wash the same way, *and I do it,* here behind the house. To this very day. . . . So *we could see freedom, but it was unattainable.*"[29] Henny makes a link between her observation (the clothesline) and something that, in the world of her imagination, can take place at a later time, when the war is over. This serves as a space for thinking, which in turn makes it possible to endure an otherwise unbearable situation as a captive. Moreover, she actually does what she promised herself that she would do (hang up her wash the way she saw the woman doing it). This can be seen as an expression of the fact that the memory is always present in her mind, even if she is not always aware of thinking about it.

The aggressors' "unpredictability": the advantage of "being little"

Sometimes space creating seems to have coincided with a moment of benevolence on the part of the guards. The youngest children who had somehow managed to get through the selections risked being found out later. This was especially true at roll calls, when their "smallness" alerted the guard to the fact that they *were children who were not supposed to be there.* Oscar explains: "I was a child, and maybe they thought it was strange and were asking themselves how I got there, but they actually showed partiality towards me. After some days they said, 'You can help out and cut the bread.'"[30] The children's smallness—*"the little ones"*—appears in such cases to have appealed to the German guards' softer side. Interaction with the child brought forth a *little* space. Sonja tells of a march in the severely cold winter, during which they ate frozen potatoes: "You understand, that we had to survive." The guard "who walked beside me . . . actually took me under the arm, because he saw that I was about to fall, and then I would have been shot."[31]

Henny also gives an example supporting the finding that the aggressors' unpredictability seems to have been one of the most common reasons that the children managed to create a space for themselves during their time in the camps: "And there came E, he was going to give me a lighter job, don't ask me why." As Elias explains: "I was, you know, rather young then, and I was given certain favours. I helped out there in the barracks. The man in charge of those barracks, I took care of his clothes, polished his shoes, cleaned his room. He brought some extra food for me."[32] He also managed to remove Elias from a group of children headed for death.

Anna tells about how the guards wanted some entertainment and asked who could sing: "I had a friend in the camp who sang really well. She was like a sister to me. When the guards said that, I said to her, 'Klara, I am going to say that you can sing', but she was very scared. But you see how I am, I went right up to the guards and said, 'Die Kleine ja singt wie schein' 'gute singen'." And they put us up there in front. She sang like a bird, and she got a little bread, which she shared with me. Otherwise I would not have survived."[33]

Being together with a family member

Sam states that if he had not had his father there by his side, he would not have made it: "I was so unbearably tired. I held my father's hand (during the death march). That way I could march and sleep at the same time."[34] Because Oscar was so young and little, only nine years old, he was always worried when the guards and the SS soldiers seemed to be looking at him, examining him. His father was always there by his side.

In contrast, Janina felt that she managed best when she was alone. She felt that she was rather egotistic when she cried for her mother, but at the same time refrained from contacting her in the camp: "I understood that it was every man for himself and that I had a greater chance to make it alone than if we were together [and had to share the bread ration]."[35]

Linking objects

It was not usually possible for the children to keep things of their own. Lilian says, however: "I have no idea how I managed, but I got to keep my shoes."[36] Sonja draped her "coat over her shoulders" and she had a "bag from home". There were a few things there, "The most important things I had there were *pictures of our parents when they were young* and of us three [siblings]. Those were my treasures." Nomi comments: "We also had a wine-coloured bowl from . . . yes, some sort of metal bowl, wine-coloured. We were supposed to use it to fetch our ration . . . our soup."[37] The bowl became an object of focus for all of them.

In the final phase of the time in the camps, when people were dying, there were survivors who miraculously managed to keep their clothes on. One of them explains, "I had a turtleneck sweater with a zip here [demonstrates], which I had taken with me from home. It had many colours, was knitted in different colours. I wore that day and night, day and night."[38]

According to Winnicott (1953), if a mother has been physically absent for a time period that extends beyond a certain point, the memory will fade of the inner representation of her (or of him, in the case of the father). Transitional phenomena gradually become meaningless, and the child can no longer experience them. The object, the mother, loses its power of attraction. Just before this occurs, we can sometimes see an exaggerated use of transitional objects as an element of the denial that the original object is in the process of losing its meaning.

Memorizing family traditions

Lilian had a special liking for pessach: "We got new clothes then. *We got patent leather shoes.* We wiped them off every step we took."[39] Sandor has vivid, detailed memories of traditions as inner positive experiences that he had taken with him and that have contributed to his being able to survive with his "sanity intact". His memories of sensory images in the following account include *"the air"*, *"the tablecloth"*, *"the sound of the prayers"*, *"the silence"*, *"the taste"*, and *"the children's laughter"*:

"When I think back on it, I can really feel the *air* in our home just as it was on Friday evenings when my father and I came home from the temple, from the synagogue. Mother had always *set the table very exquisitely* with a white tablecloth and candelabras and beautiful place settings for all of us, for the whole family, for all the children. Mother said the prayer and lit the candelabras while father washed his hands. From that moment no one was allowed to speak or to say even one word. It was dead silent. Then father poured the wine and blessed it and blessed the Sabbath and took a sip. After that he passed the glass around to the whole family, and everyone took a sip. There was this whole long tradition of all these moments, which were repeated inexorably every Friday evening and every holiday. When I think back on it, it feels as though the very air was so holy that you could cut it with a knife. What I mean to say is that it was a beautiful experience and a wonderful feeling.

"After the wine, father said the prayer over the bread. It was what they call in Sweden 'Jewish twists', with poppy seeds on them. There were two of them arranged diagonally to each other, with an exquisitely embroidered cloth over them. [Sandor gives the blessing.] *I remember that, even though I have never said that blessing myself during all these years.* Not one word was to be uttered, not by anyone in the family. It was totally silent. It would never have occurred to anyone to say anything until everyone had been served a piece of the bread, which father cut. *As soon as mother had taken a bite, all the action broke out. The children laughed, and we talked, and we ate that delicious meal with all the courses,* including carp laced with red peppers and a superb chicken soup with vegetables. Every Friday we sang the same songs between the courses. All, all of this has been, quite simply, *a rock of salvation* for me in my hardest moments. I *always thought back on this when I was in the camp, and I am sure that it contributed to the fact that I survived with my sanity intact.*"[40]

During the interview Sandor recites a Hebrew blessing over the bread, a blessing that he has not said in all the years that have passed since he sat together with his family as a child. The memory is brought to the surface in the course of the interview. According to him, "during the entire time in the camp, these memories were sustenance for me in whatever situation I found myself. Not a day passed that I did not return to these memories."[41]

Thinking/taking action

Hiding places

Hiding places were virtually nonexistent. Two men tell how they hid in the toilet area (the latrine). Noa hid in a drainpipe, in a well.[42]

Trying to have a high place

Henny tells how she was herded "into the barracks, and *my first thought was that I had to get a place high up.* That was in any case a place where you knew that no one would fall on top of you and nothing else would fall on you either. Yes, it was terrible, but remember that it was just the beginning." Sandor explains that "we didn't have our bunks along the wall or our heads by the wall but, instead, we had to have our faces towards the aisle and we were like sardines, a large number of us in each section, most of the time on boards and sometimes with blankets. You had to have your face towards the aisle."

Cooperating with a fellow prisoner

As mentioned above, Nomi was six years old when she was transported to the concentration camp together with a woman she called "Auntie B".

She recalls, "We stood out there, and the German women with their rubber truncheons in their hands walked past. I was scared to death to say the least. Ugh! It must have been cold, because Auntie B *told me that I should stand on her feet when we have roll call because otherwise my feet would freeze off.* At that time she seemed fairly okay, I didn't know any better, you know, but then I started to see that she was doing poorly. But she struggled to the bitter end, so that she could go to roll call. *Was it for my sake?*"[43]

Culture

It was very unusual but it did happen that the head of a work camp was "harsh but kind". Sonja tells how they used to put on plays and wanted *"to show that we were human beings, that we had cultural values.* The head was very impressed and got us a Christmas tree for Christmas and put it in the bunkroom. She had no idea that we did not have Christmas trees. She wanted to teach us to sing 'O Tannen-baum'. Shirley Temple films and Snow White came to Poland early, so we got up there in the bunk-room and tried to tap dance."[44] Anja tells how the Blockältersten "came with candles every Friday. Our guards were Jewish girls, and so they asked us if anyone wanted to come and light candles on the shabbes."

It is customary for mothers to sing and hum lullabies for their babies (Duhl, 2000). Humming and fantasizing could give moments of feeling, of feeling alive.

Thinking about and getting food

As mentioned above, Oscar tells how he got to "help out and cut bread, and it perhaps sounds terrible today, but in this case we are not talking about honesty. What I wanted to do was cut the bread into as thin slices as possible so that when my uncle or my father came along, I could give them a proper slice of bread."[45] He gradu-ally became a "full-blown expert" at cutting bread so that there would always be some left for him.

Sonja describes the head of her camp as "human, she got us something that we had not eaten in a long time, warm sausage. We got one each. We couldn't just eat it up, but *we sat there licking it instead, because we wanted the taste to last as long as possible.*"[46] The chil-dren constantly had food on their minds. Bella's dream was to get some white bread. She says: "to this very day, I do not eat any kind of bread but white bread. Yes, I know those health food breads are dark, but I can't bear the thought of them because they remind me too much of the bread in the camp."[47] Most of the interviewees tell of occasions when they took a risk and ran off with a piece of bread or a potato peeling that they had found.

Being combed for lice

In the final phase of the war, Sonja had the good fortune to be sent to a cottage hospital, where she was treated well. She explains: "They washed me and combed me with a louse-comb. *I thought it would never end.* But for me it was a great relief."[48] Bella mentions that she and her mother occupied themselves during the daytime by picking the lice off of each other.

To lick sausages and to pick lice off of each other can be likened to Anzieu's description (1985) of the continuing influence on the function and development of the organism of early tactile stimulation. He emphasizes the importance of tactile contact between mothers and children, as organic stimulation and social communication. As examples he mentions licking and combing, delousing with the fingers, touches, and caresses.

Age distorting

The survivors show many uncertainties about ages, their own and others', during the time at the camps. Nomi says: "No, I didn't understand that at all. I had no thoughts about anything like that [age]."[49] Oscar does not remember his father's age. He comments that "the thing was that he had to be younger and younger, and I had to be older and older. *So age was changed according to the conditions.*"[50] He returns to the question of age many times and remarks that "it's damned lucky that I know how old I am myself".[51]

Depersonalization/emotional stunting

Interrupting of thoughts

Elias points out how "strangely enough, we became numb. We didn't react like we would today. Today I am sure that I would react differently, but then I just thought, 'what luck that they're not doing that to me'."[52] Bella tells how she and her mother just sat on the edge of the bunkbed but still felt the nearness of each other. She adds that "one time when we were delousing each other, my mother suddenly nudged my shoulder and said, 'Wake up, what are you thinking about?' I must have been lost in my thoughts. I remember her alarm about what was happening to my mind. She told me that she could only see the whites of my eyes."

The children were subjected to heavy labour despite their young ages. Abraham underlines how he became "tired and apathetic. . . . I was done in . . . no feelings . . . what can a person expect? I had nothing to think with."[53]

Having intimate things stripped away

In many examples it is apparent how depersonalization was carried out systematically by stripping away the children's bodily attributes. Hair was shaved off, and the children *could no longer be recognized by others*. Glasses were ripped off, making it *hard to see others*. Jewellery, which normally served as significant links to parents and also to their own birth (earrings), was taken away and never returned. Ester gives the following account of this process: "The commanding officer cut off all my hair . . . all the hair on my body. This was, you understand, a very frightful experience, because we became totally transformed into other persons than we were before. Our identity disappeared by having all the hair on our bodies, on our faces, and on our heads taken away. It took a long time for us to recognize each other. Of course, I still knew who my mother was, but even so . . . it was grotesque, close to insane, like completely different people. My first reaction was that I almost felt like laughing at those people who weren't the same any more, until I gradually realized that I was one of those standing there naked."[54]

Sam experienced it as that he himself was dehumanized.[55] *Dehumanized* has become a concept that the survivors, in a retrospective construction, use to refer to the changes in themselves. Bauer (2001) takes exception to using the concept of dehumanization to describe what happened to the prisoners in the camps and the ghettos, because according to him the expression best fits the Nazis: they "dehumanized" themselves. What they did was to project their own abandonment of all earlier norms that had been accepted as "civilized" onto *truly* civilized people, Jews and others. The normal way of using the term "dehumanizing" makes it look as if the aggressors were "human" and the victims less human, and that was precisely what the Nazis wanted to achieve.

Being small enough to fit under the cross-bar

In the words of one of the interviewees, "When they put up one of those cross-bars and told all the children to see if they could walk upright under it, I hid, because those who could were sent to the gas chamber."[56] Many child survivors shared similar experiences.

Taking responsibility/precocity

Deliberately changing one's age and confronting the perpetrator's
unpredictability

Changing of age was sometimes a deliberate act that gave a respite,
a space. When Oscar was moved from one camp to another, he had
reached the age of fifteen, but he said that he was nineteen: "I don't
know whether they believed it, but I made myself nineteen. You can
be a rather small nineteen-year-old, after all."[57]

Generational fusing and disintegrating:
"If we have to die, we will die together"

Bella describes how crowded it was in one freight car, and how someone suggested putting the children where there was more space. She
continues: "At that point my father objected very noisily and said,
'No, the children are not going over to that car. We are going to
stick together. The children's place is here with us.'"[58] When Jacob
looks back, the painful reality overwhelms him: "My whole class was
obliterated . . . everyone is gone except one single girl."[59]

F   Liberation

"And so I was alone, and I just went with the flow"[1]

Outer threats / Experiences	Anti-semitism/ Racial laws	Deporta-tion	Ghetto	Hidden/ Fugitive/ Partisan	Camps	Liberation	Encounter with Sweden/ Post-wartime
Perforating							
Space creating							
Age distorting							

Auschwitz was liberated on 27 January 1945. Bergen-Belsen was liberated on 15 April 1945. Peace was declared in Europe on 8 May 1945.

The interviewees were still to spend some time in or near the concentration camps or in the places in which they had been hidden. They would soon be transported to orphanages, hospitals, and, in some cases, to Sweden. The majority were on the verge of death. Their legs could no longer support them. Their body weight was around 25 kg. The very small minority who had any strength left tried to get to their former places of residence in order to see whether any of their relatives were still alive. Significant persons in this historical period are fellow prisoners and helpers—that is, personnel from the Red Cross. Confrontations with the dead take

148

place continually. Many of the interviewees tell how they themselves lost a parent during the very period of the liberation. The food that was given to them often had an adverse effect upon their recovery because of the lack of knowledge of what was suitable for the survivors to eat. Child survivors have strong memory images of chocolate, sweet biscuits, and soft sheets.

Perforating

Invading of the senses

Generational breakdown reaches its culmination

Paradoxically, in a sense liberation brought with it the greatest pain. As Sandor expresses it: "It was after the liberation that I first understood what fate everyone in my family had met. That's when the whole truth became clear, and they were nowhere to be found. I saw in front of me that mass of human beings, my sisters and brothers and my mother, I saw the direction they went in and where they went. Then the realization of everything hit me, and I think it was from that time on that I had the greatest difficulties in my life, both in Switzerland (where he was sent for treatment after the liberation) and later here in Sweden."[2]

Bella describes herself and her mother: "We were so broken. I could just barely hold my head up. I was too weak to do anything else. My mother could not move at all. I did not even have the strength to care. I could become motherless, but somehow I didn't think about that. Those thoughts came later."[3] Edith notes: "I saw my best friend sitting on the barrack floor with her mother. We recognized each other, but no one said or did anything, we just gave each other a nod of recognition. After a few days, they had disappeared."[4] Now people were forced to realize the totality of their loss.

Dead people everywhere

Memories of the liberation in the concentration camps also include the difficulties the survivors had in orienting themselves after having been cut off so long from the outside world. Sandor remembers when the Germans retreated. He was in a feverish state at the time, lying on the ground under the open sky. It was raining, and he was overwhelmed by dizziness. Apart from these memories, he also has memory images of dead and apathetic people and his own body memories of being totally finished. He says that he would not have been able to go on living for more than a few days longer.

Never-ending sounds

According to a typical account from an interviewee who was hidden, "We had a few seconds to get downstairs to the air-raid shelter. We were afraid that the house would collapse. We heard the siren, someone shouted something on the loudspeaker. At that time we happened to be together. I hear my parents discussing something excitedly *but it was over my head.*" Sonja remembers when the Italians capitulated: "They went around whistling a tune that went 'Bella mi'" [she sings a little tune herself].[5]

The Russians barge in

Mirjam, who lived in hiding, remembers that the Russians barged in and "were brutal and looked frightening". They "rushed around and took everything they could get their hands on". She continues, outraged, to tell how they raped women, "and one of them was my aunt. For her this trauma became impossible to go on living with [she later committed suicide]. It happened in a room very close to ours." Mirjam also recalls that "many of the soldiers thought that I was little and cute and came up and hugged me. I didn't know if it was out of friendliness. I was totally at their mercy. They patted me on the head and said, 'Come sit in my lap.' It was terrifying when this rough, strange-looking giant put his hands on me."[6]

The children's suspiciousness and feelings about food

The experiences that the children had had of the aggressors' "refined methods" made them suspicious of the Red Cross nurses in their white aprons. As Sonja describes it, "We had to be showered and then disinfected. When we came in to be disinfected, they had some sort of steam on, and we assumed that it was gas. This horrified us, because we no longer trusted anyone."[7] Sonja also tells how she hid biscuits up her sleeve, still believing that food was very difficult to come by.

Survival guilt as a further cause of anxiety

It has been typical for the interviewees to feel "pangs of conscience" because they had survived and to feel that they "must make something" out of their lives. Moreover, parents who had lost their own children could show envy towards the survivors, and these memories are very painful for the interviewees. Just at the time when they were experiencing their own massive losses, they had to be confronted by people who seemed to be questioning their right to existence. As Bella remembers it, "It was both good and bad to be a child. Some people looked at me with affection, others almost with hatred. Young women who had lost their children in one way or another were bitter towards me or towards my mother."[8] Anna describes parents who had lost children and who "condemned me for surviving instead of them. That was a terrible feeling [cries in agitation]. They did not mean any harm, they did not want to hurt me, it was envy. Their children had not survived [breathes a heavy sigh]."[9]

Tearing away

Parents die during the liberation

Oscar and his father had succeeded in staying together throughout the entire war, up until the liberation. Oscar gives this account of what happened after he and his father had been put into the same sickbed. "My father kept saying to me the whole time, 'you understand, son, that this is the end for me, but you . . . *try to survive, survive, survive.*' Then I don't know what happened, because I was more dead than alive. I just know that *they took me away from my father.* For a time I simply did not have the strength to move, but I kept thinking, 'How can I get to my father?' Finally I got down on all fours and crawled to the room where we had been together, but the bed was empty. And then they told me that my father had died. The day after they took him away from me, it was my *birthday.*"[10]

Helpers die

Helpers became replacements for parents and in many cases served as the only link to the past. An account of Nomi and Auntie B, who met and were put in the same concentration camp when Nomi was six years old, has been given above. As mentioned, Auntie B was like a mother for Nomi. She dies just before the liberation.

Being "deprived" of significant objects

Significant objects that the interviewees managed to hold on to have served as linking objects with a survival value. However, some of these were taken away even during the liberation, as in the following description by an interviewee. "A Russian soldier came in, and everyone was overjoyed. But what did he do? He snatched all the jewellery that anyone had on. He wanted it, and he plundered it. *I had a little silver ring, which my father had given me on a birthday, so I put it in my mouth, and I got to keep it. But now I don't have it any longer.*" The moccasins that had been made for Marysia out of her mother's bag have already been mentioned. She too had held on to them throughout the entire war, but, as she explains, "Now they stole my shoes, which I had taken such good care of. They stole those shoes that I had hardly dared to put on my feet, my black moccasins."[11]

Searching for relatives

Many of the survivors started to search for their relatives as soon as they could. Those who were physically able tried to travel through Europe to their former place of residence, where they expected to find others who had survived. Only in exceptional cases did they succeed. Painful as it was, things often did not turn out as they wished. Nor did the neighbours welcome the returning survivors.

Body marking

Lesions in the skin

The interviewees remember how lice still caused them to have lesions in their skin. As Anna comments, "Can you imagine that lice attacked us even though they washed us? Small, small lice continued to attack for two weeks. They were there *under* the skin!" Marie remembers that "I had sores all over my body."[12]

Space creating

Thinking / fantasizing

New sounds on the radio; bombardment as "music"

Julia remembers that she could listen to the radio again: "They were broadcasting marches and a lot of strange Hungarian poems." Lisa emphasized that "we heard the cannons more and more, and [laughs] it was the most beautiful music for my heart. To this very day I cannot imagine more beautiful music than the Russian cannons [cries]."[13] Something that sounded like good organ music blended with a memory of the fear that *things would not go fast enough, that they would not be saved in time.*

Caring women

The women who nursed the survivors back to life were looked upon as angels. Sandor remembers "a blond angel in the form of a woman in white clothes, who is smiling at me. That was the first joy that I felt."[14]

Being able to think

Alice tells about what she experiences as her first conscious memory of what it is like *"to be thinking"*. She is sitting at a place with a view, at a window, and she recalls she is doing something with her fingers. She is meant to "replace" the family's own children, who were lost, and this can be seen as one of the many examples of *generational distortion* that arose in connection with the liberation. The eagerness seems to have been great to *maintain provisional links* as well as to *construct new links* very rapidly.

Here is Alice's account: "I was placed with a Jewish family, an older couple who had lost their own children. They were going to emigrate to America, but I don't remember very much about that. I remember *suitcases*, I remember *rolled-up carpets*. I remember that they packed their paintings and books and *they spoke like this the whole time:* 'In two weeks we're leaving. In nine days we're leaving', and so on. I remember that many, many people came to visit this family, they had a large apartment. And *I sat on the window seat* and *fiddled with the lock on the window.* They were talking and telling each other lots of things, and then one of them said, 'I wonder what she is thinking about.' *I remember that my reaction was, 'What do they mean, thinking, I'm not thinking anything.* What do you do when you think? What does that mean?' Then it suddenly occurred to me that 'maybe that's what I am doing after all, when I sit here not saying anything but still talking to myself in my own head, maybe that's what thinking is.' I remember this moment because I suspect that it was *the first conscious thought* that came up for me, pretty late in life, but I had not been able to exchange thoughts with anyone earlier."[15]

Being reborn

The majority of the interviewees point out that they were too numb to feel anything in connection with the liberation. In certain cases they allude to the relief that they felt once they had had a chance to gain a bit of their strength back. They say it felt like they had been born again. A number of them appear to have experienced the *actual fact of being taken care of* as positive, even if the painful realization that they were perhaps the only ones in their families who had survived overshadowed everything else. Bella tells about an English soldier who laid his hand on her head. She says: "When he did that, tears poured from my eyes. I cried without knowing what was going on. It just hit me. I don't even know if I had cried at all before, but I did then."[16]

Thinking / taking action

Feeling at home with the camp children

The children had a sense of belonging to their groups. As someone expresses it, "It was my home, after all, I had always kept to my group."[17] To be moved from the group of children from the camp to a foster home felt very threatening for Nomi. As she explains, "I heard that a man had seen me and was thinking of adopting me. So

I ran and hid. I wanted to stay with all the children from the camp. That was where I felt I belonged."[18]

Freedom: being able to ride a bicycle again!

Noa tells how the Americans gathered up the survivors and made a dormitory for them in a school, "and then we started to run again. We went out to see what we could find. *I found a bicycle. I did not know how to ride a bike, but I took that bike into the school, where there were long corridors. I got on that bike, and I made up my mind to ride it.* But the corridors weren't so wide, so I would bump into the one side the first time and the other side the second time, but I just kept right on pedalling. That's what I did, and finally I could ride the bike, that's how I taught myself to ride a bike."[19]

Being able to move about freely is included in many of the memory images. Alice tells about how the air attacks could continue even though the Russians had liberated certain areas. She remembers how she ran quickly into the forest with several others, wearing a new dress given to her by her helper. She comments, "I was having a hard time running fast enough, but *I remember the feeling of that dress swirling around as I ran,* that memory is firmly intact."[20]

Seeing for the first time what parents looked like

Sally says, "Right when I was staying at that orphanage, a letter suddenly arrived for me. When I open it, it turns out to be from an old relative on my mother's side who lived in America and who had found me. He went through his pictures and found these of my mother and me and my father. I still have all of them, and this way I know what my parents looked like."[21]

Linking objects

Bella had managed to hold on to a little bag with her father's belongings from the time when they had been separated. "There was a *guard* who was human and let me keep this bag with documents in it. *I have kept everything to this very day.*"[22] Marianne mentions her "first shoes after the war. Okay, they were only made of cloth, but they were warm and without defects, I remember that."[23]

Age distorting

Depersonalization / emotional stunting

The children saw their parents becoming ill and dying. Bella says: "The strange thing was that my father looked fat and that his face was swollen, so you didn't see how skinny he was." She notes that "Now I talk with a memory of a twelve-year-old—that is, as I remember it."

Feelings of helplessness

One of the interviewees illustrates how nakedness and vulnerability continued into the time of liberation. In this instance they are being picked up by an ambulance, "and *we were not allowed to have a stitch on our bodies.* Everything had to be left behind. *They had blankets. They spread them out, put us on them, rolled us up, and lifted us.* We were naked, completely naked. We were not allowed to take one single thing with us." "We just went with the flow. There was no other way" (see below).

Lost womanliness

Their bodies were emaciated. Possibilities for normal bodily development had been severely undermined. Liv remembers how it was after "the Russians liberated us". She notes, "I met a cousin who was my age, and I was fascinated by the changes that had taken place in the two years that we had not seen each other. She had breasts, her body had curves. She sat with her legs crossed, and I saw that she had proper thighs. When I crossed my legs, it was just flat. I was pitifully thin. I was at the beginning of puberty and obsessed with becoming a woman. My cousin had been in hiding with her mother on a farm. She helped out there and looked like a Polish farm girl. She had muscles."[24]

Taking responsibility / precocity

The children "become adults"

Many of the children describe how they "aged", how they took care of dying parents, or how they realized that they were completely on their own. According to Nomi, "We were all lying there when the

English soldiers came in and took us away. *I just had to go with the flow.* There was no other way, obviously. *I don't know what I thought, what I felt.* I just followed. *One thing is for sure, I entered adulthood there, in a manner of speaking, I became an adult.*"[25] When Oscar tells about the death of his father after the liberation—his father whose last words to Oscar had been an exhortation to his son to go on living, to survive—he says, "and then something very remarkable happened. Suddenly I felt this formidable force within myself."[26] Eva talks about her wish: "I wanted to be a surgeon so that I could give my father a proper operation!" She adds that she and her father were going to protect her mother: "Mother was always the weakest card in the family."[27]

Choosing a pair of shoes

Eva tells that the Americans sent clothes, and "so we had to stand in line a long while, and then we got three things to choose from. I got a three pairs of shoes to choose from. One of the pairs was transparent with a high heel. It was winter in Poland then! Another pair was too small, and then there was a large pair, maybe size 42, dark shoes, black shoes, for a man, and I chose them!"[28]

G   Transport to Sweden: the first encounter with the new country

"My health was dangling by a thin thread"[1]

Outer threats / Experiences	Anti-semitism/ Racial laws	Deporta-tion	Ghetto	Hidden/ Fugitive/ Partisan	Camps	Liberation	Encounter with Sweden/ Post-wartime
Perforating							
Space creating							
Age distorting							

In order for the interviewees to survive after the liberation, it was imperative to transport them to field hospitals and temporary quarters; some were taken on Swedish "white buses" or trains to Lübeck, for further transport by boat to Sweden or Denmark. "Altogether between 10,000 and 12,000 Jews were rescued and brought to Sweden in the spring and summer of 1945" (Wroblewski, 1995). Sweden carried out a general rescue mission in concentration camp and prison areas at this time. The mission included, but did not prioritize, Jews. Probably more than 5,000 Jews were saved by the Swedish "white buses" in this mission (Persson, in Cesarani & Levine, 2000), for which the official representative and negotiator from Sweden was Count Folke Bernadotte.

Perforating

Invading of the senses

Legs that would not bear them up

The survivors of the concentration camps were ill and in an extremely weakened condition. The majority of them had difficulties in standing and walking. They had to be "disinfected, sprayed, and showered". They needed to be helped to discover that what ghastly images might come to them in their memories, now that there was no longer any real outside threat.

Feeling abandoned

Bella tells how "we waited and waited in a huge room. I sat alone on my little baggage, while my mother sat at a distance from me. I felt very abandoned and was angry with my mother for abandoning me."[2] She did not experience her mother as being psychically present.

Quarantine

A number of people had the good fortune to be transported to good hospitals or to reception centres for further placement in foster homes. At the same time as the interviewees thought it was "totally fantastic" to have come to Sweden, they comment that they did not "find the freedom that we had hoped for" all at once. They had to spend time in quarantine first.

"A confused world"

When Nomi could not finish her food, she hid the leftovers. In her words, "Of course, I did not leave the food on a plate, I hid it under my pillow."[3] Oscar was given a knife and fork and bread, "and of course I hid the bread. I was used to not knowing when I would get food again. And I hid a potato. I saw children trying to cut their mattress open so that they could hide something in there. All the knives disappeared. I hid my knife too. We did not know anything. . . . people have no idea about how all of this was . . . it *is a confused world, not a normal world.*[4] Invading affects concerning persistent hunger cause the children to try in panic to protect what they have just received.

Differentness

Sonja remembers how she felt after her arrival in Sweden, and her observations are similar to those of the other interviewees. She felt she was very different from the Swedes, and she wondered what vibrations she was sending out from that box of experiences in which she found herself enclosed. "We were still of different nationalities there in the stadium. And *people stood along the fence to get a look at us; of course we were so very strange in their eyes.* Some people wanted to talk to us, those who could speak German."[5] Those interviewees who came one–two years after the liberation also remember seeing themselves as some sort of beings who were different from the Swedish people. It was difficult to be accepted into the group in a school class. Liv remembers: "It was completely appalling at school. I just cried. They were so snobbish, and they looked down on me. There was no one who would even want to get near me with a pair of tongs. And I was, you have to admit, totally different. I had plaits, two thick plaits that hung all the way down to my bottom, my clothes were completely behind the times, and I could not speak the language. I was one of those typical . . . the lowest chicken in the pecking order."[6] The teacher was sensitive to the situation and fetched Liv from the lavatory where she was sitting and crying during the lesson. Bella says that she was a "total oddball". She and her mother "had very little money" and did not know what "normal behaviour" was. She describes her period of growing up in Sweden as "very hard" years. I was ostracized, bullied, and alone in my teenage years. I couldn't speak Swedish. I was the only dark person in S town. I wore a winter coat without buttons, which I had grown out of. I prayed to God to find me a friend."[7] The survivors report having no memories of anyone who openly teased them for being Jewish. However, one woman remembers how, as a newly arrived child, she was called a "damned Dane", and "I thought the ones who said that were obnoxious, so I had a fist-fight with them. They claimed that it was the Danes who had started the war."[8] She adds, "I felt that I was different. I felt like an outsider."[9] The experience of differentness after the war seems to have been interpreted by the interviewees as an extension and an intensification of the catastrophe. Moreover, the interviewees were often the only children with war experiences in the group in which they found themselves.

Lack of knowledge

Teachers could be attentive to the children but at the same time insensitive towards the children's war experiences. Nomi depicts how she as a third-grader was asked to tell about her war experiences during "fun hour" at school: "On Saturdays we had something called *fun hour*, the class's fun hour. During those hours I got to tell about my situation and what I remembered. And, after all, for them it was a story. I was so young then, so *I just went on and on and on telling my experiences*. It's much harder for me to tell now, the older I get."[10]

Her classmates had been curious and had wanted to hear what Nomi had to tell. While the teacher gave Nomi a space in which to tell about her experiences during the war, she asked her to do this during "fun hour", a time for entertainment. This can be seen as an example of the cultural clash that prevailed, the ignorance that existed about what the children who had survived the Holocaust had been through and about their need for professional care. Nomi's memory can also be said to illustrate the child perspective and the adult perspective, respectively, with regard to what was happening in the inner world of the children, their feelings of being outsiders, and the feelings of shame that thus resulted.

Feelings of shame

Nomi recounts her memories of eating problems. She felt more "at home" with people who had had the same experiences, her fellow prisoners. The custom where she lived in Sweden was "to take a sandwich with you to school, and then you got a little bottle of milk there. Yes, for me all of that was strange. I had been separated from . . . [the group of children who were my fellow prisoners]. They were my family in my mind, so I was wondering why I had to be there in a Swedish school. I didn't get it. But I remember when I drank milk. *All of my classmates, they drank so neatly,* and they didn't spill anything, but when I would drink, *everything just ran down my face and clothes.* So they showed me, as a matter of fact, my classmates. All of them knew that I came from the war."[11] Nomi's memory is revived when she hears herself say, "milk". She continues and elaborates on her invading experiences of hunger: "I remember that we were given a little plastic bag with a bar of soap, a toothbrush, and toothpaste, but I didn't know what that was, a toothbrush! I had never known that in my life. *So I started to eat the toothpaste and the soap.* I took it to be food, everything was food for me, you know."[12]

Being reunited in their country of origin: a recurring thought

Elias recollects, "our plans were to go to Sweden first and rehabilitate ourselves and then to go back home again, where we had come from."[13] The interviewees often speak of their incapacity after the liberation. Those who had the energy to "think" wished to travel back to their native countries in order to be able to see their relatives. As we noted in the previous section, this was usually not possible, partly because their physical and psychic condition would not allow them to travel on their own and partly because in reality few of them had relatives who had survived.

Keeping silent about the past

The majority of the interviewees do not recall talking after the war about the atrocities to which they had been subjected. It was common that children who had been in concentration camps were urged to keep silent about their experiences. At that time in history, the concept of crisis treatment, of working through a crisis, was virtually unknown. People generally thought that they could protect the children by avoiding any reference to what had happened.

Space creating

Thinking/fantasizing

To Sweden: a dream-like awakening to a return to life

Sofia shares her memory of her first impressions of Sweden: "We saw the beautiful city of Malmö from the bus. People were well dressed. Children had white socks, and we could not believe that it was true

that we had come to such a place. It was as though we had awakened and found ourselves in paradise. That is exactly how I felt. The
thought occurred to me that now all of us could have white socks
again, knee socks I mean."[14]

The survivors thought that it was "very cold here". They made
much use of the warm clothes, ski boots and ski-pants that they had
received during the rescue mission. Leon, who came to Sweden from
Shanghai, saw snow for the first time.

For Henny the first encounter with Sweden meant getting something to eat. She laughs when she thinks of the so-called Göteborg
cookies. Other first impressions include bunk beds with soft mat-
tresses and clean sheets, chocolate, toothpaste, toothbrushes, or-
anges, clean, well-lit streets, and the Swedish summer.

Being reunited with mother in Sweden

A number of the children had the good fortune during the months
after the liberation of receiving a notification that a relative had
survived and had come to Sweden. David was only six years old when
he was separated from his mother in Ravensbrück. When they were
liberated from different camps and at different times, they were both
transported to Sweden. David's mother found out that her son was
being treated at a hospital. David explains, "I remember that I woke
up in the middle of the night, and there was a big chocolate bar in
front of me, and behind it there stood my mother. And I remember
that I screamed, 'Mamitska', which means 'little mother' with all the
strength I could muster. But to tell you the truth, the main thing was
the chocolate bar. I saw that first, and then behind it my mother.
That is a scene I will never forget."[15]

Hearing the Swedish language

While many tell about their experiences of differentness and their
feelings of shame for being awkward and not knowing how to act
in a "normal" life, many of their accounts are also accompanied by
a sense of humour. They can see the *humour* in situations that were
surely unpleasant when they occurred, but that can be transformed
into amusing anecdotes. This is most probably an important skill
for mobilizing the strength to go on living. During the interviews

it has clearly meant much to them to speak and mimic the new language as they had experienced it as children during their first years in Sweden. Sandor still remembers the melody of the Swedish language as it sounded to him when it first reached his ears, and he demonstrates, *"tralalalallala."*[16]

Sonja comments, "We had lots of fun with those *Red Cross nurses.* One of them tried to teach me a little Swedish, and I thought she said, 'Don't speak parsley with me.' We did not understand a thing. It was a totally different language, and I wondered how we would ever manage, we didn't have a clue."[17]

Thinking/taking action

White buses and cooperation with helpers

For the survivors to be able to act in this phase of the Holocaust, they were totally dependent on the efforts of their helpers and their cooperation with them. According to Edith: "The Swedish drivers started approaching us, and the way they took care of us made us understand that this was something else. We still didn't know anything except that they were very gentle with us and put us in the buses. The ones who could sit did so, and the others lay on stretchers."[18]

Protective shield

In preparing for the transport to Sweden, much emphasis was placed on the care that the children needed in order to feel whole again and to feel as secure in themselves as possible. Ester says: "There were, of course, Red Cross personnel there. I could actually communicate with people around me and be clean and comfortable. What I mean is that I had clean sheets, no straw, not there, not that scratchy straw mattress. And I could add a little . . . a few kilos to my body, so that it wasn't so painful to lie down any longer."[19] Jacob gives a similarly positive account, "In Lübeck they received us, the Swedish Red Cross workers, deloused us and gave us *proper food.* They gave us proper sweaters, jerseys, and they are almost like underwear, fine underwear, which I had never had on my body, which was covered with scars from typhus fever and so on. It was so silky, it wasn't silk, it was jersey, but it was as *soft as silk.* Trousers, *blue ones,* they were the fashion in Sweden then. All of this naturally made me feel like I had come *into contact with heaven.*"[20]

Age distorting

A question that often arises is what it meant to be a child, a youth, or an adult, respectively, during and after a war, during the Holocaust. We have seen how children who had not reached puberty acted spontaneously, while teenagers may have been more cautious. It is possible that the teenagers were more aware of what they were going through. Elias says of his survival, "I have not been struck by psychoses the way many of my fellow Jews, both men and women, have been. Perhaps this can be attributed to the fact that *I was rather young. It was a little harder for me to take things to heart and to bury myself in all the difficult questions.*"[21]

Depersonalization/stunting

A small stature

Oscar asks, "Should we show some pictures of me when I was thirteen, and I mean. . . . How big do you think I was then? I was about like a normal nine-year-old. At last I was starting to grow up, I thought, since I had received proper clothes."[22] When David's mother found him in the hospital in Sweden, he was six years old, but he was being treated in a ward for three-year-olds, as he was so "little and skinny".[23]

Taking responsibility/precocity

Taking responsibility for parents

As has been made clear already, even if the fathers survived the concentration camps, it was not unusual for them to die right before or during the liberation. Some truck drivers who were taking the ill and wounded to Sweden for care refused to take Sam's father, who was mortally ill. Sam then flagged down an ambulance and had it pick up his father. In his words, "*I was one hundred years old in my head, and I took care of both myself and my father.*"

The post-war period

Refugee facilities in Sweden in 1945

A number of refugee facilities were set up for the survivors. Some of the interviewees have told about their time at the Sigtuna Foundation facilities. There they were given a chance to form an attachment to a caretaker, and in certain cases, as in Ester's situation, they could be moved to a foster family. Sofia thought that "the people at Sigtuna were unbelievable . . . the food was very good . . . it isn't possible to describe what a reception we got."[24] Sofia also shows a photograph of herself at Sigtuna, taken when she was not yet able to sit upright. She comments, "Here is where my life actually begins." In another of her pictures there is "Mutti" who took care of them. She was "exceptionally sweet".

The psychoanalyst and psychiatrist Ester Lamm was called to the foundation as a medical consultant for the survivors. She reflected on how the young people could have survived the concentration camps. Her conclusion was that it was primarily a matter of random factors, and not "elbows". Moreover, it was her impression that those who were lucky enough to be able to maintain certain contacts in the camps, a mother or a sister, had better prospects, as did those who succeeded in cementing new contacts so that they could help each other in groups (Ester Lamm, audiotaped interview, 1988).

Not being able to return to their native countries

The survivors were warned against returning to their native countries. They heard things like "It's not just a matter of opening the door and going in. Totally different people live there now." Sofie recalls that her reaction was, "I do not want to go to Sweden, I want to go home, *straight home. . . . I want to see my brothers, maybe they are alive.*"[25] Ester comments, "They enticed us with things like, 'if you come to Sweden, you can have all the chocolate that you want', and that decided it for me."[26]

Those who do return experience new perforating

A number of the survivors in this study went through great hardships in order to return to their native countries. They hoped to see their relatives again, and perhaps they dreamed of recapturing their previous way of life. But the post-war period in their native countries usually consisted of dashed hoped that made new perforations in the psychic shield and even led to physical attacks. During her first time in Poland after the liberation, Liv heard someone say, "Look, now the bedbugs have crept up to the surface again." She comments, "and this was, note well, the first welcome after we were, so to say, liberated. This is something that *can never lose its sting* [clears her throat]."[27]

Those who returned "home" usually stayed for only a short while before continuing to Sweden. However, there were those who stayed so long that it was difficult to get out again. In Poland anti-Semitism was still strong. The interviewees who went back there do not appear to have expected the reception that they got from their neighbours. Marcus describes this: "I remember so well, I had been to pick up a hat that I was going to wear on my trip . . . and I was suddenly pulled into an entryway by two large blokes, and they smashed my nose just because I was a Jew. It was my last memory of Lòdz before we left for Sweden."[28] This brings to mind the expressive description by Igra (2001, pp. 131–132, my italics), *"New faces now looked through the windows* of the homes in which they had lived before the catastrophe." He discusses the "thin veneer that separates barbarity from culture and cruelty from kindness." He points out that he is not using this metaphor for the purpose of regarding "culture as a thin varnish over primitive animal drives which can break forth at any moment". Instead, his aim is to show how near to each other "the destructive and the life-affirming elements exist in the human being". He puts forth a further metaphorical description by giving the veneer a "door": it is as though we can never be sure about what is going in and out—obviously sound norms or meaningless actions. Perhaps the former neighbours who stand there looking through the window can serve as models for the uncertainty about what passes through the veneer of a human being and what passes out through the window. Through the window means through the boundary to the outside world and also the boundary for the kind of neighbours that we ourselves constitute in the society in which we live. However, what I wonder is, the thin veneer of culture to which Igra refers, which I see as a good upbringing and strength in generational linking—can this play a role in determining in which direction the balance will go?

Living with surviving parents

To have parents who were still alive after the liberation was naturally of immeasurable significance for the child survivors, but it was not without its conflicts. As Lena comments, "It was hard to get used to everyday life, we could not avoid conflicts at home, and everyone was understandably equally nervous . . . sought . . . help because I thought that I was different from everyone else. That help led to my moving away from home. My mother *over-protected* me of course . . . it was a *reflex* on her part, but *I could not live with being kept closed in any longer*."[29] Child survivors felt a pressure to fill a role as the hope for the future. Julia explains: "I think I felt it . . . that I received an incredible amount of attention, and so much hope was invested in me."[30]

Aspects of what it means to be the *first and the second generation of survivors simultaneously* would be an interesting subject to investigate further.

Being reunited with a sibling after many years

Janina travelled to the town of her birth and searched "desperately" for her sister, who had been in hiding. Suddenly she saw a *window with her "mother's handmade curtains"*. She wanted to present herself to her sister, but now there was a "musulman who weighed 29 kg who said she was my sister. I don't know if she was scared of me. But we have thus been reunited."[31] David's little sister was murdered. He has a photograph of her, and he says, "I don't have any memory of her at all, not the least . . . she has been erased from my memory. She would have been 54 or 55 years old."[32] Edith saw her sister again in a mental hospital. It was a very painful encounter. She laments that "there is nothing left of my sister but an outer shell".[33]

Making up for lost teenage years

In a very small minority of cases the interviewees allude to memories of how they avoided thinking about the war. They wanted to enjoy their youth very fast because it was about to slip away from them completely. Marysia, who was left in Poland and who had entered her teenage years, explains: "I did not want to know anything. I went to idiotic films, I danced, I drank vodka, I went out with my friends. I did not want to hear about, did not want to read about the ghetto, did not want to read about any camps, I did not want to take in anything whatsoever about all that. *And it's quite possible that that is why I can talk about it now without suffering too much anxiety, because for such a long time I did not want to talk about it at all.*"[34]

Returning to their homes later in life

The idea of returning to their home turf, to the house and to the street where they had played as children and where they had been with their families, has met with great resistance in the minds of many of the survivors. Many are planning now, in connection with the interviews, to make such a journey. Emilia says, "that is something that I thought of doing. Now I feel that the time is right, that I am ready for that. I am sure that no one is still living there. But I want to see the house, the places. I want to do that."[35] In connection with the follow-up interview, Emilia reveals that she has been there and that she found it to be "frighteningly the same as before".[36] Such an experience has been confirmed by a number of others.

New separations evoke a feeling of catastrophe

Right after the war some children were sent to youth camps and so were again separated from their parents, who had survived the Holocaust. Julia recalls how "I just cried and cried, and my mother had to come and get me . . . so everything [that had to do with] *keeping my mother in sight and the belief that she is going to disappear, that I am going to disappear, all that came, you see, later.*"[37]

Leaving out the most painful parts, which are kept "in a box", and trying to "accept"

Many do not want to speak of their past. Others are willing to speak of it but they want to be able to omit the most painful parts. Sam sums it up like this: "I am going to tell about Auschwitz, but I do not want to tell . . . a person can't tell everything, so I will tell about . . . some episodes."[38] Ester says, "It is there in several layers, in the background there is much of the concentration camp . . . but I accept, yes, that's the way it is . . . but looming there silent and dark somewhere . . . belongs to me, but I do not need to take it up, it's there in a box . . . somewhere inside me, so that's what it is, *acceptance.*"[39]

6

Rwanda genocide, 1994

Rwanda is slightly smaller than the US state of Maryland—a small country of 26,338 square kilometres. An extremely poor country with a population of about eight million, it is situated north of its twin Burundi and wedged in by Tanzania, the Democratic Republic of the Congo, and Uganda, in the middle of Central Africa up on a lush green plateau.

The first time we landed in Kigali, we had flown over a vast number of green hilltops. Rwanda is often called the land of the thousand hills: "*milles collines*". Kigali consists of small, unadorned houses. Most of the streets are unpaved, except in the districts where the homes of foreign professionals, embassies, and governmental buildings are located. The city is spread out among the hills, and people carry heavy loads from place to place. Because of its location on a high plateau, Rwanda's temperature is mild the day we land, about 25°, and there is a mid-day rain shower that lasts about half an hour.*

The contents of chapter 6 are also presented in T. Böhm & S. Kaplan, *Hämnd—och att avstå från att ge igen* [*Revenge—and refraining from retaliation*] (Stockholm: Natur och Kultur, 2006).

*During study visits in 2003 and 2004, Rwandan researchers, trauma therapists, and teenagers were interviewed, as well as international genocide scholars.

During the genocide in Rwanda, from April to June 1994, be-tween 800,000 and 1,000,000 Rwandans were killed within a time span of 100 days. Those murdered belonged mainly to the Tutsi ethnic group, writes the investigative journalist Philip Gourevitch (1998). About 75% of the country's total population of Tutsis were murdered. The murderers were fanatical Hutus, who had gained huge popular support for their movement, "Hutu Power". It is es-timated that over 120,000 people took an active part in the killing. The Tutsis made up 15% of the population and had long been the well-educated elite. They were mainly cattle-owners. The Hutus made up 85% of the population, most of them landless farm workers.

The expert in African history and politics Mahmood Mamdani stresses that the more colonization and the more settlers there are in a land area, the greater is the violence perpetrated upon the natives, because of the inevitable scramble for land (Mamdani, 2001)! In 1904 the Germans wiped out 80% of the Herero people in Southwest Africa (Namibia) within a period of one year—this can be seen as the twentieth century's first genocide with a claim of racial superiority used as a legitimizing rationale. In most instances colonialists politi-cize the fact of a people's ethnicity, their identity as natives of the land, at first negatively, and then the native people themselves take it over and politicize it as positive. The Tutsis were set up as a privileged group by the Belgians and then, after 1990, labelled negatively by Hutu Power as "non-native". Mamdani argues that the genocide in Rwanda was a genocide carried out by those who saw themselves as native Rwandans against those they saw as settlers. For the Hutu, the Tutsi was an alien, not a neighbour.

In the 1920s the Belgians defined Hutus as native-born Bantus and Tutsis as "Hamites" of foreign descent. Direct rule was combined with indirect rule via the Tutsis in order to divide and conquer. In a similar fashion, people in other African countries have been divided by the colonialists into so-called subject races, which were then po-liticized—that is to say, assigned different statuses, such as coloured, Asians, Arabs. Julius Nyerere of Tanzania is described by Mamdani as the only African leader who has worked for a unified citizenry.

While Rwanda was a Belgian colony during the first part of the 1900s, Hutus and Tutsis were played off against each other, and the Belgians exploited the leadership role of the Tutsis. When the Tutsis demanded independence in 1959, the Belgians changed their tune and supported the Hutus, who seized command. Thus when liberation from colonialism came in 1962, a Hutu-run government was in power, and restrictions were put into place against Tutsis with regard to work, education, and equality with Hutus.

The most important means of communication in Rwanda was the radio. As early as 1990, Hutu extremists started broadcasting their ethnicity-based hate propaganda. The now so well-known hate propaganda broadcasts started in 1993 over the radio (*Radio Télévision Libre des Milles Collines*). The Tutsis were called cockroaches that should be sent back to where they came from. The successive steps to get people used to the idea of wiping out the Tutsis, defined as alien vermin, are now being documented in the literature (Mamdani, 2001). A number of concepts served as buzzwords. A political indoctrination process and the killing of Tutsis took place between 1990 and 1994.

Massacres of thousands of Tutsis took place recurrently in different parts of the country; nevertheless, most of the surviving Tutsis stayed where they had been. The Tutsi-dominated liberation army, RPF, trained in Uganda, tried to remove the Hutu dictator in 1990. They advanced as far as the outskirts of the capital, but the Hutu government was then rescued by means of a telephone call to France's President Mitterrand, who saw Rwanda's French-speaking government as part of the Francophone world (Melvern, 2000). Paratroopers, weapons, and money flowed to the Hutu government from France, and the Tutsis were forced to retreat.

The origins of both ethnic groups are shrouded in myth and unclear, writes Gourevitch (1998). Such myths and uncertainties seem to contribute substantially to revenge ideologies. The dominating Hamitic myth claims that the Tutsis came from Ethiopia several hundred years ago, while the Hutus migrated to Rwanda from other parts of Central Africa.

The ethnic groups are now, and have long been, greatly intermingled. They have always intermarried and shared a common social and community life. However, the government that was put in power in 1962 made everyone obtain ethnic identity papers. They had to be classed as Tutsi or Hutu, depending on their father's ethnic background. The question of ethnic background was thus kept at front stage, in a way reminiscent of the methods used by European fascists. As time went on, this emphasis on ethnic belonging developed into racism on biological grounds. Measurements were made of nostrils and head size, just as in the Europe of the 1930s. Tall, slim people with slender noses were classified as typical Tutsis, while shorter people with darker skin and broader noses were classified as Hutus.

Rwanda is an extremely organized country, while at the same time it is extremely poor. The population is kept in check by means of a rigid hierarchical system. After four years of a smear campaign against Tutsis, an aeroplane carrying Rwanda's Hutu president and Burundi's president was shot down, and both men were killed. A prevailing belief is that the Hutu fascists orchestrated the attack in order to have cause to incite genocide in revenge. In addition, they were ready to get rid of their president, who had shown too much willingness to negotiate with the Tutsis and the United Nations. It was in April, well known to be the poorest month, when they could count on whipping up the support of hungry, desperate people, excited by a chance to plunder.

The no-holds-barred massacres that led to genocide had started at this time. Rwanda has a history of civil obedience, and people tend to trust what the authorities say: this contributed to the rapid escalation of destruction, described by anthropologist Jet Pagnier (2004). Violence was trivialized and normalized without any intervention by the authorities. The aggressors used expressions like "pulling out the roots of the bad weeds" to refer to the killing of women and children. All the chances for a new generation to live were to be eliminated. The idea of a final solution reached general acceptance. When President Habyarimana's aeroplane was shot down, it seems that all obstacles in the way of a full-scale genocide were removed, and the *genocidaires* felt free to carry out their plans.

The entire political opposition was murdered within the first 48 hours, and after a relatively short time 50,000 moderate Hutus as well. The genocide was not stopped by the United Nations, or by any other international organization, or by efforts by other countries, even though there were a number of reports and warning signs about what was in the making. On the contrary, the French kept on supplying the Hutus with weapons. After intense pressure from the United States and France, the United Nations also withdrew its protection troops two weeks after the genocide had begun. Boutros Boutros-Ghali, UN Secretary General at the time, who was responsible for these troops, must bear a great deal of this fiasco on his conscience, writes investigative journalist Linda Melvern (2000). The Canadian UN Force Commander in Rwanda, General Roméo Dallaire, expressed his firm conviction several times that the 5,000 UN troops who were there before the withdrawal would have been able to stop the entire genocide if only he and they had been given a mandate to intervene. However, he was not given this mandate, and the several hundred UN soldiers who remained in the country could only watch while the tragedy unfolded.

Tutsis and neutral Hutus were sometimes shot to death, but most often they were murdered with machetes, clubs, arrows, and axes. The methods were bestial. What made this genocide unique was that it was carried out by over 100,000 civilians, many of whom were organized in militias. The majority of the country's population is Roman Catholic, and priests and bishops took part in the genocide. Congregations of Tutsis were locked into churches that were then set on fire or bulldozed to the ground. Doctors murdered their patients, teachers their pupils, neighbours their neighbours. All of these examples show that large masses of ordinary people supported the genocide.

When the Rwandan liberation army finally invaded the country from Uganda, they were able to put an end to the killing. A new government was appointed, with General Paul Kagame, a Tutsi, as president, and several Hutus included in the regime. The rule that a person's ethnic group had to be stamped on his ID papers was revoked. The new leaders emphasized that the Rwandans had to unite, and at the same time they launched into the extremely difficult task of implementing a reconciliation process or—as they preferred everyone to call it—an "acceptance" of history.

As late as 2003, there were still 120,000 criminals from the genocide in jail: to try them all through the normal court system would have taken hundreds of years. There was a shortage of everything after the war, including lawyers, judges, and courts. At that time Rwanda was the poorest country in the world. The United Nations set up a court in Arusha, in Tanzania, where some of the most barbaric of the leaders were put on trial. Millions of dollars have been spent, but so far only a small number of sentences have been passed. The new government in Rwanda took another approach and brought the old village court councils—the Gacaca courts—back into existence (Pagnier, 2004). It was decided that cases related to the genocide would be dealt with via a system based upon the old one, and in 2000 a Gacaca law was enacted. All genocide-related crimes committed between 1990 and 1994 would be tried within the Gacaca framework, and the judicial process would involve all of Rwandan society (Gacaca with a capital G refers to the tribunals that work with genocide issues) (Pagnier, 2004). Thousands of judges and other personnel have been given a fast course in how to make the Gacaca courts function. With thousands of newly established village courts broken down into smaller geographical units, it would be possible to try the more than 120,000 persons suspected of genocide. A process consisting of eight different phases has been set up, in which the new officials find out who has died in a province, who is still living there, who has disappeared, what the present residents have seen and heard about the murder victims, and what they know or have heard about those who had murdered them. This is an example of justice and restitution, the necessary conditions for bringing about reconciliation as opposed to revenge. The name "Gacaca" for the village courts comes from the word for the plot of grass where the villagers sat for their traditional judicial processes. Disputes were settled by a council in the presence of the entire community.

One of the leading Hutu fascists was Théoneste Bagosora, who was also called Africa's Hitler, as the writer Lars Berg (2001) stresses. Bagosora was one of those who appeared before the UN International Criminal Tribunal in Arusha and was identified as the mastermind behind the genocide in Rwanda. He and his cohorts had been planning the genocide down to the smallest detail since the autumn of 1992—more specifically, two years before the genocide was actually incited. They imported half a million machetes and had them distributed. They built up Hutu militias. They were the ones behind the radio-broadcast propaganda that incited people to prepare for the final extermination of the Tutsis—"the cockroaches".

These leaders provided the genocidal process with a destructive ideology that functioned as a driving force. The role they played in instigating destructive processes in a sufficiently large part of the population was devastating. This was especially true because counterbalances—such as intervention by the United Nations or other countries—were not in place or had been eliminated, as in the case of the opposition within the Hutu group itself.

Because of a long history of repression and a culture of suspicion, Rwandans are quick to let themselves be absorbed into groups in order not to risk having their heads cut off, either physically or socially (Pagnier, 2004). This creates an atmosphere of social conformism. Groups with little or no power adapt out of fear that their oppressors will otherwise take revenge on them. They also fear being criticized by members of their own group.

However, we cannot assume that people obeyed in a simplistic manner when they participated in the genocide, even though they were part of a culture with a long heritage of fear and obedience. There was also resistance. Whenever there is power, there is always resistance.

The atmosphere in Rwanda

Pagnier, who has lived among Rwandans for considerable periods of time, argues that the strongly hierarchical and control-based society has generated an atmosphere of distrust (Pagnier, 2004). Rwandans often describe themselves as suspicious. A woman says: "If someone asks you the way to get to a certain place, why should you tell him? You don't know why he is asking you, or why he wants to go there. It's not good to tell the whole truth."

Also, Rwanda is still a country ridden with ideology, an ideology communicated from the top—from the state—to the people below. The state preaches about morals, rules, and good versus bad habits. People must follow the rules and attend village meetings, or they risk being fined. "Solidarity camps" or *ingando* have been set up as rehabilitation for former prisoners on their way back into society as well as retraining for people coming into new administrative positions. Unity and reconciliation are key concepts in the government ideology of today. However, together with a tendency towards blind obedience and social injustices, there is a risk for new explosions of distrust.

We know that one million people were killed some years ago, but this knowledge can remain rather abstract when we are far away. Those of us who have had an opportunity to spend time in Rwanda, however, to meet Rwandans face to face and to visit key places—churches, museums—that in their very existence bear witness to history, have experiences that are momentous and change our perspectives on life. Everything in Rwanda bears the imprint of the genocide, and thus the tension between revenge and reconciliation is present in the atmosphere.

There are also stories of heroism in Rwanda, though they are few and far between, considering that three quarters of the entire Tutsi population was wiped out. However, there were Hutus who found ways to resist genocide on moral grounds. There were those who risked their lives to save a Tutsi. We can say that almost every Tutsi who survived did so through help from a Hutu (Pagnier, 2004).

How can people go on living after they have seen all hell break loose? Everything in Rwanda was destroyed—one million dead. Streets, houses, schools, and the infrastructure had gone. Hundreds of thousands of children live in households run by children who are in many instances just slightly older than they themselves. We visited Josephine, fourteen years old, who was taking care of three younger siblings after her mother, the only remaining parent, had died of AIDS. In a mature, caring way she managed the household and made it possible for her siblings to go to school. We can ask ourselves how this forced premature adulthood, this "age distortion", is going to affect the youth as they reach their true adulthood and their parenthood-to-be. J. is dressed up and says: "We wake up early in the morning, fetch water, clean the house . . . (*silence*), I prepare for the day and porridge before going to school. Later . . . meet together for a pray, teach word of God, and . . ." I ask: what are the greatest demands or worries? Josephine is quiet. She bows her head (no answer in words).[1]

A teenage boy whose parents and siblings were murdered and who has lived the major part of his life on the street said to us with a gesture towards his heart: "In my heart there will always be grief and anger. I will never be able to reconcile, but I have to accept."[2]

We see the concepts that the authorities have put into place and expect every citizen to adopt and to live by. The words of honour are reconciliation and national unity. The authorities are against talk about Hutu and Tutsi. Now they want everyone to see themselves as Rwandans. Tutsis who have survived are called survivors (*rescapés* in French). Hutus, who had been called *genocidaires*, are now called non-survivors, *non-rescapés*. At the same time, argues Pagnier, who did her research and lived with people in a part of Rwanda where acts of revenge were especially common, it is impossible to talk about the genocide or questions related to it without talking about the two categories—Tutsi and Hutu. We can ask ourselves whether it is a constructive policy or a way to pretend that nothing happened—or at least a way to cover up remnants of feelings that would need to come out into the open and be worked through. Pagnier focuses on the relationship between an authoritarian state and an obedient society. Comprehensive studies of the Rwandan genocide give us one picture, she argues, while the historical narratives of individuals give us another. Those who were up against the murderers face to face harbour a strong distrust, and the population as a whole is far from ready to establish a collective picture of this historical tragedy. In addition, people parrot "prepared" phrases handed down by the authorities. Genocide, Gacaca, and reconciliation are sensitive subjects, and there is much that is never said. In addition, Pagnier's experience is that Rwandan culture in general frowns upon the showing of feelings, and faces are hard to read. The true experiences sometimes come out first when the tape recorder has been turned off.

We visited the Kigali Memorial Centre, a museum in Gisozi, a part of Kigali, where documentation of the genocide has been collected. This is also the site of the mass graves of the 250,000 people murdered in Kigali. By means of foreign aid, it has been possible to build an impressive memorial that joins the past with the present. It helps visitors to understand where all the beggars with missing limbs, all the frightened expressions, and all the sombre soldiers have their background.

Leadership and group phenomena

We should emphasize once again that genocide never develops from spontaneous actions on the part of a group of individuals or a population. Individual or social psychological factors are not enough. Impulse-driven group destructivity is limited in time, and riotous behaviour ends as soon as the outburst of rage has cooled down. Genocide, in contrast, must have leadership, ideology, and organization. People who participate in genocide have had time to undergo a change, to be trained in specialization and mechanization, as well as dilution of responsibility. There is an interplay between ideological organization and blindly functioning group phenomena, so that the ideological leaders know how to get their supporters to rally around them blindly. Also, political power struggles are often recast as ethnic struggles in order to gain supporters. This strategy can be a part of the leadership's way of organizing and setting up the scene ideologically. Large-group repression can be manipulated by leaders either to make the large group function more efficiently or to enhance the large group's regressively blind faith in them, which is described by the psychoanalyst Vamik Volkan (2004).

The social psychologist Ervin Staub (2000) describes the social psychological forces that lay the foundation for genocide in terms of the following points:

> degradation—directed from the top down;
> destructive ideology—absence of a complex shared truth;
> unhealed wounds, resulting in a defensive feeling of superiority;
> unquestioning respect for authority and a shared one-dimensional view of history;
> a monolithic society;
> social injustice;
> passive bystanders, regarded as support by the aggressors;
> superficial contact with neighbours, involving shared simplistic goals (as opposed to deeper contact).

As shown in this chapter, a cross-scientific discussion concerning genocidal processes is of decisive value.

III

HOW ARE MEMORIES BEING RECALLED?

7

Two boys—one event:
how memories are recalled
in interviews about massive trauma

In this and the two following chapters I return to the interview situation, which I introduced in one of the opening chapters. I accentuate those phenomena that concern *how* memories are recalled and thereafter present a theory that has emerged in the work with the interviews.

Disrupted thinking and affects

One could not "imagine the unthinkable, the inhuman and unthinkable thought of the fate that was in store for most of us",[1] Sofia recalls: "We didn't even know if it was night or day . . . we were completely brainwashed, and in a way that was good, because otherwise we would not have . . . we could not have endured it."[2] Food serves as a constant reminder, David says: "When you don't get food, your head doesn't function, you don't think."[3] It has not

---

Chapter 7 is a revised version of S. Kaplan, "Two boys—One Event: How Memories Are Recalled in Interviews about Massive Trauma". *Scandinavian Psychoanalytic Review*, 25 (2002): 108–116.

been formulated at any time; it is "something that I carry around like a hump", says Bella.[4] Sam says, "it was hell on earth ... it is a *package* that you carry with you the rest of your life, as you perhaps understand."[5] Krystal (1968) describes what the child survivors went through: The "automatism" surrounding the phenomena described, the act of "not thinking", is most probably rooted in the fact that "the Nazi brutality was systematically changing the self-representation of the prisoners from self-respecting individuals to commodities".

The concept of affect is applicable here. It is used to describe the bodily aspect of the feeling that is elicited by external or internal stimuli (Lerner, 1999; Nathanson, 1992). For the interviewee this means that there are both unconscious and conscious aspects of the affect. The original affect can take various pathways, and it seems as though the affect can also arise instead of a thought. The established expression "invading memories" seems a contradiction in terms, since memories are something that a person could think around and neutralize. What seems to be invading is the affect, the anxiety. My conclusion is that the concept should be "invading affects". Earlier studies have made it clear that traumatic experiences have come to be recorded in a specific way in the minds of survivors: as a result of such traumatic upheaval, experiences have not been recorded as memories in the usual sense of the word, but as a disruption in thinking and as a more-or-less distinct affect that may intrude later in life, in the words of H. Enckell (personal communication, 2002). The trauma is thus imprinted as an affect, and the "memory" is a reproduction of this affect.

The memory images are brought to the surface and are experienced at moments in the present that bear traces from the past. Affects can "spill over" the self (Matthis, personal communication, 2002). The decisive factor seems to be the extent to which the individual can differentiate between the present and the past when emotions seems to be of the same nature. The degree of integration of the trauma appears to determine the form that the memory takes. A split in the self may also appear as a result of the difficulty of coping with memories from massive trauma. If survivors try to remember things as a whole, they most probably cannot avoid realizing the totality of it all, and this pain can be absolutely excruciating. When, as children, the survivors concentrated their attention on some object such as a hat or buttons, these could function as linking objects and also as a way of diverting their attention from what was most painful. At the same time, as mentioned above, these perceptual images may function as cues to the traumatic event.

Retaining the significance and core of outer reality

Memory researchers now agree that we do not store objective snap-shots of our earlier experiences but retain, instead, the significance, the atmosphere, and the feelings that these experiences gave us. At the same time, it is commonly agreed that even if recalled memories can be a restructured psychic reality, they still reflect a "core" of outer reality, of the historical events that took place. A characteristic of false memories is that recounting them is seldom accompanied by feelings of dread, horror, and anxiety—that is, the traumatic experience itself (Christianson, 1994). Memories of emotionally traumatic events, such as extreme repeated traumas, are often more correct than memories of single traumatic events (Sandler & Fonagy, 1997).

I have assumed that massive trauma has influenced the child survivors in similar ways, in interaction with previous personality structures, due to the force of traumatization. At the same time, at another level, the developmental phase of the child at the time of the trauma, as well as experiences after the war as children and young adults—among other things the capacity to express painful experiences—may influence the recounting of their life histories in adulthood. Thus the life histories reflect both a historical reality and each person's psychic reality. Through the testimonies we can get a picture of how traumatic events are transformed in individual ways into memory images and affects.

Two boys: one event

In the interview material of 40 child survivors of the Holocaust, sequences with two of the interviewees seemed to concern the same event. As boys, both were involved in this event, which concerned the deportation of a group of children. That the descriptions are of the same course of events is verified through significant clues in both accounts, in addition to the fact that they refer to each other by name. There are both similarities and differences in the pictures from their memories. It can be said that when the two men bear witness to an event that has taken place, they do so based on *experiences* in their respective psychic realities. The interviews were conducted independently of each other, at different points in time, by two different interviewers, with me as the coordinator. First I present the interview sequences concerning the event as verbatim as possible, after which I discuss similarities and differences in content as well as aspects of reconstruction and construction—"historical truth" as well as "narrative truth."

The interview sequences concern the deportation of a group of children from the Kielce ghetto. Kielce was a town north of Krakow, which was occupied by the Germans in 1939. At that time about 24,000 Jews lived there. The Kielce ghetto was established in April 1941, and thousands of Jews were forced to move there from small towns in the surrounding area. The Jews worked for the Germans, but the Jewish population was reduced to 2,000 as a result of the elimination of the ghetto in 1942. Jews who were ill and younger children were put to death before deportation to death camps and concentration camps (Gutman, 1990, pp. 801–802).

I will now present the accounts of the two boys. I call them Noa and Sam. Even though they escaped, they were later recaptured and taken to Auschwitz. After liberation they were sent to Sweden.

According to the accounts below, one of the boys was twelve and the other ten years old when the event took place. The two of them succeeded in hiding together with a third person. Both men describe there having been "some third person there", but at the same time it is with regard to this point that the life histories differ most markedly.

Two accounts

Noa, the younger boy, gives his account

"It was a sawmill. So they were going to close it, and they sorted out everyone they did not need. And they lined everyone up . . . with the old and the ill, women and children by themselves, children they thought were too little. And little by little they started to transport the children away somewhere, I don't know, but those children [snuffles]. What did they transport them with? It was with horse-drawn wagons, or they had some sort of truck. It is Germans, that is, who picked them up and gradually transported them away as soon as they could fill up the wagon. So I tried to be last [silence]. When I saw that . . . I understood, you see [silence] that I had to run for my life . . . or hide [snuffles] . . . one way or another. So we stood . . . I stood not far from a house there, so I. . . . It was open, so I moved slowly, and on the way there I saw a couple more children I knew [silence] and asked them quickly if they . . . wanted to come and hide [cries]. No, they didn't want to, but instead a boy went into that house with me. We ran in there fast and started searching for a place . . . to hide. It was a fairly tall house, so I mean there were stairs going up, so we ran, and I took the other guy with me. His name was Sam. And when we went into that house, we were surprised. We *found an older man* who was already staying in there in the house. He couldn't walk. He was alone, no one with him. You weren't allowed to be in those houses, but he had tried to hide. So he stayed seated on the staircase. We ran around and looked all over to find a possible hiding place. So we ran up as high as we could, and there was an attic on top of another attic that was open. So we looked up there and we . . . Sam, he lifted me up, very hard, could look in there. We thought that it was a good place to hide, just then, to escape the transport. We took the older man with us, and we went . . . one went up first to the attic and then we pulled up the older man. Don't know, he had a leg injury, so he had been thrown out, left to die. And we helped him get up to the attic, and we hid there. After a while it was quiet outside. They had taken all the children away, all the adults, everything in the work camp was totally silent, silent as the grave [sighs]. Then it was night, and we lay still up there, all three of us, myself, Sam, and the older man. And there were dormers jutting out, openings that we crawled into. Then, as we lay there, an SS man came into the house and started searching around, to see whether anyone was hiding inside. I don't know if he suspected something or if it was just a routine check. And we looked out and we squeezed ourselves in—we weren't so large, so we squeezed ourselves into those openings, and then we saw a soldier stick his head through the opening into the attic. And he looked around, and as luck would have it he was alone, and he concluded that no one was up there, so he went away [sighs]. And that was on that day, you see. And then it was totally silent, and we were there and lay still during the night and we heard lots of shooting, the first night. It was probably people who had hidden and then tried to flee from the camp, and that camp, you could not flee from that camp. All of it, all around it, it was enclosed and secured with barbed wire and fences. Soldiers were placed everywhere around it, so that no one could flee from the camp late at night. But we heard shots coming from different directions. So we lay there that night, and then we lay there the whole day, the next day. Then it was night again, and we heard scattered shots now and then, yes, that's right, the shots were from . . . but that camp was guarded the whole time. Of course we got hungry, so Sam and I went down from that attic at night, we crawled on our stomachs, crawled on all fours, so to say, and looked in. . . . We searched the houses, they were utterly empty. We looked for something we could eat. The only thing we could find was old bread, very hard, it was as hard as a rock. But we found . . . could take, or drink water then, when we were down there. And we crept on all fours as far as we could. We crawled around and did not dare to go upright, you understand what I mean, because then we could be found out. So we went on like this as far as we could, and we fetched a little food, or bread, for the man who was still in the attic. We went back up, and by that time we had eaten, I mean we had time to eat a little down there, and then we took a little food up with us. But we could not take very much with us and what we found in those houses was very little. The people who lived there, they had very little for themselves. So night came again, and we went down again, Sam and I, and crawled our way forward, through houses, other houses. And then we went on all fours around the fence and tried to find a hole that we could possibly use to escape, because we did not know how we were going to get out of there. But we did not find anything. Everything was closed off, with steel wire and barbed wire, the whole fence. So we went as far as we could, and then we fetched food again for the other man. We lay still up there in the daytime and only went down at night. Then on the third day, we lay there three days, you see, on the third day, in the afternoon, we saw . . . *we heard sounds.* We heard a horse-drawn wagon come in. They were sent to fetch something from this camp, I mean some things and what not, because they were moving everything over to the ghetto, you see, to the other place.

So we looked down, and I saw that the two people with the wagon who were loading things were Jews. So we ran down to the wagon, he and I . . . Sam and I. I don't remember if the older man was with us. We hid under. . . . I think he was there, too . . . and we hid under all those things they had piled on the wagon, and they drove out of the camp. They were stopped by guards, but they just looked around on the outside. We heard them speaking German, you see, and they just looked, but they weren't so careful about checking the wagon, so we got out of there and could get to the ghetto, or the other camp. After we got there, we had to hide the whole time until that whole ghetto had been eliminated."[6]

Sam, the older boy, gives his account

"And . . . I must have been twelve years old, I suppose. A rumour got started in the camp that we were going to be moved, because the adults had seen them building barracks with barbed wire by the factories. Here we were still living in proper houses. And one day we had to line up in that place there. This camp was built around this place, you see. And then we lined up there, and an SS guard came and grabbed me by the nape of the neck and dragged me to a house and threw me in there. And over 100 children had been gathered there. Those children whose parents had a function—out in every camp there were lots of capos. Their children, ten children more or less, got to stay with their parents. There were over 100 children gathered in that house . . . [silence]. I went up to the guards and said, 'I want to go back to my parents.' I got my ears boxed, and maybe that woke me up. In any case I had a feeling that something that was not good was going on. There was a second storey so I went up there. There I found a friend of mine named Noa and he asked me what I was doing. I said, 'I am going to hide', and he said that he was, too. And there was another child, *a boy who was six or seven years old*, whose name was Matthias. We were . . . I must have been around twelve and Noa eleven, or I don't know, something like that, maybe ten. And the other children were screaming or sitting there in apathy, so I just climbed up went up to the other storey. And there we saw an opening to an attic. The ceiling was very low and from the stairs was one of these wooden railings. So we got up on the railing and Matthias helped Noa pull himself up. Then he took Matthias up again and the two of them pulled me up into the attic. And then we saw that the roof stuck out like you know a dormer with a window with a little roof of its own on top of it. We saw that there was a little hole that we could climb into and get under that little roof. So we climbed in there, and it was so little that I lay beside Noa and Matthias lay on our backs. We lay there, and we did not see anything, but *we heard*. We heard when the adults marched away, and after some time we heard the trucks come and fetch the children. I say trucks, we found that out later. I heard car motors, *I hear children screaming and it gets quiet in the camp.* Through Christian Poles who lived near the burial place we later learned that the children were driven out directly and shot down into freshly dug graves. Well, that way we knew that we had lost many other friends. We lay there the whole day, and we wondered, could we go on lying there, because the camp was completely empty, but there were blankets and things left, and there were guards around who were keeping watch. But we knew that at a certain place, where the train tracks ran, there was a hole. Children know things. There was a hole in the fence, so we decided to try to go out at night, to try to sneak out and try to find the factories where our parents worked. So we went down at night and tried to sneak in that direction. And it was really hard, because they had searchlights sweeping over the camp so we had to inch along out under the windows. We waited until the searchlights swept by, and then we crept to the next window and sat and waited. And finally we came to a place where there were ruins left by a house. We went in and found what was left of three rooms and there was a wall with an opening where a window had been. It was dark in there, and if we looked out it was light. And when we were about in the middle of the other room, a guard came along and stood in the window opening with his back towards us. It was a wonder that we did not have a heart attack. We all said that [reaches for air]. But Noa pressed his hand over that little boy's mouth so that he could see that something . . . and I remember that I tried to stop my heart because it pounded so hard that the guard must be hearing it. Yes, he stood there maybe two, three minutes but *all three of us aged by about 20–30 years in that short time* because that's how long it seemed to us before he went away again. We

saw that we could not get out any other way than to crawl all
the way back up to the attic. And we lay there for about four
days and nights and on the fourth or fifth day, I don't remember exactly, we heard voices on the stairs speaking Yiddish. It
was a work group who had been sent to clean up and take blankets to the new camp. So we peeped out from that opening in
the attic, and we saw three of our people and no guard beside
them. So we made ourselves known. They looked up, and they
turned pale, because they thought they were seeing ghosts. In
any case news travelled on the jungle telegraph that children
had been found alive, so that they had. . . . Everyone was, you
know, taken to Auschwitz, and the ones who had a watch or a
ring, they gathered them all together and buried them as far
away as they could from that house at that place. They said to
the guards that they had found a buried treasure. They went
there, and then they took us down from the attic and laid us
in the wagons with lots of blankets over us, and in that way we
were taken to the new camp. And they would not allow me to
see my parents right away, because my parents, after all, had believed for several days that I was dead and had recited the Kad-
dish for me—you know, the prayer for the dead. And so if I just
showed up all of a sudden, I would . . . maybe they . . . [laughs].
But after some hours I got to see them, and it was, of course,
absolutely wonderful."[7]

Discussion

Similarities in the two accounts

Even if the two men do not say the same thing word for word, what
they say does convey similar phenomena in connection with the
persecutions. What their accounts have in common is the description of persecution, of their vulnerability. They have experienced
being violated both physically and psychically. They were both "lined
up"—"children by themselves". One of them was roughly "grabbed
by the nape of the neck" and had his ears boxed. Both note that
they were transported or dragged into a house and felt the threat
of being separated and taken away from their parents. Both "heard"
the silence. They also heard sounds. Noa remembers the sound of

shots being fired, while Sam remembers motor sounds and children's screams. Both of them mention a guard by whom they felt
threatened.

As children, the two men had a preparedness to act together as
friends. They state that they saw each other and that Noa was the
one who initiated the contact and brought up the idea of hiding.
They describe themselves as agile, and they seem to have been able
to orient themselves spatially. They understood what was high up and
far down, as well as the nature of holes and openings, such as in the
attic area. They helped to "pull" each other up. They squeezed their
bodies together and made themselves small and supple. Both speak
of holes in the fence that enclosed the area, of Jews loading things,
and of blankets when they made their escape, hidden in wagons.

They remember their respective ages when this event took place.
Sam adds something significant: that he experienced that "children
know things", which in this connection assisted him in creating space,
in thinking about a route of escape. Children who are subjected to
massive trauma have, as stated earlier, a distorted conception of age.
Sam experienced that he himself aged quickly, "all three of us aged
by about 20–30 years". It is probable that children see both things
that adults do not see and things that adults do not know that children see. In addition, the children were forced by the situation to
see things that children should not have to see, and they became
precocious and adult-like, which can have led to their experiences
of age distortion. Age distortion seems to have occurred with regard
to the conception of the third person's age: Was he a little child or
an older man?

Differences in the accounts

The interview sequences give a picture of the same course of events
with relatively similar affects, though at the same time there are differences. Sam remembers the crying of the older children who were
deported, while Noa remembers the silence that followed. Noa said
that "they were looking for something to eat". This is not mentioned
by Sam.

*Noa remembers the third person as an older man and Sam remembers him
as a little boy six or seven years of age.* I can only speculate as to why the
accounts differ in the particular case of the third person. A third
person was there, but the awarenesses of this third person are dif-

ferent. To make the third person older, as Noa did, could be rooted in his memory of longing for a safety-creating person, while at the same time this older adult was injured—"thrown out". Noa does not mention missing his parents in this connection, whereas Sam does. Sam, who was older, had possibly had more time to stabilize links to an inner object.

Both experienced the sudden appearance of a guard. Both seem to remember this event, so it is very probable that it did, in fact, take place, even if Noa remembers it as taking place in the attic while Sam remembers it as taking place beside the window on the ground level. Noa, the younger, gives the impression of speaking from a "child's perspective". It is as if he is being invaded by affects during the time that he is recounting what happened. Sam, the older, seems, by interweaving information that he received later about the course of events in Kielce, to be able to maintain more of a distance to the trauma. Affects seem to be more restrained in connection with this particular interview sequence.

Perhaps their respective ages at the time of the trauma have significance for their ways of remembering, as do their respective degrees of capacity to put their experiences into words, then as well as later. Because of his age, Sam possibly had a greater sense of geographical orientation, whereas Noa, with his greater nearness to affects, remembers other details in the sequence of events. Noa says that he "hides" in a house, while Sam mentions going upstairs in a house. The said phenomena illustrate the complexity of the survivors' life histories.

Psychoanalytic listening

A central task of psychoanalytic listening is to gain an understanding of the narrator's *experiences*—that is, the psychic reality that emerges in the manifest memory. It is possible that an historian pays close attention to this as a factor to be taken into consideration, perhaps as a bias, which calls for additional material from other sources. The approach of the psychoanalyst is to try to find clues that increase the understanding—in this case concerning, for example, "the third person"—by using the information that is available in other parts of the life histories. Generally speaking, by paying special attention to contradictions or apparently irrelevant material, a trained interviewer and listener to the recorded interviews can find surprising information of both historical and psychological value.

My starting point is that Noa and Sam are two completely different individuals of different ages and with different world-views rooted in their own personal histories. However, in spite of this, they spontaneously recounted several situations from the war in similar ways. Apart from mentioning the hiding place in the attic, in which they were both present, there are two situations when they were apart from each other. One of these occasions concerned being forced to see people they knew in the ghetto being hanged. Both of their accounts of this painful situation were accompanied by strong affects when they were being recalled. The other situation had to do with avoiding a routine procedure in Auschwitz, to which each of them was transported without knowing of the other's fate. They managed to get out of having to walk under a cross-bar that would have revealed their short height and young age. There is obviously congruency in other memories as well.

To return to the third person, whom they remember in completely different ways, Noa speaks of an older, injured man who had been "thrown out", whereas Sam speaks of a boy six–seven years of age, whom he also calls by name. They see the same thing but obviously interpret it in different ways. In later parts of the life histories I find out that on his first day in Auschwitz Noa was placed in barracks, together with other children and people who were old and ill, probably awaiting further transport to the crematories. In the morning he discovered *"an older man* who lay to the side of me and . . . was dead".[8] Later, with the help of some older boys, Noa was able to escape miraculously from the barracks through a roof window. The account of this flight, which in certain respects resembles the sequence of events in the attic in the ghetto (escape up towards the roof), can give clues leading to an hypothesis concerning a shifting and condensing of various memory pictures. The dying man beside Noa in Auschwitz seems to "melt together with" (become condensed with) and be shifted to "the third person" in the attic, whereupon the third person becomes old instead of being a child. In Sam's later life history there is no corresponding memory of a boy that could have provided the substance for remembering "the third person" as a little boy. The two men's memory pictures from the ghetto can thus have to do with how the memory is constructed based on each individual's personal experiences after this trauma and on the extent to which each of them has verbalized what happened. It can be assumed that the incident with the "third person" made different "imprints" in their personalities, both in the past, when it occurred, and when they remember it now.

Reconstruction and construction of memories

Historical truth and narrative truth are established concepts today in research in the social sciences. In psychoanalysis there is a parallel conceptual formation designated as the reconstruction and construction of memories (Reeder, 1996) or the repeating and retranscribing of experiences (Modell, 1990). When the interviewee has shown strong affects, it is probable that the affects were also present on the actual occasion—something that has been confirmed both by cognitive memory research and through experiences from work in psychoanalytic practice: if "construction seeks to join various elements in order to form a whole, it is because it always has a historical slant" (Etchegoyen, 1991). However, the question is posed as to whether the affects are always related to the same event that the person experienced when he or she shows them during the recounting process. Matthis (2000) makes a comparison with dreaming: it is not certain that the affect is connected to the history that the person is recounting, "but it is connected with something, something is awakening the affect, but exactly what it is which awakens a violent affect, that is not possible to know". Matthis stresses that in order to understand the affect, one creates a picture of reality or a dream picture that can explain, for example, why I am so afraid. Something has happened, symbolically or literally. This representation of it is something that both can be partly reconstructed and is usually constructed to a great extent. Against the background of Freud's trauma theory, she formulates a differentiation between reconstruction and construction: "Reconstruction can take place on the basis of repressed memories—that is, the memories were conscious at one time, while construction is built upon vague evidence, like a new building established with 'rubbish'" (p. 224). The patients' histories are thus always true at one level, but whether or not they reveal a factual historical truth cannot always be ascertained solely on the basis of what the patients consciously relate. Theoretically it seems easy to keep reconstruction and construction separate, but in practice difficulties are inevitable. Both elements are present all the time. The one never excludes the other. Spence (1982) stresses that there is no clear line where reconstruction stops and construction begins. He says: "language is always getting in the way between what the patient saw or felt and the way this experience appears in the analytic conversation" (p. 286).

It is hardly a coincidence that certain words appear in both life histories—for example, in connection with sounds and silence. With reference to Damasio (1994), who has studied autobiographical memories, Matthis points out that

> when we are subjected to certain stress, the cortex of the suprar-
> enal gland starts to produce glucocorticoids and this contributes
> to enhancing our memory of significant events. However, when
> we are subjected to excessive stress—which . . . in war situations—
> the release of glucocorticoids by the cortex of the suprarenal
> gland increases to such a level that the hippocampus, instead
> of being stimulated becomes inhibited, yes, it can even close
> down completely. Experiences a person goes through in such
> circumstances leave only *vague traces*, perhaps only in the form of
> excitement and uneasiness, but the link to a specific place and a
> specific time is lost" [Matthis, 2000, p. 224]

Memories of strong anxiety "can only be constructed, never reconstructed". Findings from the work with life histories show that perceptions from traumatic events have, as mentioned, "made imprints"
of such depth that they are kept "active" in a part of the self as invading affects. Reeder (1996) states that

> construction may fill the gap in the historical accounts of the
> analysands [here, the interviewees] about themselves when there
> is no longer any memory to latch onto—construction intervenes
> in other words entirely on the narrative level and serves the
> purpose of achieving coherence in the self-understanding of the
> analysand. [Reeder, 1996, p. 243]

This can be compared to the interviewees' endeavours to create meaning in their own life histories. There are examples of discus-sions between historians and psychoanalysts concerning the assess-ment of life histories. Felman and Laub (1992) describe an example of historians not being able to grant credibility to a testimony con-cerning the blowing up of chimneys because the survivor remem-bered fewer chimneys than were actually present where the event took place. The psychoanalysts' understanding was that the survivor was giving testimony about something else—something radical and urgent: that one chimney in Auschwitz was blown up was just as unbelievable as four being blown up. The number was of less importance than the fact that the event had actually taken place. The survivor bore witness to an event that crushed all thoughts—Jewish resistance just could not happen here. She gave testimony to the breaking of a frame, which can be seen as the historical truth. In summary, it is necessary for us to keep an open mind as to how the situation actually was in reality (at the time of the historical event). However, we can make observations and reflections and formulate hypotheses based on the survivors' life histories from experiences of massive trauma, such as those presented by Noa and Sam.

In my presentation of a theory in the following chapter, I bring together *how* the interviewees recounted their life history (affect regulating) with *what* they conveyed (content).

IV

FROM CONCEPTUAL MODELS
TO A THEORY

8

The "affect propeller" as an analytic tool for trauma-related affects

There is an ever-increasing interest in the interdisciplinary aspects of understanding the roots of genocide as well as its consequences for the traumatized. Until now, studies of affect regulation of the victims and, specifically, the psychic experiences of children after genocide have, however, been under-represented in research.

My interest began when I conducted the two extensive interviews with Anna and Emilia, who survived the Holocaust. They were both eight years old at the time their native countries were occupied. The traumatization seems to have been a central factor in their attitude towards having children of their own. They actively abstained from giving birth. One of them, Anna, said in a loud voice: "I did abortions twice *because I was a child myself.*"[1] This statement is the basis for posing a question that has remained of great importance: What was the significance of a child's own age and conception of age during

Chapter 8 is a revised version of S. Kaplan, "Children in Genocide—Extreme Traumatization and the 'Affect Propeller'". *International Journal of Psychoanalysis*, 87 (2006): 725–746; also presented at the 44th IPA Congress, Rio de Janeiro, Brazil, 28–31 July 2005, and at the 45th IPA Congress, Berlin, 22–29 July 2007 (Hayman Prize, 2007).

and after the genocide when it came to the possibility of maintaining the feeling of having inner links to significant persons, and how might these inner links serve as a lifeline to allow the creation of links to the next generation? The theme of reproduction seems like a "focal point" with links to different traumatic experiences during the persecutions, resulting in the child survivors abstaining from giving birth—or, conversely, choosing to have many children, which I interpret as two sides of the same coin. This issue led me to study more life histories recounted by women and men who had survived the Holocaust as children (Kaplan, 2000, 2002a) and, later, by teenagers who survived the 1994 genocide in Rwanda. What I saw as a break in reproduction manifested itself later as being an important aspect of a "*generational collapse*".

In analysing the interviews, an opportunity has arisen of becoming aware of psychological phenomena for which the survivors might not have "thought of" seeking psychotherapeutic help—even if they have had the opportunity—since their life history contains invading affects and memory images that they only want to forget. The interviews can thus be seen as a complement to experiences from psychoanalytic work. It is about situations that we cannot imagine experiencing ourselves—"unimaginable primitive affects", in the words of Grubrich-Simitis (1984).

Children are persecuted

Children were afflicted particularly severely during the Holocaust (by the Holocaust, I mean the entire Nazi period from 1933 to 1945, since the final persecutions were built on earlier preparations). Only 11% of the Jewish children in the Nazi-occupied countries survived this period (Dwork, 1991).

Anna, who was eleven years old at the time, talks about being pushed into cattle cars:

". . . she [a woman] had a pillow with her. Everyone was very surprised. She asked me if I wanted to stand next to her. She came into the car with that pillow and stood there, you couldn't sit down. We couldn't really all stand next to each other. Everyone was shoving. It was horrible. You can't imagine. Everyone tried to get some air. The only possibility was to get close to a little opening in the side."

—"Do you remember what you thought in the wagon?"

"You didn't think, one was scared . . . Everyone wanted to get close to the opening, but you couldn't, . . . And then, when we got to Latvia, to Riga, the cars stopped, and the big doors opened. Then Russians, Ukrainians, started screaming, I can't describe it . . . and they ran into all the cars. Get out, get out—like wild men. And can you imagine, a little girl [the pillow had, in fact, been a little girl] woke up. The woman had a daughter whom she was putting to sleep, and she woke up and started to cry. Everyone was surprised. A small child! And then a Ukrainian came and pushed and shoved and wanted to know where the crying was coming from, and he trampled that little baby with his boots until she died. And when we got to Estonia, the mother took her life. . . . She took her life."[2]

In Rwanda, a genocide was orchestrated, led by Hutu extremists, which in many ways resembles the Nazi atrocities during the Holocaust. The central aim was extermination of a people (Melvern, 2000). Human Rights Watch (Rakita, 2003) reports that 400,000 children—more than 10% of Rwanda's children—are estimated to be orphans today. This is because of the genocide and HIV/AIDS, resulting from rapes committed during the genocide. Seven Rwandan teenage boys who lived in the streets after the genocide were interviewed in depth twice, with a one-year gap between interviews (Kaplan, 2005a). (The interviews were conducted with the help of an interpreter. The boys' answers in the local language, Kineyarwanda, were later translated in detail and transcribed into English by a Rwandan translator.)

Frédéric, nine years old during the Rwanda genocide, talks about incidents at the road-block:

"There they stopped people and asked them if they were Hutu or Tutsi. When we got there, they asked us if we knew what ethnic group we belonged to. One of them told us to show our hands, because they could tell from the palm of our hands. He said that Hutu do not have the middle line in the hands, while Tutsi have the middle line straight. As I bent to open my hands, one of them grabbed my sister's child. . . . They turned to me, took the baby from my back . . . grabbed me and threw me in burning coffee husks, and I got burned everywhere while they were just laughing. After some time, they took me out of the fire and threw me in a pond that was nearby, thinking that I would drown. It was good that the baby had been taken from me—I would not have been able to carry him, as I had been burned all over. I cried loudly, and one of them said, 'Why don't we finish that fool and stop having him making alarm for us?'"[3]

The extreme cruelty of these actions—where the selections are the most painful acts—may have affected child survivors, both men and women, in their identification with the needy child. I have assumed that extreme traumatization on the occasion of a traumatic, un-expected, abnormal event is *experienced* in similar ways, regardless of culture. Each individual's vulnerability and personal life history does, nevertheless, have a bearing upon how one *regulates anxiety* in connection with the traumatic moment and afterwards. This view ap-plies especially to manmade trauma and, to a lesser extent, to natural catastrophies. Sgofio and colleagues (1999, quoted in Schore, 2003a) write about social stressors being far more detrimental than non-so-cial aversive stimuli, and therefore attachment or "relational trauma" from the social environment has more negative impact upon the infant brain than assaults from the non-human, or inanimate, physi-cal environment. Thus, the importance of obtaining a psychic space follows as a thread in this presentation.

A single traumatic event, cumulative trauma, continuous trauma

This book concerns manmade trauma, which especially evokes feelings of humiliation. I differentiate between a single traumatic event—for example, when a child is being attacked and humiliated in the schoolyard, where caring adults may be available and thereby help the child find words for what has happened—and prolonged, repeated trauma, such as genocide, where the victim has no access to such *psychic space.* In the first case it is possible to talk about what has happened, to work through the event. In the second case children only register what has happened as a panicky feeling in the body. "You didn't think"—as Anna said—is a frequently heard comment from the interviewees. An interruption in thinking occurred. A perceptual image or sound like the perpetrator's voice can be imprinted in the body, and the event cannot be left behind as a memory in the way we think about memories. Instead, it remains as an inexpressible discomfort in the body. A split in the self appears as a result of the difficulties in dealing with the anxiety. Individuals with experiences of early childhood abuse may develop more dissociative responses to subsequent traumas (Bremner, 1999, quoted in Schore, 2003a). Dissociation refers to a compartmentalization of experience, which is stored in the memory as isolated fragments, sensory perceptions, affective states, or behavioural re-enactments (van der Kolk & Fisler, 1995). From a psychoanalytic viewpoint, the relationship between inner and outer reality should be stressed (Varvin, 2003). This might explain the fragmented narratives and sudden bodily reactions triggered by clues in everyday life. As Schore puts it, "the person would not be aware that his fear has any origin in space, place and time" (2003a, p. 258). This could be described as a traumatic re-enactment encoded in implicit memory.

In many countries there are continuous, ongoing traumas. Children have no other experience than of living in political conflicts and being witnesses to violence and death, and this may add a new dimension to trauma theory.

Method

By applying psychoanalysis to the survivors' life histories, we get a conception of the way memories have become a part of the survivors' life world. Rubovits-Seitz (1998, p. 294) differentiates between two levels of psychoanalytic theory that facilitate an understanding of what is meant by applied psychoanalysis. The first level concerns basic methodological core concepts, such as the unconscious, defences, meaning, and the importance of childhood, which form the basis for interpretations both clinically and non-clinically. This is the basic way of analytic listening. The second level concerns specific "clinical" theories, which are tentative constructions that might be applied (e.g. *Nachträglichkeit*) clinically or in other applications, such as interviews. Listening at this level seems to be more "applied" with preconceived conclusions. However, these thought models might interfere with the individual's construction of unique personal meanings. In this study, despite my preliminary preconceptions, I have made an effort to be open to the material in order to allow myself to be surprised by each interviewee. This also connects with my interest in cross-scientific viewpoints. Thus, I use hypotheses generated from the core concepts, as well as relevant thought models in relation to the interview material (Kaplan, 2000, 2002a).

As described in the introduction, by using the method-grounded theory (Glaser, 1978), I have been inspired to "think conceptually". This method aims to create theoretical models from the development of hypotheses well grounded in data and formulated in concepts, the relationship between concepts, and theories about social and psychological processes. There are similarities with psychoanalytic work. I have emphasized the interviewees' ways of expression— both contents and affects. An analysis has been started of how these concepts relate hypothetically to each other within associative fields about *what* and *how* the interviewees present their life stories. Below, I summarize themes and concepts developed in my studies.

Themes emerging in the interviews

Especially notable phenomena in the interviews are based in sensory perceptions from the partly fragmented descriptions on persecutions and in the affects that become tangible in the room at the moment the interviewees talk about these experiences. Significant persons, as well as a number of meaningful linking objects that were mentioned, have been of great importance for my understanding. Repeated statements have often been connected with "looking into the faces of adults" and "looking out through windows". These statements I have interpreted as significant borders for experiences between the inner psychic world and the outer world. These observations are in accordance with Schore's (1994) extensive studies on the significance of the primary caregiver's affective response—mutual gaze transactions and the mother's facial expressions. Older children's vulnerability to the mother's gaze probably means they regain its immense importance during traumatic events. The expressions of affects in the interviews oscillated between sudden wordless crying to sometimes cohesive narratives with more relaxed eye contact.

Generational collapse as a core process

The major concern of the survivors, the core process to which most of the clues in the life histories seem to be linked, I have called "generational collapse". This process is built up by two core concepts, which I designate as "perforating" and "space creating", and the dynamics between these. "Perforating" comprises the inconceivable cruelties to which the Nazis subjected the Jews, and the Hutu extremists the Tutsis, in connection with their, respectively, systematic persecution. All forms of outward actions carried out by the aggressors and described from the perspective of the persecuted belong to this category. "Space creating" is my term for the inner psychic processes through which the persecuted created their own space for thinking and acting in spite of conditions being minimal, and which they described in the interviews. By using the active form in the generated concepts below, I want to emphasize the ongoing process.

Perforating

The facial expressions of adults and the atmosphere in the home changed radically. Through parents' "discussing"—or the opposite, "being silent"—the children understood that something was about to happen, but not what it was. Something "diffuse" worried them. There was a feeling of "danger and vulnerability . . . the danger was creeping closer and closer to the skin", said Sandor.[4] Generations have been destroyed, dissolved, when the psychic shield was perforated by sensory perceptions. The psychic membrane has figuratively and literally become "full of holes" by *invading the senses* (something—for example, a frightening voice—forces its way in and destroys), *tearing away* (something—for example, family members, important objects and routines—is taken away and leaves a vacuum) and "body marking" (both actual and symbolic, such as being abused and having to mark the clothes with the Star of David or "T" for

Tutsi in the identity card, or fabrication of a race difference, as was the case with Frédéric's hand). Sensory perceptions have made "imprints" in the personality.

Space creating

The children's preoccupation with the facial expressions of the adults probably constituted, as well as spatial orientation, a way of examining the possibility of creating a space and *recapturing life* as it had been when it "was normal". *Space creating* refers to a psychic room that an individual, as a child, creates according to his or her needs. This phenomenon can have a link to a real space where they, for instance, could hide for a short while. Despite minimal space in the living conditions that predominated during a genocide, glimpses of experiences from the children's fantasizing in connection with the traumatic events were recounted associatively in the life stories. These experiences were probably a prerequisite for continuing to exist at all and for constituting meaningful themes for human existence—a mending of the trauma. There could even be moments of "excitement" in new situations, even though the situation was full of fear. Edith fantasized as a child about a tree far away that she saw through a little hole in the wall of the train wagon in which the victims were transported to the camps. She could thereby mentally "move herself" out of the terrifying situation and feel "alive" for a moment. To highlight these moments gives us a sense of how the interviewees may have used mental strategies in creating links to inner pictures of important persons and events to fend off perforating and the fear of dying. Certain pieces of clothing, small things, stuffed toys, dolls proved to serve as essential *linking objects*. Culture and religion may support this process. By "strategy", I mean situations in which the strategic/creative process is something that first and foremost emerges on the spur of the moment, based on existential needs. *Thinking/fantasizing* and *thinking/acting* are the phenomena that I see as the basis for space creating.

I asked Jean, a Rwandan teenage boy, what constantly comes back into his mind. His answer illustrates the dynamic between perforating and space creating. In the beginning he is extremely agitated and has his fingertips pressed against his forehead.

"The thing that constantly comes back to my mind is the way my sister died. . . . While I was in Kigali roaming about, sleeping any-where, jumping over dead bodies, and so on, and when I would think of my sister and how I could not find her, yet I was told that she was alive, I felt very bad. She was not old when she died, because we used to play together while going to church. They told me how she died. She was hit on the head with a hammer, then put on a motorcycle and taken very far away and thrown there. What hurt me most was that the man who killed her used to be our neighbour, roasting meat near our home. I always think that if I could only see him, I would also kill him—that is what disturbs my mind most. During those days, they were looking for young people to join the army, and whenever I remember that man who killed my sister and was close to my father, I feel like joining the army so that I could also hunt him and kill him. I feel that even if they found me out there and killed me, I would also have revenge for my sister. When I was still on the street, smok-ing bang, we used to go to a place . . . and there they would try to stop me from thinking about revenge, they would bathe me, feed me, and I would start behaving like a normal child. I would then sit down and tell them all my plans, and if they tried to stop me, I would run away and go back to the street. While I was still at this place, I met a certain lady who liked me and would take me to a place for prayers. She even gave me plastic bags to sell so that I could get some money to live on. She was very happy to see me afterwards off the street and to hear that I am now at school, studying. I no longer think like I used to, because those who are dead cannot come back to this life we are living in. I only hope for a better future, with a wife and children. I will tell them the things that happened to me."[5]

We can observe the rapid affective shifts. The probability of surviv-ing psychological damage/humiliation and abstaining from acts of revenge may increase if there is a support for developing mental space. Jean's narrative is an example of this.

Age distorting

Age distorting contains aspects of both perforating and space creating and can be seen as an aspect of the self-image. "Distorting" is used here in the sense of "reversal" or "twisting". The child survivors express a feeling of not being of their chronological age. To claim to be older than one's biological age in order to pass the selection could give a psychic and real space, a hope for survival. But the need to lie is a strain for the self. Sam said: "I was 100 years old in my head and took care of both myself and my dad."[6] Anna, who was quoted above, gave a crying expression of the signal anxiety that was triggered when she thought of her pregnancies. This emotional statement may imply a traumatic link to her experiences in the cattle car next to the woman with a newborn baby, and may also show that child survivors in general lose their teens and became precociously adult. Thoughts of having children seem to create confusing links between different time dimensions. Fragmented life histories indicate a difficulty in experiencing the past as something one has left behind in order then to get on with life—lacking life continuity. Subordinated categories are *depersonalization/emotional stunting* and its opposite: *taking responsibility/precocity*. I perceive associative connections between *perforating, space creating,* and *age distorting,* which have led to a conceptual model (see Table 4.1) that functions as an analytic tool for the contents of life histories about trauma (Kaplan, 2002a).

What is said and *how* it is told: content and affects in the interviews

During the study, I became more and more attentive to the interviewees' emotional expressions. The affects and also the lack of shown affects served as signals and guideposts. *How* something was said and the interviewees' facial expressions came to be just as meaningful to me in my understanding of what the victims had been through as *what* was said. A web of memory fragments and affects came therefore to constitute the base for a number of hypotheses concerning affect regulating that seems to be the essential aspect of the core process generational collapse. These hypotheses form the base of a developing theory concerning the psychological phenomena that I call *trauma linking* and *generational linking* and which constitute one of the axes in Table 8.1, with a number of categories concerning *affect regulating*, constituting the other axis. In summary this means:

1. perforating and space creating constitute elements of the narratives;

2. trauma linking and generational linking constitute associative connections to these elements, respectively; and

3. these connections are based on affects regulated by the individual.

Trauma linking is thus an inner psychological consequence of perforating and means that traumatic experiences are "easily awakened" associatively in the interview and in conjunction with events in everyday life. The survivors appear to live with a sort of "doubling"—a "vertical split" in the self. The past and the present are in different compartments, with no associative connection between them—that is, the trauma is constantly kept present in one part of the self while the person lives an ordinary life and appears untouched.

Generational linking, the result of successful space creating, means that the interviewees have their attention directed towards significant persons and objects in the past and in the present that strengthen the feeling of living in a context, and that also can be seen as an aspect of resilience. Through the sensitive attention of the interviewer, the ability to associate is increased. In analysis, the analysand is less afraid of "opening the channels" between trauma experiences and the "normal" course of life. These different tendencies—trauma linking and generational linking, respectively—can dominate in different stages of life as well as in different stages of an analysis for each individual.

The affect diagram (Table 8.1) shows the process in trauma linking and generational linking within *each* individual—that is, the diagram says something about the time perspective and something about the process between different categories of affects constantly going on within the individual. In certain persons, some categories of affects will dominate over others. The transition between trauma linking and generational linking is, hence, buoyant. Hopefully, generational linking will have developed over time, so that this process,

Table 8.1 Affect diagram.

Hypotheses about affect regulating in trauma- and generational-linking processes within each individual

AFFECT REGULATING

LINKING	Affect evacuating	A Affect invading	B Affect isolating	C Affect activating	D Affect symbolizing
Trauma linking	*Transported link*	A1 *Affect as link*	B1 *Encapsulated link*	C1	D1
(Perforating)	Perception of trauma—may lead to *revenge*	Perception of trauma—retraumatization, which may be shown in body language and *repetition*	Perception of trauma—retraumatization, which may lead to somatizing and *distancing*	Representation of trauma/verbally expressed—perforating to small extent—may lead to (optimal) *anxiety*	Representation of trauma/verbally expressed—perforating to small extent—may lead to (bearable) *pain*
Generational linking		A2	B2	C2 *Normalizing as link*	D2 *Metaphor as link*
(Space creating)	Illusory space creating. Demand on personal rehabilitation. *Pseudonormalizing*	Minimum of space creating. *A cry for help*	Partial space creating. *Maintaining control of* the trauma	Expanding space creating—may lead to *recapturing of a* 'normal' life	Flexible space creating—may lead to *creativity*

Reproduced, with permission, from Kaplan, 2005a, p. 176.

decades after the Holocaust and the genocide in Rwanda, dominates over trauma linking.

Trauma linking dominates

Affect invading (A) can be seen when the interviewees openly express feelings by, for example, crying or laughing in a panic-stricken way. The memory images seem to be interwoven with strong expressions of emotion and are characterized by repetition compulsion. This can be exemplified in Anna's desperate crying as an answer (a cry for help) when she thinks of her abortions—affects that may have associative connections with earlier traumas. The affect is the link, which may be compared to Klein's (1975) concept of "memories in feeling". If the individual is overwhelmed by affects that go beyond the threshold for psychic pain, the risk of psychosis increases through what I call an *affect imploding*, which could correspond to memories being "erased" (Laub, 2005) and "attacks on linking" (Bion, 1959).

Affect isolating (B) is characterized by a distanced narration, with which the majority began their interviews. The interviewees tell the "known story"—the one usually told when someone asks. This may seem to be a completely locked position but might also, in generational linking, mean that control of the trauma is maintained, thus establishing a certain acting space. One may, however, reflect on what happens with the affects when they are totally encapsulated—what the consequences may be, for example, in chronic states. Perhaps the affects are manifested as physical symptoms. This extreme phenomenon is called "affect encasement". Imploding and encasement (Kaplan & Laub, 2007) are discussed in the next chapter.

Generational linking dominates

Agreeing to being interviewed can be seen as an aspect both of *affect activating* (C) and *affect symbolizing* (D). One exposes oneself to the risk of becoming moved and possibly feeling anxiety and pain when talking about traumatic experiences. The effort of regaining a "normal" life, of leaving a main identity as a "survivor" and, instead, feeling creative, is dominating. The interviewee may, at these moments, *feel more free in relation to the past*. One could say that the trauma no longer exists only set apart, contained in a closed part of the self, but also to a certain degree conforming in a time perspective in one's course of life.

Affect evacuating

Table 8.1 illustrates an ideal development from a lower to a higher level of integration (from A to D), but in reality the regulation of affects probably oscillates between affect invading and affect symbolizing during different stages of an interview and in an analytic process as well as in situations in everyday life. One may imagine a alternating between, for instance, bodily stiffness with an "empty" gaze during the interview and "lively" eye contact and bodily/metaphorical descriptions and back again to possible somatization. In summary, affect invading and affect isolating are more primitive defences that distort and are inefficient; affect activating and affect symbolizing are more adaptive defences and are thereby more efficient.

To what extent is it possible to achieve lasting "open channels" between trauma experiences and later "normal" experiences? It is probably best to talk about experienced traumas early—something that it would be possible to carry out in Rwanda today. At the same time, fantasies of revenge may be more open, as in Jean's case, and the risk of projective identification is great—that is, projecting the feeling of humiliation on the aggressors in order to create a "pseudonormal condition". *Affect evacuating*—projections—the most primitive level in the integration process presented in Table 8.1, is shaded and appears in the first column (without a letter designation). However, this destructive form of affect regulating should probably be placed within each of the other categories of affects, as aspects of these, which is illustrated in the next step of the affect diagram, the "affect propeller."

Dealing with frustration and anger

In Rwanda the Hutus and Tutsies have to deal with living side by side in the same country. After the Holocaust, the survivors were spread out all over the world, and the real distance to the aggressors became greater. There may be many reasons for the more common expressions of revenge phenomena in interviews with Rwandan survivors compared to Holocaust survivors. There are aspects of trauma-related affects, like Jean's revenge fantasies, that naturally emerge more clearly in interviews with survivors from Rwanda compared to survivors from the Holocaust. It had only been 9–10 years since the genocide at the time of the interview. For the Holocaust survivors revenge may emerge in more sublimated forms, like not buying German merchandise. The extreme poverty in Rwanda—the lack of satisfaction of basic needs for the majority—probably plays an important role in how people deal with their feelings. The history of the region is important, and extreme poverty should be considered as the central factor in the start of a genocidal process (Staub, 1989).

The "affect propeller"

I want to show the possibility of further understanding trauma-related affects via a continued theorizing and development of the affect diagram (Table 8.1). I have chosen the shape of a propeller (Figure 1) to further emphasize the dynamic process within each individual (Kaplan, 2005a). The blades of the propeller pivot around the central point: "affect regulating". Each blade consists of three different levels of linking processes based on my earlier categorization. On each blade there are two levels of *trauma linking*: one deals with the acting-out processes, *affect evacuating*, revenge; the second deals with trauma-related affects that are felt and experienced by survivors; and the third level is the more constructive *generational linking*. The blades rotate around their pivot and may cover each other or lie separately from each other, similarly to how emotions fluctuate. Sometimes one affect category dominates, sometimes another, and sometimes there are mixed forms. Some modes of expression may have been abandoned, since they are no longer used because other, more adaptive modes have taken their place. A consultation may start at any blade and level. Affect evacuating, which I discuss in greater detail here, is marked to show *the different roads that revenge may take*.

In affect invading there is, for instance, a risk of being overwhelmed by unbearable feelings, and *actions of revenge* may be the result. By thinking of revenge, one may feel as if one gets a "personal restoration" (Igra, 2001)—a pseudospace for a "normal" life. But, in

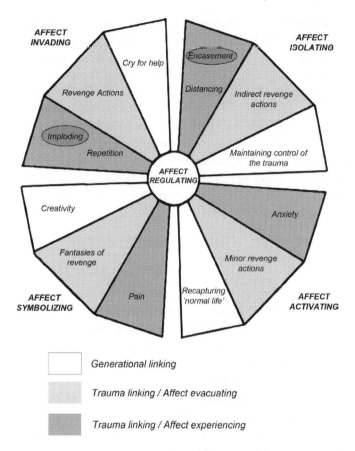

Figure 1. The "affect propeller" as an analytic tool for affect regulating within each individual (adapted from Kaplan, 2005a)

fact, the victim turns into a perpetrator. Within the category of affect isolating there is, for example, a risk of *indirect actions of revenge*: the "elimination" of trauma by flight into exile, or psychologically. There might be a risk of self-destructive behaviour.

Further, within affect activating there is a risk of *minor revenge actions*, such as when one looks for (negative) "satisfaction"—for example, by letting an audience listen to traumatic life histories without space for reflection and possibly with an accompanying thought: "they won't escape"—as one survivor expressed it. In affect symbolizing, we may suppose that there are *fantasies of revenge*. There may be a revengeful wish to reach a larger audience, by, for example, writing a book about one's experiences and, in one's mind, directing it at the aggressors. At the same time, such acts may have another side. It may be a way to "share the pain", with the emphasis that "all people are involved" in the genocide that is carried out—that is to say, genocide is a global problem. However, it is, on this level, essential to underline that there may at the same time be a healthy relief in the survivor—that there are people who want to listen and be witnesses to one's experiences—to share the feelings. I interpret this as the converse of revenge, as a step in the effort to live in a context, generational linking. Herman (1992) expresses this phenomenon as the victim asking the bystander to share the burden of pain.

While we remind ourselves that a conceptual model is always a simplification of reality, it may also be seen as an analytic tool for the temporary present focus of the affect regulating of an individual as part of the trauma process. The affect propeller as a whole may also be seen with different expressions of affect regulating in trauma—that is, as an illustration of how complex affect regulating is for traumatized individuals. Hopefully, in the long run, trauma linkings will be "covered", conformed behind generational linking processes that become the dominating ones.

Revenge and revenge fantasies are phenomena that seem to be taken for granted and are therefore comparatively rarely studied and described psychoanalytically. However, they are very much present psychologically and widespread in acted-out violence. There is thus also a great need to study the conditions of refraining from revenge (Böhm & Kaplan, 2006). As we can see, the blades with revenge are placed between trauma linking and generational linking experiences. The revenge may contain at one border destructive acting out and on the other the effort at reparation, to restore one's own dignity.

The generated concepts
in relation to contemporary theory formation

It is necessary to integrate the perspective of closely connected disciplines in the study of human emotion (Schore, 1994), and it might also be useful to compare concepts generated in this study with established concepts.

"Perforating" in relation to established concepts

Anzieu (1985) notes how intense chronic pain may bring the psychic apparatus into disorder, threaten the integration of the psyche into the body, and disturb the ability to wish and to think. The perforating concept connects to theories by Anzieu, who stresses Freud's (1920g) fruitful metaphors of a wound, a puncture in the *psychic shield*—that is, internal bleeding resulting from psychic trauma. There is agreement today that the concept of trauma does not have a clear and well-defined meaning. The concept is used for different experiences of psychic strain. Krystal (1978) emphasizes after-effects regarding both affective and symbolic functions. There is an increasingly accepted view of memories as something not stored statically, but as something changeable. Central concepts within current research are *symbolizing* and *mentalizing*, understood as mental processes that transform bodily/affective experiences into mental representations (Varvin, 2003). Children's vulnerability to a changed atmosphere included seeing a frightened and aggressive expression on the mother's face, which is imprinted and later appears as a *flashbulb memory*, extensively investigated by Schore (2003a). He also refers to clinical research emphasizing a possible link between childhood traumatic experiences and somatoform dissociation in chronic post-traumatic stress disorder (PTSD) (2003b). The relevance for the PTSD diagnosis, though, is increasingly being questioned. Children affected by war must not be stigmatized as permanently damaged, says Summerfield (1998). There has, however, been a shift in the key focus of defining PTSD: today the label is best understood in terms of what an individual brings to the traumatic event as well as experiences afterwards—not just the traumatic event itself (Schore, 2003a). This coincides with results of an extensive study of child survivors by Keilson (1992).

"Space creating" in relation to established concepts

An increasing interest has been shown in developing thought models about *mental space*—how to transform sensory perceptions into psychic content. Theorists have, from various perspectives, addressed the development of thinking and its connection with the child's active search for a containing object (Bion, 1967), with the focus on the significance of the transitional phenomenon (Winnicott, 1971), and with the skin as the starting point for theory formation about thinking (Anzieu, 1985; Bick, 1968), as well as the importance of the child's ability to bond with a caretaker, attachment theory, which is highly relevant in this context (Bowlby, 1988; Fonagy, Gergely, Jurist, & Target, 2002; Schore, 1994). Winnicott (1971) describes how the transitional object constitutes a defence against anxiety, which can be compared with Segal's (1957) and Modell's (1993) view of anxiety as a background in symbolizing. The use of objects may be significant out of the need to have something to "hold on to" (Bick, 1968). This "something to hold on to" is unconsciously constructed so as to strengthen the feeling of being an integrated, "contained" person (Bion, 1967), of not "falling apart" when confronted with the persecution or memory images from the trauma. It seems to be a phenomenon with significant survival value. The links are created to connect everything that supports the self with the feeling of one's own existence and are thus a central aspect of space creating and generational linking.

Winnicott (1971) writes about a potential psychic area that constitutes a bridge between isolation from and closeness to the mother. He distinguishes between the use of the object as comforter (strong bond with the mother) and as provider of calm (transitional object). Space creating and the child's use of linking objects may include both symbolizing (with a creative link to the object/ the mother) and different fetish processes (anxious clinging to the object). The objects may be used in an oscillating movement characterized by, on the one hand, experiences of a secure infant period and, on the other, the trauma situation, with a long separation from the mother. Fantasies of objects seen at a distance, as Edith's thought game of the tree, may—from a *dimension of connectedness*— create a space from the function of symbolizing to connect and unite contradictions, which is Winnicott's contribution. The fetish may also be seen as space creating because it diminishes anxiety in clinging to or controlling the object, as, for example, when the victim holds the object tight in the hand or the mouth and sometimes even swallows it.

The interviewees seem to have had good early relationships with their parents and thereby most probably have been able to create symbolizing (transitional) objects. Good symbolizing objects may, though, be destroyed and deteriorate to fetishlike objects if the mother does not return in time, before the longing turns into trauma. The only function of the object is, then, to provide the child with a certain amount of protection against frustrating anxiety. Whether the symbolizing object leads to one or the other psychological phenomenon depends on the time the mother has been absent (Deri, 1978). Elias, thirteen years old at the time, remembers

> ". . . the gathering of the things that we considered to be the most important . . . I had a . . . little piece of jewellery or whatever you might call it. It was not really jewellery either; it was a calendar on a chain to be worn around the neck. It looked like a necklace. That was the only thing I took with me. I dragged that with me all the way to Auschwitz. But that is the only thing that I have a clear memory of having."[7]

This "jewellery" may have functioned as a fetish with possible symbolic value (Winnicott, 1971), and thereby a connection to Elias's own body, his neck (Ferrari, 2004), and to his previous life. Ferrari's hypothesis stresses the fundamental role of the body for the development and realization of mental functions.

Fonagy (1998) argues that an alienated self exists in us all as the consequence of normal caretaking with its inevitable deficiencies. This self is normally covered by other self-images that we can create from good new experiences. The alienated self becomes most dangerous when later traumatic events in the family or the close surroundings force the child to dissociate, to split off a part of the experienced pain by identification with the aggressor. In these cases the covered deficiencies in caretaking—the empty spaces—will be filled with images of the aggressor, and the child will experience itself as destructive and, in extreme cases, as monstrous. Brutal behaviour from attachment objects generates intense shame; I imagine that this applies also to close neighbours as an extension of one's network, as shown in Jean's narrative. Early parenting deficiencies might create a vulnerability in the child that can be very destructive if later experiences are unfavourable, either as failed mentalizing or in order not to feel the powerlessness (Fonagy et al., 2002).

"Age distorting" in relation to established concepts

After extreme traumatization, the time concept and the time-related memory function are damaged. It is as if the trauma happened not a long time ago, but again and again every day. Laub and Auerhahn describe this phenomenon by showing how fragments " . . are recalled without the individual knowing that the 'I', or the subject who experienced the event, is different from the one who recalls it . . . there is a collapse of the two at the moment of recall, with no reflective self present" (Laub & Auerhahn, 1993, p. 291).

The past and the present exist simultaneously within the experienced self, which coincides with my impressions in this study. Winnicott's studies (1984) show that child survivors preserve those qualities that belong to the so-called latency period, or return to these values after an imperceptible attempt to attain a more mature developmental level.

Grubrich-Simitis (1984) focuses on the ability of the ego to use metaphors, as well as the related ability to structure time in the past, present, and future. A number of the life histories include memories of the mother's vulnerability to shock, which the home raids and the deportations brought with them. "My mother became . . ." "paralysed" . . . "speechless" . . . "totally at a loss" . . . "blind", said four of the interviewees. Psychic development may have become complicated, particularly because children were the target of persecution, especially if early attachment bonds were weak (Bowlby, 1988). In addition, parents who were child survivors themselves in areas with continuous political conflicts are more at risk of transferring trauma from one generation to the next via sudden interruptions in their natural web of emotions towards the infant. This corresponds to Faimberg's (1988) discussion. Schore (2003a) stresses the effects of the caregiver's stress regulating and dysregulating interactions on the infant's maturing coping systems. Both in Nazism during the Second World War and at the time of Hutu power in Rwanda, reproduction was attacked through rape, experiments, and torture. The phenomena presented seem to go together into an anxiety about childbearing and being a parent.

"Affect regulating" and "memory" in cross-scientific light

"All descriptions of the phenomenology of trauma include a disturbance in affectivity, but the precise role of affect ... is not clear", stresses Krystal (1988). Affects may metaphorically be seen as "glue" or as something that "brings energy" by binding together and facilitating the formation of connecting links. Our earliest psychic world is created by this process, as affective processes can be said to be in the core of the self. Clinical practice has shown that people who do not have access to their affects do not seem capable of integrating their experiences to a cohesive experience of their own life history and the self. The ability to symbolize may be seen as the basis for thinking and creating. Segal (1957) underlines symbol formation as a process in which the inner is brought together and integrated with the outer, like a self with significant others, and earlier experiences with later ones. She says that the formation of symbols is an activity in which the ego tries to deal with the anxiety arising in its relationship to the object. Specific categories of affects are awakened, according to Modell, who develops ideas about affect categories: "Split-off aspects of the self are centered on specific affective memories of the traumatic interaction between the self and the other ... Both the self as a victim and the self as aggressor are internalized as split-off aspects of the self" (Modell, 1990, p. 46). Like Segal, Modell (1993) states that symbolization means that a person has been able to work through his or her experiences and, through a recategorization of traumatic memories, has been able to deal with the anxiety. Emde (1999) describes the early childhood transitions and illuminates particularly the processes whereby affects promote integrative connections. The degree of integration of the trauma determines which way the memory traces go—to bodily expressions or to thought contents (Matthis, 2000).

The regulating of affects is thus a central organizing principle of human development and motivation. Loss of the ability to regulate the intensity of feelings and impulses is possibly the most far-reaching effect of trauma and neglect (van der Kolk & Fisler, 1994). The concern is to see how early patterns of individual adaptation evolve into later patterns—that is, the individual's coping system (Cicchetti, 1994, quoted in Schore, 2003a). The right brain is centrally involved and in control of vital functions that support survival and coping with stress (Schore, 1994; Wittling & Schweiger, 1993, quoted in Schore, 2003a). According to Tutté (2004), the most useful recent findings, which come from neuroscience, concern encephalic structures that are linked to emotion and memory. He emphasizes the current view on memory in terms of separate multiple systems—the difference between declarative and non-declarative or procedural memory—and stresses that "there is no disputing today that there is a sharp difference between what can be thought of, represented in images or put into words and what is inscribed in terms of affect-charged procedures, or affect-motor schemes" (Davis, 2001, quoted in Tutté, 2004, p. 912). Nathanson emphasizes that we all have innate, relatively similar affect mechanisms, and we also have our own "unique" ways of understanding or "remembering" our experiences of the innate affects: "Very quickly, as the growing child accumulates experience, affects become intertwined with memory" (1994, p. 50). He points out that an outside listener needs therefore to know about the history of our affective experiences but also how memory influences perception of current emotions. Pally (1997, 2000, quoting Tulving & Thompson, 1973), who describes the encoding of an event and subsequent factors that facilitate the activation of the memory of this, even states that the impact of emotional arousal on encoding is mediated by stress hormone activation of the amygdala (cortisol, etc.). She says that what enhances memory retrieval is the degree of similarity between the retrieval situation and the encoding situation. This is why memory is state-dependent. We are more likely to remember an event that was encoded during a sad mood if we are feeling sad while recalling it.

Modell (1990) regards Freud's concept of *Nachträglichkeit* in a more universal sense. Memory is not a permanent tape-recording in the brain that imitates the real event but is, rather, a dynamic reconstruction that starts out from the context and is created with the help of categories, which is confirmed by a neurobiological interpretation of this concept.

If one is unable to remember a specific event, this may be because one has not perceived a retrieval cue that awakens this specific memory (Schacter, 1996). If one cannot translate traumatic experiences to the developmental phase in which one finds oneself, they remain unassimilated (Emde, 1999). The experiences cannot be given a meaning and thereby cannot be contained by the individual. The probable consequence is a repetition in the next developmental phase.

In summary, then, there is, on the one hand, the repetition of intrusive memory fragments associated with bodily sensations/affects that may be triggered by clues in the present and, on the other hand, the remembering process built on the traumatized having had a possibility to verbalize in connection with the traumatic event (to symbolize) and thus put it behind him or her. This should be compared to aspects of the implicit procedural memory and declarative explicit semantic memory, respectively (see Tutté, above). The established term "invading memory" thus becomes a contradiction: it must, rather, be a case of "invading affects".

9

Trauma linking and generational linking: applications of the "affect propeller"

The paired concepts of trauma linking and generational linking have been introduced in order to show two possible pathways that the inner psychological process can take. In this chapter illustrations of these are presented.

Max: a clinical vignette (Kaplan, 2006)

Max, a latency boy, had been adopted at the age of three. He was referred for four-times-a-week psychoanalysis because of sudden major outbursts. He had been deeply traumatized during his first years of life in several orphanages, where he had been repeatedly abused. When the adoptive parents came to see him, he was "black and blue all over his back". During his first sessions Max showed *affect isolating* by stressing, "I don't want to remember—I want to forget", and he simultaneously repeatedly communicated his psychic state by bodily movements and comments on his sensory perceptions. He said, "I am overheated"—an expression of *affect invading* probably evoked by the analytic frame. During one session Max wore a sweater with a hood. He took it off and put it on back to front, with the hood over his face. He turned around on the couch frantically and said in a loud voice, "I have a problem coming out of this beehive ... I like bees, but not their sound." I hear "over-sounds", he continued. I asked him what these sounds felt like. It "makes the neck hurt", he said. Max most probably enacted his despair at being locked in, like being blind, sensitive to every noise from the outer and inner world (bees in the hood), enveloped sound memories from early traumas stored in the body. He tries, but does not manage to, fend off trauma-related affects. Moreover, he says he likes bees, and this may mean some linking object in his inner world that makes him feel creative.

In the following session, Max was more explicit and showed tendencies for *affect symbolizing*. He told me in detail an event from school the day before. It was "the worst that ever happened to me", he said. He had met his friend, A, and his worst enemy, B. B had said that A "had normal intelligence" but that Max had "an intelligence like a seagull". Max became more and more upset while talking about B's comment and exclaimed, "I hate him, I will kill him." On the one hand, a positive transference, a *generational linking* process, seems to develop—a trustful attitude towards the possibilities of the analysis, which I designate as *affect activating*. He verbalizes his concern and shows his vulnerability. And, on the other hand, he wants to "kill" his enemy, an expression of *affect evacuating*.

During the sessions that followed, Max brought two plastic figures, which he placed on the couch. He hit the cover of the couch, and the figures fell down, and he laughed with mockery in his voice. He repeated this sequence during the next two weeks. An acting out of fantasies of revenge in the *trauma linking* seemed to be taking place.

At the end of one session before a weekend break Max did not want to leave. I told him that the 45 minutes had passed. He said, "Forty-five minutes! Can't I order a full hour?" The concern for the analysis had grown, and he was upset that I had limits. I perceived his statement as a "cry for help". Now, Max started a period of repeatedly and concretely investigating the consulting room. He stood on the couch and felt the structure of the walls with his hand hour after hour. He was upset when he felt uneven spots in the wall. He returned to certain spots to feel whether the unevenness was still there. During one session he suggested that I should have walls that are even and sound-isolated. I wondered what that would be like. Max exclaimed in a seemingly ambivalent way that "then I could hear noises in my head, and that would not be so nice".

In my understanding, Max shows initially that generational linkings are cut off—no drawings, no playing, hardly any narratives. Simultaneously, he shows longing for space creating and being "contained" within a safe frame, and taking the risk of feeling the anxiety that is connected with the noises in his head, finding a language for his affects—*affect symbolizing*. Max's way of presenting himself actualizes Ferrari's (2004) hypothesis that the body has a fundamental role in the realization of mental functions. Frightening noises and faces have been imprinted. To quote Klein, "In taking the analysis back to earliest infancy, we enable the patient to revive fundamental situations" (1975, p. 234). It is a revival that is spoken of as "memories in feeling". The pendulum of affects is clear. There is a lack of sufficient capacity for emotional self-regulation (Toth & Cicchetti, 1998). Max fights against his sense of being "overheated", associated with feelings of being humiliated and, simultaneously, longs for the presence of an attachment figure, which creates hope for future dominance of generational linking processes.

Jean: Interview 2 (Kaplan, 2005a)

When I carry out my follow-up interview with Jean—the teenage Rwandan boy I presented in chapter 8—he has been living, since our last interview, for a little over a year at the home arranged by the paediatrician who is helping street children. The particular day that I interview him is a special day of commemoration. It is April 7th, exactly ten years after the start of the genocide in 1994. Jean is wearing a beautiful multicoloured shirt with an African pattern. He is calm and serious. He does not look at all "dangerous"—the way he did during our conversation the year before. He gives me a friendly and polite smile from time to time and looks me in the eye. He has a blue cap in his hand, which he balances on his fingertips (the previous time, his fingertips were pressed against his forehead).

Ever since he came to live at the doctor's, "things have been going in the right direction". What he "thinks about most—that's school." "There's lots to do in the future in this world," he says. His dream is "to get work at a hospital". "I hope I can be a doctor." "And I want to work for my country," he adds.

Today's ceremonies in commemoration of the genocide are being held at Kigali's big stadium, and the ceremonies are also being broadcast on television. The television is on all day in the room next to us. Jean looks sad. He says that he doesn't have the strength to sit too long in front of the television. He goes into the television room and comes out again, back and forth.

"I can't stay there by the TV . . . I leave the room to keep from thinking too much." When he is asked later in the interview if he has been having nightmares, his eyes dart around, and he avoids my gaze. Even though his dreams about the future are to some extent a defence strategy, my impression is that there is hope for Jean, hope for constructive development—a generational linking, which in the long term will dominate over trauma linking. He can let himself accept help, he completes his schoolwork, and he can adequately regulate the affects that are evoked when he sees pictures and hears sounds on television that remind him of the past. The oscillating between trauma linking and generational linking may in that way be part of a healing process. The more traditional view about working through is to deal intensively with the trauma itself. But the attention I give to generational linking has to do with seeing it as a central part of the working-through process itself.[1]

Chronically hospitalized Holocaust survivors: further research

I am currently (December, 2007) working in cooperation with clinical professor Dori Laub on a study that will eventually be published. This "work in progress" is described briefly below, and I demonstrate how the "affect propeller" can be used as point of departure for further theorizing (see also Figure 1).

A 1993 survey of approximately 5,000 long-term psychiatric inpatients in Israel identified about 900 Holocaust survivors. Trauma-related illnesses were neglected in diagnosis and decades-long treatment. In 2002 and 2003, 26 videotaped interviews were completed in Israel by Dori Laub and his colleagues. They found that certain common features regarding the memory of the Holocaust experience could be detected. There was an underlying common thread to all of them, which Laub names *erasure*. Strategies widely adopted by these survivors included claiming to have forgotten it all, doubting that it ever happened or what precisely happened, and claiming that their traumatic experiences were neither extraordinary nor unique, and therefore did not matter and did not merit being spoken of.

Eight of the interviews are now analysed in detail, with the affect propeller as an analytic tool. An overall first impression of viewing and listening to these survivors, mostly with a diagnosis of psychosis (schizophrenia, bipolar, etc.), reveals an experiential landscape that is quite different from that found in the testimonies of survivors who had led a "normal" life after their liberation. This is already evident when comparing a page from a transcript of a testimony from each group, without even examining the content. The quantitative differences between two such pages are blatantly obvious: whereas the page of the normal testimony is filled with words from the survivor's testimony organized in full sentences and paragraphs, the one transcribed from hospitalized survivors is much more sparsely worded, limited to brief utterances and statements, and punctuated by many more comments and questions put by the interviewer (Laub, 2005). Our impression is that in chronically hospitalized Holocaust survivors the affects seem to be encapsulated in an especially strong way—a notion which will be explored in detail in the ongoing study. The question arises if new linking phenomena (even if it is expressed as warding-off) concerning different time dimensions will become manifest.

The aim of this study is to learn from this particular population what additional characteristics need to be added to the trauma-linking processes to thereby further deepen and enhance the understanding of extreme traumatization. What distinguishes the testimonies of this group of trauma survivors from testimonies of non-hospitalized survivors is the persistent decontextualization of their overpowering affect fragments, which completely explode any containing narrative frame. Whereas in normal testimonies (fragments of) intense affects are key nodal points that convey meaning and drive the narrative while simultaneously creating its impasses, in this group the flow of narrative has come to a halt. Affect fragments are like immense volcanic icebergs both completely adrift and colliding with the witness on the one hand, and solidly encased in stone on the other. In either case, processes of symbolization and free association are virtually nonexistent.

Extremes

To reflect this phenomenology, two more categories have to be added to the "affect propeller" (see Figure 1), which can be characterized as extremes of affect regulating.

(a) *Trauma affect imploding* as an extreme of trauma linking within affect invading

(b) *Trauma affect encasement* as an extreme of trauma linking within affect isolating

It should be noted that whereas in other traumatized populations the use of the various categories is flexible and interchangeable, in the group of so-called psychotic survivors the range of categories used is drastically narrowed. It is as though the pressure and threat of the memory affect fragments is far greater, and the venues of their expression more impoverished. Imploding and encasement are close to each other, since there may be quick oscillations between these positions during an interview. Both mean an interruption of thinking. These categories could hypothetically be understood as *attacks on linking* (Bion, 1959). Bion's theory could be an alternative way of understanding the phenomena of erased memories. The "attacks on linking" may be inherent in the experience of extreme trauma itself, or they may be the result of a lack of earlier assistance in verbalizing traumatic experiences within a safe environment (Kaplan & Laub, 2007).

Trauma linking and generational linking in clinical work

Dialogues with colleagues—as in seminars, team work, and supervision—are especially important in working with extremely traumatized individuals. They are also of great value when applying developing theoretical models—to see how they work. With these patients one has to be fully present—in Laub's words (personal communication, 29 Dec. 2007), "turn to the resonances awakened within oneself in order to provide all that the survivor cannot produce". Focus should be on the therapeutic relationship, though transference interpretations should be avoided (Pearlman & Saakvitne, 1995). But the countertransference is an important source. In a discussion about the "affect propeller", Hanke says (personal communication, 20 Jan. 2008): "The analyst, when reflecting on his own reactions, will discover that he himself is also oscillating between trauma linking (being touched deeply by what the patient describes) and generational linking (trying to regain thinking space and creativity in himself). From the experience of this oscillation the analyst can help the patient to oscillate more easily between these two states of mind and gradually widen the space for generational linking."

In summary, trauma linking and generational linking, phenomena that I have introduced in this book, may be helpful in orienting oneself in the analytic work with traumatized individuals. These two tendencies can, as presented above, be seen to alternate in domination. By assisting the patient in successively becoming conscious of disturbing reactions that may appear irrational—triggered by associative links to traumatic events—the survivor may become less anxious and fixated with the trauma. The possibility of living one's life with a history of trauma is facilitated—"to go on surviving", as one survivor expressed it. Simultaneously, by listening to underlying themes associated with generational linking phenomena, highlighting these and also assisting the patient in connecting these kind of experiences—including what appear as subtle examples—the analyst may show the individual's personal preconditions for creativity and life continuity. (This is, in my view, quite different from "supportive therapy", where defences are stressed and exploring is not aimed at.) My concepts are a way of emphasizing important affective shifts in the analytic process.

Concluding remarks

Life stories recounted by survivors who were children during the Holocaust and during the genocide in Rwanda in 1994 have constituted the core of my research. Each individual life story has made a powerful impression on me, as have the interviewees as people. With the help of the video-recorded interviews, to which I have returned many times during the research process, I can see each and every one in front of me, which has also facilitated my psychoanalytic listening. My overall aim was to learn about children in genocide: to find indicators for, and to analyse, psychological phenomena that emerged in the life stories. My studies also aimed to find a generality in the phenomena that arise when children are subjected to massive trauma.

With the background of the increasing traumatization of children in different war zones—where we know that the civilian population are not only victims but are also used for strategic purposes—there is much reason to refine the theorizing about the after-effects on the victims when it comes to affect regulating. It is about perforating situations that we cannot imagine experiencing ourselves—"unimaginable primitive affects", in the words of Grubrich-Simitis (1984). I want to emphasize the importance of not stopping at listening to single cases, which are themselves unique, but also of lifting oneself above (theorizing) what we may hear and feel when encountering the traumatized individual, to create a possibility for our own thought space in order to refine our own concepts and approach, which may give a possibility to act.

I have reached an opinion on how various affect-regulating phenomena in the individual are related to each other—how one concept may be built on another within the frame of an emerging theory about trauma-related affects. Variations in affect regulating have existed within each individual. Thus, there are variations in the ability to symbolize in different phases of an interview, clinical sessions, and in everyday life. The *"affect propeller"* is intended to illustrate the dynamics of these trauma-related processes. This model may be seen as an *analytic tool* for the temporary present focus of the affect regulating of an individual as part of the trauma process. It may also, as a whole, be seen with the different expressions of affect regulating in trauma as an illustration of how complex the psychological processes are for every traumatized individual.

I especially want to underline the importance of "space creating" for traumatized children—to create a psychic space for all kinds of thoughts. To work through feelings of revenge may change the self-image of the victim and also his attitude to the world around him. To reach a state where you feel more free in relation to the past demands that you put words to your rage and your feelings of humiliation, in order to develop the image of what you have experienced, to symbolize the events. Early life experiences and the experiences immediately following the traumas seem to have greater importance for recovery than the kind of traumatization the individual has endured, which corresponds to Keilson's discussion (1992).

The process of mentalizing may change one's self-image and attitudes (Fonagy et al., 2002). Symbolizing is needed to diminish anxiety-driven behaviour. This psychological work can be done in a lay context (out of necessity in poor countries) but may have to be done within a professional framework. Both kinds of work are necessary. To create space for expressing all sorts of thoughts is also important for eliminating the breeding grounds for political extremism. Moreover, it is important to identify manipulation on the part of activists of groups of young, vulnerable, traumatized victims in order to avoid the risk of escalation of a destructive spiral of revenge. From this perspective, we have to be aware of what humiliating feelings will be passed on from one generation to the next, and what the consequences may be.

An overall conclusion from this study is that past traumatic experiences are recovered not as memories in the usual sense of the word, but as affects invading the present. Accordingly, affects seem to tell the story of the past traumatic experiences. The theory developed in this book constitutes a unit that can serve as an analytic tool and may provide a foundation for an increased understanding of young people who have been affected by extreme traumatizing processes.

Two different tendencies, trauma linking and generational linking, respectively, can dominate at different stages for each individual. Hopefully, in the long run, trauma linking will converge into generational linking processes that can then dominate in a more enduring way. Generational linking—the possibility of resilience—calls for the presence of certain steps on a societal level, such as a functioning judicial system and school system. Cultural values that have been destroyed must be highlighted. Documentary projects may be invaluable in providing information for research, museums, and other places of commemoration. Reconciliation is usually associated with transformations in relationships that go further than just being able to exist together: it is a process that takes time, probably several generations.

APPENDIX A

The interview with Emilia, which I conducted, is presented here in its entirety. This gives the reader an opportunity become familiar with an entire interview at any time while reading the main text. In the previous chapters I presented some of Emilia's memory images and discussed these in connection with quotations from other interviewees, and the reader may recognize these sentences (I = interviewer, E = Emilia).[1]

Tape 1

I: Today is 23 March 1997, and I am going to interview Emilia. What is your name?

E: Emilia.

I: When were you born?

E: I was born on the 24th of July 1931, in Lublin, Poland.

I: When you were a little girl, did you have any nicknames?

E: Yes, they used to call me E and F . . . that was all, there weren't any more . . . .

I: Who was it who used to call you by those names?

E: Everyone, those were typical nicknames used in Poland.

I: Can you tell about your very closest family members, those you lived together with?

E: I was an only child. My father's name was E. He was an ear, nose, and throat doctor, and my mother was a housewife Her name was X. And I was their only child.

I: Do you remember the house—what it looked like where you lived, the house?

E: Yes, I remember it. We lived on the second floor. My father had his private practice there. I often made visits there. There was a waiting room for the patients, and then there was the part where we lived. I had my own room. And then there was a b-i-i-g-g! dining room and my parents' bedroom. And the kitchen and the bathroom.

I: You often went to your father's private practice, you said.

E: Yes. When my father was attending child patients, I seemed to have a calming influence on them. I went to them and said, "You don't have to be afraid. It won't hurt", etc. Then if my father had a little free time, we talked a little right there in his office.

I: How old do you think you were at that time?

E: Well, my first memories are perhaps from the time when I was three–four years old. But these are just fragments.

I: What do you see before you?

E: That I am sitting in a baby buggy, and I am crying because I want something and cannot have it. I don't remember what it was. I wasn't a nice child!

I: What do you mean by that?

E: I was stubborn. That's right, I wanted to have my way but . . . I would be punished right off by my father. He would stop speaking to me. That did it. That was the worst punishment for me. I tried to be nice.

I: Can you elaborate on your relationship to your father?

E: He talked with me a lot. We very often took long walks. He treated me like a conversation partner, like an adult, not like a child. I could ask him about different things, about religion, about politics, about ideas, and he treated me well, with dignity and tolerance, and I think that was what helped me to survive. And later! To deal with everything afterwards. I never felt inferior. I was always myself.

I: Can you remember in actual fact what he said about politics?

E: Yes, all ideas have something beautiful about them, and it doesn't matter if they are political ideas or religious ideas, but behind the words are people who are only human. Do not believe in words, do not believe in authorities. Trust yourself. Listen, think, and make up your mind. Never hurt others, but don't let them step all over you I can't repeat the words but . . . it was his way of being that I took on.

I: At the same time, was it possible for you to see whether he sympathized with a certain political line?

E: No, he felt that humans are not mature enough to reach up to the beautiful mottoes that the various political parties put on display. He was right.

I: What about religion?

E: No, we did not talk very much about that. He always said, "We are Jews" . . . and he . . . the first time, . . . I didn't know I was a Jew, I must have been very little, I was playing somewhere in the park, and the children called after me "Jew, Jew"—then I thought I was some kind of strange creature. I didn't know what it was. I went home and said that the children say: You are a Jew. And they said, "Yes, you are. You are Jewish, they are Poles, there are Hindus, there are Chinese . . . and we are all alike as human beings." That was the first time. I don't think that he was very religious, and I don't think he usually observed the traditions; I know that he went very seldom, but he did go to the Synagogue. But I was never in my life in the Synagogue. We did not talk about God. I think that he was an atheist.

I: But he did go on exceptional occasions?

E: I think because it was tradition, it was out of respect for the family, that was it.

I: Was there anything at home, Jewish symbols or the like?

E: No, he told about Esther [the story] and other old Jewish stories. Judaism had value as a tradition but not as a religion.

I: And your mother, how would you describe her? [She leans her head back.]

E: Remember nearly nothing at all. She didn't take care of me, because there was an nanny who took care of me. I don't remember that we talked with each other. I didn't know her. I remember nearly nothing about her.

I: Do you remember how she looks? [E. gazes a little to the side.]

E: Yes, but I don't know if I remember it because I have only one photo of her and that I remember, but not her face. Only Pappa has stuck.

I: Do you know anything about the nature of the difference between your father's family/parents and your mother's family/parents when it came to Jewishness?

E: I don't know . . . I guess that my father's family were educated so-called assimilated Jews. My mother's family were simple people, her father sold sausages, was in the sausage trade, rather simple people. I don't know anything about their religiousness.

I: You said that you had a nanny who took care of you.

E: Yes, she was a very young girl by the name of Estera. Very cute. Very nice. I don't know what her last name was. I know that she was from a very poor family and that she was the eldest of a large number of brothers and sisters. *I idolized her.*

I: Did she live with you?

E: No, she lived with her family. She came every morning and then left in the evening. I know that she enjoyed her job. She was a very important person for me.

I: What was the name of the street where you lived?

E: It was Staszica no. 3 . . . in Lublin.

I: The surroundings, the part of the city where you lived, how would you describe them?

E: It was fairly close to the hospital district where my father worked. The people who lived there were middle-class. There were no poor people there but . . .

I: How large a part of the population was Jewish?

E: I don't know. We had contact with a couple of families. And afterwards I realized that they were all Jews. I didn't think about it then. But we kept company with Jewish families only and all my childhood acquaintances were Jewish children, but they were all Polish-speaking, all of them.

I: Those children that you encountered in the park, that was the first time that . . . ?

E: That I got to hear that I was Jewish. And then I suppose that my parents protected me so that I would never again land in . . . and that is why I went around with Jewish children only.

I: How old do you think you were that time in the park?

E: Five or six years old.

I: Do you recall the next occasion when someone outside said or did something that pointed to your being Jewish?

E: Not before the war, because we kept company with only Jews before the war came.

I: How old were you when you started school?

E: Six. I was pretty stupid. I was not mature. It was early for me.

I: In what way did that come out?

E: I couldn't read. I knew all the letters, but I couldn't combine them into words. I thought that I must be an idiot, because the other children could read. I remember that my father was very worried. And then suddenly my problems disappeared, and I was like all the others!

I: Your classmates in that class. Were they Jewish children, or was the class mixed?

E: I don't know. I think they were Jewish children, but I don't know.

I: Do you remember any classmate?

E: I don't remember anyone from school, but there was a friend . . . because there was a Jewish family who had a daughter, from a family that we spent all our summers, all our winter vacations with, so we were always two. She was a little older. She was very pretty. I looked at her. I was a little jealous. That's her.

I: What was her name.

E: Her name was Ester Stein. I don't know how she spelled her name, but I have a picture of her.

I: Do you know what happened to her?

E: Unfortunately, yes, I know. She was the one who . . . they took her father first and killed him. He owned a large tannery in Lublin. They were very wealthy. So he disappeared first. Then her mother disappeared. Two people hid her in their house, it was two elderly women, sisters. Then I don't know what it was, if they were afraid, because they wanted to get rid of her. This is when I was already at Luvisa's. Luvisa had put her there. Luvisa came with her and couldn't find any place for her. Nowhere. And I didn't dare ask too much. *And Ester said that she would rather die than be . . . so we got hold of some poison . . . and Luvisa went away with her. We said good-bye to each other, and . . . and when Luvisa came back, Ester was dead. If she had been the first to come to Luvisa, then she would be sitting here, alive. I came first. I got the place, she didn't* [very disturbed].

I: So that is what you think!

E: Yes, absolutely. She had better chances, because she was blond, blue-eyed—she was good-looking . . .

I: If we go back in time again, because we have come forward some-what into the time when the war was going on. Do you remember the first signs that you detected, signs that now things were serious?

E: First it was not like that, because we were—it was summer vacation, and we were at a summer place, mother and I. Father was working, and Ester and her mother. And we talked about it, that now the war was coming. We found out that they were mobilizing. Father had to take everything and go home.

I: Which year did this happen?

E: It was in the summer of 1939.

I: Had you heard anything at all about . . . ?

E: People said that now the war is coming, but I thought that it had nothing to do with me.

I: And how old were you at the time?

E: Eight . . . I did not understand what war was.

I: Do you have any memory at all of when you heard . . . ?

E: I went into a panic when I found out that father was being mobilized. I knew that in a war people can kill, and that filled me with panic. And my mother. She did not say much. She just said that now we have to flee to our relatives in Lvov and hope that father comes there. So we fled. It was horrible. There was a wave of refugees . . . they were bombing, and there were many dead, and horses on the road, and when we heard that aeroplanes were coming, we ran and pressed ourselves to the ground.

I: Did you get ready at home to flee?

E: No, we fled in panic. We left everything behind. Everything. So there was not one thing that we . . . [silent].

I: And when you left the house, what happened then?

E: My mother arranged for someone to take us by car. So we were lucky that we could ride in a car. There were many people who walked. There were many who had horses and horse-drawn wagons, and we had luxury. They started shooting, and everyone ran to the side. Then it was just as bad for everyone.

I: How long had your father been away from home?

E: I don't remember. I just know that when we came to the family in Lvov he was away. I don't know how long it had been. Then I found out that Poland had been divided—the Russians had taken a part and the Germans had taken another part, and father was in the German part. They did not tell the children very much. And then one day there he was. I must have grown while he was away, because I know that I thought that he had become smaller, very thin. He fled. He had been in captivity [sighs]. I don't really know. I just know that I was like bursting with happiness to have him there. He didn't say much, but we were together.

I: When you said the family in Lvov, can you tell me who they were?

E: It was my father's older brother who lived there, he was a lawyer, his name was Julius. It was himself and his wife and my cousin who was a couple of years older than me whose name was H. They had servants. They were well off. My uncle was wonderful. [Emilia closes her eyes, rubs her hand against the nape of her neck again and again and leans her head back.] I loved him, and I know that he loved me. Things weren't as good between his wife and my cousin and me. They weren't delighted with my mother and me.

I: How did you notice that?

E: We noticed it . . . we knew our place. It was so.

I: Do you have any idea how long you lived with them?

E: It was August to September 1939. Then the Germans came in 1941. When the Germans came, my uncle disappeared, he was one of the first.

I: What was the address in Lvov?

E: It was J. Street 17.

I: You said for one thing that your father came there, and then later you said that your uncle was the first to be taken.

E: Yes, they came with a list of names and addresses.

I: Who was it that came?

E: Germans.

I: Did you see them?

E: Yes.

I: Do you remember what they looked like?

E: No; I know that I was very frightened. I don't remember what they looked like, because I was sent away. But I know that someone in the family made note of several names and addresses because I was sent to warn those people, and I know that I ran to the first and the Germans were already there. So I ran to the other place, and I had time to say that they were on a list of people to be arrested, but I do not remember who they were.

I: Do you remember what you were thinking as you ran from house to house?

E: I was thinking that it was not possible that they killed people, I thought that maybe they did something, prison or . . . Such horrible things were unthinkable.

Tape 2

I: You mentioned earlier about how the political situation changed. There was a division—Russians, Germans.

E: It was a division. For us it was a question of survival. We knew that where the Russians were, lives were not in danger. But later we heard that in the part of Poland where the Germans were, they had begun to kill Jews. People talked about it more and more, and they tried to talk so that the children didn't hear. But we heard anyway. We heard horrible things, and then we became really frightened.

I: What were the horrible things that you heard?

E: We heard about a man, a Jew, who was forced to wash a car. It was winter. And the Germans thought that they had hit upon a funny thing to do. And they took the hose and sprayed water all over the Jew and made him into a block of ice. And people were killed in various other ways, and we knew that it was so close, so it was—it was then that we understood that it was serious. Lives were in danger.

I: What else did you hear?

E: People were saying that maybe they were coming and also that the Russians were trying to evacuate us, I don't know why. But my parents chose to hide. So we were in hiding and were not deported. We thought that we had succeeded, but no doubt it was the opposite. More chances of surviving if we had been deported to Russia. But that didn't happen. I remember that I saw it through the window, German soldiers on motorcycles. Everyone knew . . . panic broke out. Everyone knew—now it's too late.

I: Where were you when you saw this through the window?

E: At home, at my uncle's. A short time later I heard screaming in the street, and they were beating up an old bearded Jew. *Then my cousin and I were locked into the bathroom so that we could not see, so that we could not hear. No one wanted to talk to us. It simply did not exist.* They tried to protect us, but we heard anyway.

So there was this Jewish family who had fled from western Poland, for political reasons, I think, they lived on the floor above. There was a mother, a father, and a daughter of about fourteen–fifteen years, I think. They were scared out of their minds. I did not understand how people could be so frightened. I simply could not believe that things can be so horrid. The girl, she didn't dare leave the apartment. She was called Lena. Then I heard when the Germans came to arrest this family. I stood in the big room, *and I saw something big and dark behind the window, and a scream, it was that girl who jumped . . . from the window* [closes her eyes, shakes her head]. *Her foot got caught on the balcony, she was torn apart, and she was lying down there on the street, screaming. She was still alive, and we children were locked in the bathroom again* [indicates this with a hand gesture]. *Then I asked what had happened to Lena, and they said, "She has gone to the hospital, she'll soon be well"* [she imitates a falsely calm adult voice]. *But I knew that it wasn't true.*

Then there was another family from western Poland, a mother, a father, and a daughter who was perhaps four–five years older than me. Her name was Lita, and she had a little brother. They were not as afraid. Lita was . . . she had a motherly instinct. She took care of all of the children who lived there. Played with us and taught us different things. She read books to us. They had to work. My father was not allowed to work as a doctor. So my mother and my uncle's wife baked cakes and sold them. So the adults worked, and Lita took care of us. But then they also got arrested. Shortly after that I saw a column of prisoners on the street. There were girls from the work camp, and there was Lita with a shovel [indicates with her arm how Lita carried the shovel over her shoulder]. They were, so to say, marching. When I saw her, I didn't stop to think . . . I just shouted "Lita!" and she looked at me and looked away. Then

I understood that I had to keep quiet. I mustn't do what I had just done. I will never forget her face. She was a wonderful girl. I believe that her parents and her brother were already dead. She was in a work camp. I don't remember her last name [silence].

I: She was an important person!

E: Yes, for all the children. She was like a teacher. We liked her. She was wonderful [silent].

I: You don't remember her last name. Do you remember Lena's last name?

E: No, children never ask to know last names. Lena never spoke to other children. She was afraid, she stayed at home, but Lita took care of us others. These were things that we maybe both heard people talking about but which we also saw ourselves.

I: Are there other things that you saw or heard about which you would like to tell?

E: This is something about when my parents were still alive. People started talking about the ghetto. The adults discussed it, "what can it be" and everyone that I remember came and said, "It must be work camps, it just can't be that they murder masses of people." If it is work camps, it's possible to go on living, the work part is harder . . . but possible to accept. I have no memory of anyone who believed that what was going on could possibly be pure and simple murder. So we were not so terribly afraid of it.

I: What happened then?

E: They started to organize the ghetto. And then my family found a family in that area, and they decided which apartments, and they were in the process of moving. And then my father came and said that something terrible is taking place. They are just singling out Jews. So we must not go out. We must hide. Then it was Luvisa, who was a maid employed by my uncle, she found a place without a window. I don't know where it was. It was damp and dark, but no one knew that such a place existed, such a space behind the curtains in the same house. When it was dark, she put everyone there. And I was supposed to go with them, but I had an ear infection, so Luvisa said, "No, she can stay here, because she is sick." So she was with me. They were hidden there, and at night, when it was dark, Luvisa went with water and with food so that no one would see. And I wrote small notes to them. I remember that it was after my birthday.

I: Which birthday?

E: I turned eleven, that was it. I had my birthday on July 24, and then we were together. It was normal. So it was later. It must have been at the beginning of August when it happened. It took a couple of days, I don't remember how long they were hidden. One day Luvisa came running home in the middle of the day and said to me, "Quick, under the cupboard!" and she pushed me. She was forced to push me in because there wasn't room for me, so the cupboard was almost standing on me. She said, "Put your hand over your mouth and don't breathe, because they are searching for you."

After a while the Germans came and some Polish neighbours. And they discovered some way where my family was hiding. And they looked for me. A girl was missing, and I remember that I lay there and I actually tried not to breathe and I could see their boots and I thought that when you look at a bird or an animal it doesn't move, but when you turn your head it flies away. So I should not look so that they don't feel my gaze. So I closed my eyes. [E closes her eyes.] And then they looked everywhere and a little bit by the cupboard before they left. And then Luvisa said, "You can come . . . come out." I thought "My family—they're gone!" Luvisa continued, "You can't stay here, because they are after you. You must run away, but we will wait until it gets dark. If you cry, you will draw attention to yourself, so you must act normal." We waited until it got dark, and we rode to the railway station and rode far, far, I don't remember how long.

I: Do you remember what you were thinking?

E: *I just thought I couldn't understand, I didn't think it could be true. I thought that I must be having a nightmare, that I would wake up. It is not possible, "not them."* At the same time I had to keep tight, not show anything. So we came to—I thought, what is happening now, what should I do, now I am alone. I have nowhere to go. But Luvisa was there. And she didn't say much, she just took care of me. It wasn't what she said. It was her body language that calmed me a little. Then we arrived, . . . it was dark, night, at a little Ukrainian village. Everyone was asleep. She went with me to a "serke", which is a little Greek Orthodox church. I remember that she told me to wait. And that she was going to fetch "pop". That's their priest. I think she was born in that village. I don't know, it's just a guess. She knew the priest. She came out with that "pop". She told him that I was her daughter, born out of wedlock, the result of a relationship with a Jew. She wanted him to baptize me and give me a birth certificate. Dated with my real date of birth. He baptized me. This was the first time that I was inside a "serke". It was night, and everything was strange and foreign and frightening, but even so, when he asked me, "What name do you want to have?" I said that I wanted a name that was similar to Emmi. I was thinking that if someone called out to me, I wanted to recognize that it was me they meant. So I chose a name that resembled my real one.

Then we did not stay there very long. We took the train back to Lvov, a long train trip. There Luvisa found . . . rented a room in the district of Lvov where most of the population is Volksdeutsche or Reichsdeutsche. That was very wise of her. That was the best you could find. She rented a room. Near the house was a police station. The lady that she rented from was Polish, and I am sure that she knew who I was, but we never spoke about it. She tried to act like she was mean and strict, but she was very nice. And she was in a much better economic situation than we. Because Luvisa, to put it bluntly, smuggled food. She traded with food, and that meant lots of running around, working at night, and carrying heavy sacks. She made very little money, but we never went hungry. The food was simple, but I was never hungry. And she was . . . we said very little to each other, but she was really nice. She cared about me. It never occurred to me that I should help out at home, because I wasn't used to that. So she did all the housework, even though she worked so hard. She washed my hair. She was wonderful.

I: How did you wear your hair?

E: I had rather long plaits, long plaits. I had lice. I had scabies. So did all the other children. I was never hungry, and I never froze.

I: You said something about how you thought that she made a wise choice when she decided to live in that district. Please explain what you meant.

E: Well, hmm, I thought that it would never occur to anyone that a Jew can be hiding among Germans and right beside a police station. That's a matter of fact. And who would dare, with my looks. I built on that. I had two girl-friends. One girl my age, who was Reichsdeutsch, and the other was Volksdeutsch. I was very aware of what I was doing, even though I was so young. I reasoned like this: when we play together, no one can suspect that I am Jewish, because her father, the father of the girl who was Reichsdeutsch, he was in the SS, I believe. I remember his leather boots and his manner.

I: Did you go to her home, too?

E: We lived in the same building. And I asked . . . they went swimming in the middle of the winter, there was a sign für Deutsche . . . and we went together . . . I! I went there. Because I thought that it was safest to be with them. Then in the other house there was a Polish family, and they were landlords. It was a Polish family, and they had a daughter my age. And these people were real friends. These people, they did not let on about it, but they knew who I was. They cared about me, and they were wonderful. And the father in the family, he was a carpenter. He would make a toy, a present for his daughter, and he made exactly the same thing for me, every time.

Then a prostitute came along and tried to blackmail us. She came to Luvisa. She said she was coming back the next day, and she wanted money or she was going to go report that Luvisa had a Jewish child. Luvisa was frantic. And she asked me what we were going to do. Had no money. So I said that I would go talk to Bronja's father. And I went there. I did not say that I was Jewish, I didn't dare do that. I said that when this woman comes, she wants money, otherwise she is going to the Germans. And I hear Bronja's father say, "Take it easy, I'll take care of her." And he did. I don't know what he did. We never saw her again. Never. At their place I often got a little fruit, food that was a little better. Both of them worked. They were real friends.

I: What were their names?

E: I don't know. The girl's name was Bronja.

I: And the part of town?

E: The Poles were just there as landlords, all the others belonged to the German aristocracy. Maybe the buildings were a little newer, the comfort a little better. The street was called Totochiega eight.

I: During this period of time, did you go to any school?

E: I started school almost right away. I was in the same grade as I had been in before because I had started when I was six years old. I could do that. But I understood that I have to be average, I can't be better and I can't be worse. I made a great effort to be in the middle, not to be too good. Luvisa was often away, so I thought it was wise to do as other children do. They were Catholics. They went to church. I had never been in a Catholic Church in my life. I kept a few steps behind the others and did exactly as they did. So if a girl scratched herself behind her ear with her left hand, I did that too [E. demonstrates, scratching herself behind her ear]. I didn't know what was important and what was not important. And I learned very fast. And I felt safe in the church, because is was so dim in there. I could be on my knees and hide my face [E. bends forward and demonstrates] so that people could not stare at me. I attracted attention. When I was outside, I could hear women whispering, "Jewish girl, Jewish girl." In the church I was almost invisible. I went to church a lot. And I heard the sermons, and they were very beautiful. So I started to believe. I became a faithful Catholic, even though I had been baptized in the Greek Orthodox Church. But I had faith in the priest. I knew all the songs, all the rituals, everything, but I do not remember much today. So other girls took their first communion. So I did too. Luvisa . . . we didn't talk about religion, she never went to church as far as I know, so I don't think she was a believer. But she respected what I did. When I told her that I was going to have my first communion, she borrowed one of those pretty white dresses for me somewhere, I have a photo of myself . . . I believed in it. The words were beautiful. I trusted the priests. So I went to my first confession. We had two priests. The church in our part of town was the Mary Magdalene Church, and the school where we lived belonged to it. There were two priests, one who was young, funny, liked by all the girls, and all the girls wanted to go to him for confession. The other one was older, fat, bald. He was very serious. But no one wanted to go to him for confession. But there were too many people, so I ended up going to him. So I had to go to the one I did not want to go to. The first thing I said to him was, "I am a Jew." And he said to me, "Before you make your confession, you must promise that you will not go to another priest. That you will always come to me for confession."

And I promised him. Later I found out that he helped many people and that the other priest was with the Germans. Isn't it just like something from Symborska [a poet, Nobel Prize Winner whose poem she later reads]?

Tape 3

I: You were just about to tell what it was like when you woke up every morning.

E: *Yes, I understood that I look very Jewish, and the only thing I can do is not be Jewish. So I made up my mind. I am a blond Ukrainian.* [She closes her eyes, leans her head back, and puts her hand on the nape of her neck.] *If I show the least sign of worry, it's over! One has to be happy, relaxed, and I tried to do this the whole time. Not show the least, even if I heard "Jew"! I turned around, and I could smile at them.* [She turns her head to the side, closes her eyes, shrugs her shoulders.] *I did this every day, but it was . . . torture. All the time, I felt people's eyes on me, and my dream was to be able to become invisible. But that was impossible, so I was very visible.*

I: You said it was almost like torture?

E: Yes, it was torture, every second pretending to be a Ukrainian and at the same time being scared to death of everything. That was the worst. Then I believed that they were killing Jews all over the world So I knew that I had to die, and so I thought about all the ways there were to die. I prayed to God . . . I decided that the best way was to be shot in the head. So I prayed to God that I would be shot in the head.

I: What were you most afraid of? What was the worst?

E: Pain, pain, pain, pain. That affected my choice of profession, my area of special competence, anaesthesia [she is an anaesthesiologist]. My life influenced my choice of profession. *I wanted to die quickly and painlessly.*

I: You were forced to steer your thoughts in that direction?

E: Yes. And at the same time, not show it.

I: Hmm, no. Did you dare, was there any space for you to give vent to your thoughts about what had happened to your family?

E: No, no. I tried, . . . that was behind me. Now I had to think every second about saving my own life.

I: You took one step at a time?

E: Yes, at night, when we went to bed, we slept together in a little bed, Luvisa and I, then I would think that it was dark, nobody was looking at me, maybe I could sleep through the night. Then I will have managed to stay alive one more day—that is torture the whole time.

I: And then what happened?

E: One time, we, my German girlfriends and I, were going down the street. And so a German came up to the German girl who was Polish-speaking. He said, "Come here a minute. I want to talk to you." They stepped over to the side. Then she came back. She started to laugh. "Do you know what he said?! He said that you were a Jew and that he wanted your address. Of course I gave him your address." And then I felt that now it's over. And I felt all my blood disappear, but I couldn't show it. So I sat on the street and started to fiddle with my shoes to control my expression. Now I felt my doom had come. But I got control of myself rather fast, and we spoke as though nothing had happened, and then I thought, what am I going to do, now I have to make a decision, I have to do something. So we talked a little more, and then I said I had to go. Bye. I thought like this, that now I have nowhere, nowhere to go. Then I thought of Luvisa. It's her life. She is gone right now. I know that this man is waiting. Luvisa does not know. To be taken unawares, that's the worst. I have to collect myself. And I must get there first and put on my pretence of being Ukrainian before he comes. I think that was the most difficult. I pulled myself together. I went home, and he was there. Luvisa was not at home. I prayed to God that she would not come. If I can't pull this off, it's only me, I thought. Then maybe she'll make it, because she was risking her life as much as I was.

And he was there. He was German, and he spoke Polish. He said, "Hey, you, where were you?" "Oh, me? Where? I was at school", I said and "with my friends". I was a Ukrainian. I WAS A UKRAIN-IAN DEEP INSIDE. He said, "I am waiting, because I want to speak with your mother." "Yes, of course", I said. "Of course. Please have a seat. I have to have a little something to eat, because I ate quite a while ago." I ate, and we spoke about school. And he spoke of my father. Luvisa and I, we had not prepared any story. We had not prepared ourselves, so I had to improvise. I said that my father was fighting in the war. He said, "Does he write to you?" I said, "Of course he writes to me." He asked, "WHERE is he?" I said, "I don't know if they are allowed to write any address. Some numbers are written there, I don't know. But he promised that he will come back, he will surely come back to me." "Do you look like your mother?" "No, I look more like my father, but I look most like my grandmother", I said. And then he asked what my father looked like. "The best-looking of all", I said. And then I found a photo of hers, of a man, maybe in her family, or a boyfriend, I don't know. He was dark-haired but typically Ukrainian, with one of those shirts that they wear. "He is the best father in the whole world." He sat there for maybe two hours, and when he left, he was convinced that I am Ukrainian. Before Luvisa came home. I was totally knocked out. *I said to myself that if that girl had not warned me, I wouldn't have made it.* So it's also thanks to her that I am alive. To make the whole thing even stranger—when the Germans started to flee, her family fled too. and she . . . she sent me a letter with their address, which was secret. And her picture!

I: What did you think?

E: *That I loved her!* Quite simply that I wanted to see her. She had confidence in me. They fled, they were going to be killed, and she, she was not allowed, her parents would not let her contact anyone and tell her address. And she did it. I hope that she has a good life.

I: Her name?

E: Johanna Höpting, but I don't know how she spells it.

I: But she returns to you in your thoughts?

E: Oh yes, yes, often, often. It was her warning that saved me at the hardest of times. That she later gave me her confidence, when it was she who was in danger. That is something . . . after all, we were just little girls, she was not aware of what she was doing when she warned me, she didn't know.

I: With some part of herself she understood that it was important.

E: Yes [taking a deep breath] . . . I don't know what her parents thought. I would see them several times every day, I don't know . . . we were different people. We had a German, a Wehrmachtmann, who was living in the same house, who cared about me. He did not know anything about me. But he had a daughter my age. He said that I made it, his daughter would make it. He cared about me.

I: Did you get an inside view of the German families' lives?

E: Yes, in my eyes they were living very well. They had plenty of food, lots of clothes, and lived a life of luxury in my eyes. I never heard them talking about Jews. Never about politics. Never. So I don't know anything about their opinions and ideas. I was concentrating the whole time on telling myself, "I am a blond Ukrainian." That was my task in life the whole time, every minute of every hour.

I: Were there any new events that happened later and that feel . . .
    ?

E: No more horrors. Not if you mean Germans. Not about my being
    Jewish. And when it came to Russians, I could openly say who I was
    and what my name was. It was hard for me to believe, but it was
    true.

I: You told about Ester earlier. When did Ester come to the place
    where you and Luvisa were living?

E: I don't know. I don't remember. I had already been at Luvisa's for
    quite some time. She was in hiding, it was perhaps 1943. Perhaps
    '44. The two older ladies who were hiding her, I don't know what
    frightened them. They wanted to get rid of her. She would have
    made it there.

I: And then she came to stay with you and Luvisa for a short time?

E: [She becomes very quiet, she is holding back her tears.] *Because
    . . . it makes me sad . . . because, I knew, she knew, Luvisa knew. And all
    three of us discussed it, and we agreed that it was the only thing to do. It's
    true, this is how it was.* Today this is criminal. But it was the best . . .
    she was growing, she had already started to have breasts, and what
    would happen to her, so a quick death was better. And she chose it.
    And I also thought it was best, and Luvisa also thought it was best.
    There was no choice. No choice.

    Then [another episode] there was a little girl who stood on the
    street, the one I wrote about in my letter [written to me before the
    interview] who stood on the street outside the police station where,
    where I lived. A little girl, who had been in hiding somewhere,
    she was little, she stood there surrounded by Polish women, her
    hair was bleached with hydrogen peroxide. A bad bleach job. She
    was terrified. She was just standing there, making the sign of the
    cross, saying the Lord's Prayer from beginning to end, over and
    over and over again. The women who were standing around her
    were waiting for the police. She had already been discovered. They
    were asking, "Where do you live? Where is your mother?" . . .—"*My
    mother lives in the closet.*" I was thinking, I was standing there a little
    in the background, I was thinking, these women are mothers, they
    are daughters and sisters, *and it did not occur to a single one of them
    to comfort her.* It was too late to save her. There were too many who
    knew. But they could have at least shown some care for her, to say
    "Don't be afraid. It will go fast." They said things about her right

in front of her, but said nothing to her. And I, I didn't dare come closer, because then they would have taken me. And I have this on my conscience [her voice changes].

I: In what way do you think about this then?

E: That I should have gone up to her, I should have put my arms around her, died together with her so that she would not be alone and afraid. This is the way I think. I think about how it felt for her. She was a little girl. Alone. And no one to comfort her.

I: You were also a child.

E: Yes, but I was older. I could have comforted her. . . . I just walked away. I disappeared. You don't feel right when you do something like that. I will never forget that girl. I knew that I could not do anything, but I still felt guilty [sigh, silence]. I hope that it went fast. That is all you can do, hope. You have to accept.

I: What else happened?

E: The Russian occupation. I was not happy. All the adults that were around . . . we had had a German occupation, now we had a Russian occupation. What was the difference? But for me there was a difference, I can promise you that. Luvisa said, "Now you should go join your aunt, your father's sister." I knew that she was alive. I hardly knew her at all. I had no feelings, not warm, not cold. None at all. Luvisa put me on the train. I had almost nothing with me. Luvisa altered her fine Sunday clothes for me, so I always had clean clothes with no holes in them. And she did not. She was ill. I did not understand it then. We slept together. She coughed a lot. She coughed up blood. She was sweaty. She had tuberculosis. But I did not think about that, did not understand. Children are rather egocentric. I was afraid, I thought of myself, and I thought of protecting her. But I never thought about her being ill. Never. But she was. We said good-bye, and I rode away. Now the worst was over. But not for me. Perhaps I should not say this. But they are no longer alive, so it's just as well. So I arrived at my aunt's home. She was a dentist. And her husband was a lawyer, a notary public. And they had two daughters—one from an earlier marriage, so they weren't sisters. They were ten years older than I was, young adults. They had survived in the home of a Polish family who had double walls. They lived four persons between two walls. They paid, but still. The Polish family had two children the same age as theirs, so they risked their lives and the lives of their children. So I arrived,

and one of the first things I got to hear was that it was too bad that I
had survived and not my cousin. Because he was "charmingly cute,
clever and kind" and I was not. That was true. I heard that over and
over again. It was hurtful. And they also let me know that "You eat
our bread, and we expect to be paid for it some day." So I tried to
eat as little as possible. It was heavy going. Also, I came there as a
devout Catholic. And they forbade me to go to church, but I went
anyway. In school I was Jewish. When we had religion and the priest
came, I was forced to leave the class. It didn't matter. I was Jewish.
I was not allowed to sit with all the children. I had a ghetto in the
classroom, a little corner, a little table. I had no friends, of course,
because they were ordinary, normal children, and I was tainted, I
was different. And I was ashamed of being Jewish, and I actually
thought it was something horrible to be Jewish, all those years, I
thought I was not as good as others. But that went away fast. I had
such problems too.

The worst thing of all was that my aunt forbade me to write to
Luvisa. She said to me, "You are not an adult, you eat our bread,
and you must do as I say. If you write to her, then she will make
demands. She wants me to give her money. So I forbid you to write
to her a single time. When you are grown up, you may do as you
like." I obeyed. I did not understand that Luvisa could die. I did
not think about that. I never wrote to her. I could have written in
secret. I didn't do it. I was forced to obey. I did indeed eat their
food without paying for it. Then I met a woman on the street who
lived near Lvov, and she said to me, "Do you know that Luvisa died?
She had massive hemorrhaging of the lungs." You can't go back
and do what you have left undone. I am . . . [Her face is tense, she
is silent, and she shakes her head.] I am sure that I will never forget
that.

I: You say that you can't go back and do what you have left undone.

E: No, you can't . . . Maybe she thought that I was ungrateful. I was
never ungrateful. I knew exactly how much she meant to me. But
I was too young and too foolish.

I: You had lived for many years with having to adjust yourself to all
the demands that were being made by people around you.

E: Yes [long silence] . . . yes . . . and then I noticed that there were
other Jews who survived. I had thought that I was the only one.
There was my aunt and her family, and then one more and one

more, and then I found out that there was a Jewish orphanage in P and that Jewish children lived there. Then I found out that there was a convent in X where they had hidden a number of Jewish girls. Just girls. Of course they did not dare to have boys. But all of them survived. I was not the only Jew in the whole world. And so I also started to think that it was nothing to be ashamed of.

I: What would you be ashamed of?

E: That I am Jewish. I thought it was something to be ashamed of. That I am a pariah. That's what I thought.

Tape 4

I: We spoke about the time right after the war when you started to orient yourself towards the outside world and discovered that there were other Jewish children who had survived. What did that mean for you and your identity?

E: That I was not alone. That there were others like me. But I did not seek them out, because I was a devout Catholic. So I felt a little different in the beginning. But I went to school, and I had Polish friends who were very nice. I had no problems later in upper secondary school. But I had problems at home, because . . . I was not allowed to go anywhere. I was forced to help out at home. I wanted to join the scouts, but I was not allowed to. So I went to school and then home and then did housework.

I: Did you ever hear what happened to your immediate family?

E: No, never.

I: Did you go back to your home?

E: No, that is something that I thought of doing. Now I feel that the time is right, that I am ready for that. I am sure that no one is still living there. But I want to see the house, the places. I want to do that. [Note: she did go there subsequently and found it to be frighteningly the same as before.]

I: So you lived with your aunt?

E: Yes, and there I decided that I wanted to study, to continue with my education. They were against it. They didn't think I should do it. But then I found out that there was an institute that trained dental technicians. There was such a school in V [Breslau]. Then I managed to convince my aunt that it would be good if I became a dental technician. I found out that there was a dormitory for Jewish young people, and I thought that could be a good idea. I was accepted and started my studies. There I lived among only Jewish young people. I did not feel that I had anything in common with them. It was just that . . . most of them came from Russia. Most of them had read, I don't know what it's called, komsomolska, I don't know. I was an outsider once again. I made up my mind to concentrate on school and to study, and that's what I did. It was a three-year course of study. I did well. Then I was accepted at the university and got a room in a dormitory for Jewish university students, Jewish young people again. I had a hard time making ends meet. I had a scholarship, it was very difficult . . . it did not cover my food expenses. So I worked with whatever I could on the side.

Then I got a job as a nursemaid in the home of a Jewish family. They had two little boys, and I loved them. I can't say that I contributed to their upbringing, because they did whatever they wanted with me. We had lots of fun, but I can't say that I had any teaching role there. I lived with them. That meant that I had a place to live and breakfast, and I could only read at night because I had rather a lot to do. And after I had completed one and a half years at the dental college, I found out that I had tuberculosis, and that it was contagious. My first thought was of the two boys. The first I think I did was rush in to their parents and say, "Quick! Take the children to a doctor", because I might have given them tuberculosis. But thank goodness they were healthy. I ended up at the clinic. I had rather advanced tuberculosis [E says the name of the kind of tuberculosis]. In any case, there was no medicine available in Poland. And again I thought, "the end has come". I had to break off all contacts because I had a contagious disease. So I limited all my contacts with my friends and colleagues because I did not want to transmit my disease to anyone. And so once again I was totally isolated, alone, and thought that I was going to die. But I kept studying anyway, and I did not die. My lungs got worse and worse, and I was convinced that I would have to have an operation. But I wanted to qualify for my profession first, so when I received . . . the last year, that was it! I said yes to the operation. It was in Zakopane, and it went well. My health returned, and there was no longer any danger that I would transmit the disease.

Today I was thinking, oh, to be able to live, to find pleasure in such small things that no one else understands. Appreciate them, just that the sun is shining, just that there is a flower over there, that it smells so good, small things like that, and to drink coffee, to sit and do nothing. That I can enjoy things. That is life, and I don't think ordinary people know how wonderful it is. Just to get to live. Not to be hungry, not to freeze, not to be afraid. That is the best you can have in life. I have it.

I: It sounds like this feeling started to grow when you understood that you would survive that disease.

E: Yes, and then I did not think about it so much, because I worked all of my life, very much.

I: You went on with your education?

E: Yes, first when I did not think that I would survive that illness I completed a specialist course on lung diseases. I worked with people who had tuberculosis, so that I would not give my disease to healthy people. But then when my health was restored, I could do whatever I liked. I wanted to work with anaesthesia, and I thought that anaesthesia, that's a lot, that's very involved, but the first, the most important thing in the beginning, was that people who are going to have an operation are scared, that someone is going to cut into their bodies and that it was what I was most afraid of. And so my place is here. That is how I ended up in anaesthesia. I never regretted it. I read a lot and worked very hard, I loved my job. I had satisfaction, I felt that I was doing something useful. I often had conflicts with my superiors, but I was always most highly appreciated by the patients. I never had problems with the personnel, because I had been so far down that I identified myself with the lowest, not with those in power, never. If I had conflicts, it was because I took the part of the patients, I defended them. I was maybe not always so diplomatic, but that's the way I was. Once that way, a person stays that way. But I loved my work.

I: And during this time you also met your husband?

E: Yes, I met him when they were getting me ready for the operation, taking me to the lung reception . . . It was in Zakopane, in Poland. He was a patient, but he was almost well, and I was very ill. So we met there. Then after the operation I passed my last exams, and later he arranged a job for me. I did not know anyone, so he did that. He had his family outside Warsaw. He arranged the job, and we moved in together, but I didn't want to marry, because he was a Pole. And I knew that his mother was against it. And I never wanted to have children, Jewish children in Poland. Never thought about moving from Poland, because I didn't know anyone else in the whole world. I had nowhere to go. I had to make my life in Poland. Then I will never have children. No child needs to go through what I did. I don't regret it. We lived together at first. But later we got married.

Without his mother, of course. It was horrible for her. But then, after maybe two years, I said to him that she was his mother and that he couldn't just abandon her. I told him to go visit her. She was an old woman. And so she asked if she could come stay with us, and I said, of course, welcome! And then it was she who was always on my side. Not on his. When we got divorced, he, my former husband, got a . . . he was told off by her, because she thought that I was the best. But I could never feel tenderness towards her, because whatever happened, I could never forget the first thing she had said: "We come from the nobility, a Polish upper-class family, and you are going to marry R." I understood that she was stupid, old . . . and she was his mother—but love her, that I could not do. I did everything for her when she was ill. And things were good for many, many years. And then came his 50-year crisis, and he met a young girl and came home and said, "I am in love." I said, "Well, of course." We left each other as friends. For me it was something horrible, but that's something else. But there was never any quarreling, and never any money problems, we did everything in a smooth way. He remarried, and then I was asked if I would like to take a job in Sweden for someone who was away. And I said yes, but I was very scared because I am not gifted in languages. I thought Swedish was like Chinese. It is not possible, I thought. I will never manage. I took the temporary position in Köping, and there I met the L family. The head of the anaesthesia unit tried to talk me into staying . . . but I needed time, so I went back home, and then later they asked me again, and I made my decision, in 1980. I just went there for a temporary position, and I did not go home again. I thought, okay, I'm divorced, I have nothing left. I can close the door and start all over again. And in that way I ended up in Sweden. I am very ungifted when it comes to languages. I got lots of help from the nurses in Köping, lots. I was lucky, I must say, they were kind and they were helpful and I have only warm feelings for them.

I: Yes, so people helped you orient yourself to work life in Sweden and you met a family in Köping.

E: Yes, a family where I was always welcomed. And I remember that I started going to courses at ABF [an adult education association started by Swedish labour unions] to learn Swedish. I remember that I did what I used to do in Poland. I said to the teacher, "You have to know that I am Jewish." She said, "Why is that?" And I wondered how it could be that it did not matter. That was the first time in my life that it really did not matter. She was thinking, "What do you mean by that? Do you mean you can't come on Saturdays? Or why are you saying that??????" It was shocking. There is an enormous difference between Poland and Sweden in that way. It is very important there are . . .

I: It is still very important there?

E: Oh yes! Oh yes! I can tell you a short, funny story from Poland. I was on duty, and a patient came to me, a nun, and she wanted permission to go to church, to go to Mass. Then I said to her, "You are not my patient, so I must take a look at your notes." I read the notes, there was nothing, so I told her she could, she could go church. She was overjoyed, and so she asked me, "Doctor, you know the hierarchy here. That Dr K, is he Jewish?" I told her that he wasn't, and she said, "But Dr L, is he Jewish?" I told her that he wasn't Jewish either. Then she said, "But who is Jewish here?" I said, "Only me." To see her face. She was taken aback. She became pale and looked at me and after a long, long while, she said, "Well, it doesn't make any difference to me, it does not matter at all." Exactly. That's how it was. When I looked for work, I worked there many years, as an aneasthesiologist there, in the lung surgery unit, that's what I was best at and still am best at, thorax anaesthesia, but it occurred to me . . . but it is not good to know how to do only one thing, so I thought of changing jobs, of changing to a hospital that had obstetrics and gynaecology and orthopaedics . . . all the different specialities. It turned out that this was not so easy. There were openings, but not for people like me. They needed someone, and when I called they were enthusiastic, but when I came in, it was just, no, sorry. One of them who wanted to employ me, the head of a surgical clinic, said, "I am sorry, I need you, I would like to employ you, but . . ." I told him that I accepted not being employed there, but I wanted to know why. "Because the hospital manager has said that we are not going to have any Jew working at this hospital."

That's how it is. There are many like Symborska, many wonderful people, but there are many, many of the other kind. You are not allowed to forget that you are a Jew for one second. And here in Sweden, it has no significance, none whatsoever!

I: How are things where you live?

E: I live in S-town. I can't imagine a better life than I have. I have a little house and myself. The house was very cheap because it was in great need of repair. And so I learned. I taught myself to put in a floor. Of course, I got help from my colleagues. My neighbours were a little reserved in the beginning. I have lived there 10 years, and now I belong to the "We"! It is our street. We! are going to do this. It is a community, a sense of community. I belong to this street. It is a wonderful feeling to have a house of my own, my own garden to plant things in, to see things blossoming. It is . . . well, it could not be better, that's a fact. Yes, so now, That's all.

I: Before we end, one thing I would like to ask is if there is something that you would like to say to coming generations, to young people today?

E: Since, as you say, I am pessimistic, I think . . . [E is referring to a conversation that we had during a break], but as I see it, I am re-alistic . . . Human beings live in flocks and never let foreign flocks invade their territory. Do you understand what I mean? Look at what is happening in Israel. Jews–Arabs. In the former Yugoslavia. In Rwanda. In the whole world.

I: And in H [where she lives], you have said.

E: Yes, in H there are neo-Nazis. Most of my neighbours are against them, but I wonder if they dare to be against them if they are in power??? Because then they are in danger. I understand people who are against them and keep quiet. I understand it. You have to have tremendous civil courage to speak out against them.

I: Would you like to add anything about the neo-Nazis in H?

E: No, I just read about it in the newspapers so I know what is going on. And I know that one of the teachers at the upper secondary school is their leader, and I don't know him, I have never see him, never met him, but he is talented, he has charisma, and the young people idolize him. And that is dangerous. You can't influence that. You can't do anything about it. So I, I see the future as dark, and I hope that I am wrong.

I: I would like to thank you so much for telling your life history; and before we finish, we are going to look at some photographs that you can also tell about. You also have a couple of books with you. Perhaps we should also look at them.

E: Yes.

[Pause]

Emilia reads a poem written by Islavar Symborska, a Polish poet who received the Nobel Prize in Literature in 1996. The poem is entitled "Close to the Eye."

She shows some photographs [all of which constitute various aspects of links to the past].

These are pictures of my father's parents. The first is my grand-father. It was taken in Vienna, I don't know what year it was but he died the same year that I was born. His name was E.Z. and I was named Emilia after him. That was the only thing that . . . so I never met him. And this is my grandmother on my father's side. The picture was taken in Lvov. Her name was M.Z., and she died when the war began. I don't have any close feelings for her. I did not see her very often.

These are pictures, the only pictures that I have of my father. The first is as a schoolboy, and the other is as an adult, and as I remember him. His name was F.Z. and he was a medical doctor, a specialist in . . . The picture was taken before the war, but I do not know when.

This is my beloved nanny C. who took care of me from the time I was born until the war came, and I don't know what her last name was. But I loved her, and here we are on a walk, she and I and my cousin, who is in . . . [short pause].

This is my uncle on my father's side and his family with whom we lived after the war. His name was Dr Z and he was a lawyer, and his wife. Their son, my cousin M, had been killed before the time that the picture was taken.

Both of the next pictures were taken right before the war. The first is of O.P., we were. . . . And this is the only picture that I have of my mother. The first person here is my mother. And then here is Ester, the pretty blond girl, the one whose horrible . . . fate I have told about. And this is her mother to the left, and the smallest and shortest is, as usual, me. And in the other picture in the middle is Ester and to the left of her is me.

And here it is 1943. My name here is Ee, and I am a devout

Catholic. It is my First Communion.

This is my friend, Janna. She was Deutsch. She warned me that someone was coming . . . who suspects that I am Jewish, and thanks to her warning I managed the whole thing.

Here the war is over. The Germans are fleeing, and she and her family . . . And she sends me greetings and look . . . her address, even though they are afraid.

[*End of interview*]

APPENDIX B

The International Psychoanalytical Association gratefully acknowledges USC Shoah Foundation Institute for Visual History and Education, University of Southern California, for allowing us to use the following testimonies:

Interviewee Name	Interview Code
Susanne Arvidsson	23226
Salomea Baum	25458
Dorothy Bergman	27632
Susanne Berglind	8855
Ruth Berlinger	13515
Orian Berniker	23600
Hanna Biderman	33900
Iza Bleich	34712
Halina Brill	37539
Gabryela Bromberg	45295
Susanna Christensen	30570
Robert Felszegi	22948
Bernhard Fishbein	35135
Olga Gruen	7779

Interviewee Name	*Interview Code*
Nikolaus Gruner	37470
Lea Heyman	34658
Alina Högasten	30051
Judith Korosi	48714
Elizaveta Kotliar	31100
Roza Lekach	28737
Judit Ljungberg-Miklos	49244
Marta Löwy	31973
Tove Michaeli	31424
Sala Parzenska-Zyskind	27108
Tobias Rawet	31301
Lucy Renyi	28877
Sara Rosenbaum	35338
Ervin Rosenberg	37892
Alexander Rothman	21246
Klara Ruben Tixell	32714
Mikos Schwartz	30578
Heinz Spira	25870
Maria Stein	23505
Kate Wacz	12783
Annika Welinder	26154
Egon Wolsner	25537
Stefan Zablocki	23346
Danuta Zipper-Oledzka	27838
Fajga Zughaft	29598
Kiwa Zyto	29958

NOTES

All interviews, with the exception of follow-up interviews and interviews in Kigali, were conducted in Sweden by the Survivors of the Shoah Visual History Foundation, now the USC Shoah Foundation Institute for Visual History and Education at the University of Southern California. The initial at the beginning of each entry is the initial of the family name of the survivor/interviewee, and IC = interview code.

Chapter 1

1. Z: Stockholm, 23 Mar. 1997 [IC 27838, Tape 3, 15:27:10–15:37:15].

Chapter 2

1. Follow-up Interview 34. Kaplan S. (2002a)

Chapter 3

1. R: Stockholm, 23 Nov. 1997 [IC 35338, Tape 5, 25:19:20–29:16:14].
2. Z: Stockholm, 23 Mar. 1997 [IC 27838, Tape 1, 5:04:15–6:59:10].
3. Z: Stockholm, 23 Mar. 1997 [IC 27838, Tape 1, 4:11:15–6:59:10].
4. Z: Stockholm, 23 Mar. 1997 [IC 27838, Tape 1, 4:11:15–6:59:10].
5. Z: Stockholm, 23 Mar. 1997 [IC 27838, Tape 1, 10:53:02–11:39:23].
6. R: Stockholm, 23 Nov. 1997 [IC 35338, Tape 1, 3:50:15–8:57:19].

7. R: Stockholm, 23 Nov. 1997 [IC 35338, Tape 1, 3:50:15–8:57:19].
8. Z: Stockholm, 23 Mar. 1997 [IC 27838, Tape 1, 8:56:02–9:20:20].
9. R: Stockholm, 23 Nov. 1997 [IC 35338, Tape 1, 23:26:16–28:31:00].
10. Z: Stockholm, 23 Mar. 1997 [IC 27838, Tape 2, 9:54:12–14:50:02].
11. R: Stockholm, 23 Nov. 1997 [IC 35338, Tape 1, 23:26:16–28:31:00].
12. Z: Stockholm, 23 Mar. 1997 [IC 27838, Tape 3, 0:20:12–7:39:18].
13. R: Stockholm, 23 Nov. 1997 [IC 35338, Tape 2, 16:44:02–23:49:25].
14. Z: Stockholm, 23 Mar. 1997 [IC 27838, Tape 2, 3:02:07–5:22:15].
15. R: Stockholm, 23 Nov. 1997 [IC 35338, Tape 3, 0:14:21–12:54:25].
16. Z: Stockholm, 23 Mar. 1997 [IC 27838, Tape 3, 0:20:12–7:39:18].
17. R: Stockholm, 23 Nov. 1997 [IC 35338, Tape 1, 16:44:02–23:49:25].
18. Z: Stockholm, 23 Mar. 1997 [IC 27838, Tape 1, 18:26:0919:59:02].
19. Z: Stockholm, 23 Mar. 1997 [IC 27838, Tape 3, 13:30:2115:27:10].
20. R: Stockholm, 23 Nov. 1997 [IC 35338, Tape 4, 6:51:19–15:44:05].
21. R: Stockholm, 23 Nov. 1997 [IC 35338, Tape 4, 6:51:19–15:44:05].
22. Z: Stockholm, 23 Mar. 1997 [IC 27838, Tape 4, 12:57:25–13:40:11].
23. B: Stockholm, 14 Nov. 1997 [IC 34712, Tape 7, 2:28:12–14:12:19].
24. Z: Malmö, 15 Dec. 1996 [IC 23346, Tape 2, 24:00:23–24:48:11].
25. P: Lund, 22 Jan. 1997 [IC 27108, Tape 4, 1:23:07–9:22:29].
26. S: Stockholm, 2 Dec. 1996 [IC 23505, Tape 4, 18:41:16–24:38:08].
27. B: Uppsala, 25 June 1998 [IC 45295, Tape 5:14:10:19–18:02:12].
28. Follow-up Interview 30, Kaplan S. (2002a)
29. F: Stockholm, 16 Nov. 1996 [IC 22948, Tape 6, 24:04:11–26:14:04].
30. B: Gothenburg, 6 Jan. 1997 [IC 25458, Tape 4, 8:21:10–9:43:15].
31. B: Gothenburg, 6 Jan. 1997 [IC 25458, Tape 4, 27:42:00–28:01:00].
32. B: Stockholm, 1 Dec. 1997 [IC 37539, Tape 1, 15:59:02–19:35:15].
33. Z: Stockholm, 23 Mar. 1997 [IC 27838, Tape 4, 7:40:12–9:23:16].

Chapter 5

Section A

1. W: Stockholm, 17 Jan. 1997 [IC 26154, Tape 2, 2:02:15–14:03:09].
2. R: Stockholm, 29 Oct. 1996 [IC 21246, Tape 3, 15:14:23–22:06:02].
3. Follow-up Interview 32, Kaplan S. (2002a)
4. Follow-up Interview 11, Kaplan S. (2002a)
5. Follow-up Interview 18, Kaplan S. (2002a)
6. Follow-up Interview 6, Kaplan S. (2002a)
7. L: Malmö, 15 Nov. 1998 [IC 49244, Tape 2, 18:13:07–21:50:15].
8. Follow-up Interview 4, Kaplan S. (2002a)
9. Follow-up Interview 9, Kaplan S. (2002a)
10. Follow-up Interview 32, Kaplan S. (2002a)
11. Follow-up Interview 34, Kaplan S. (2002a)
12. L: Malmö, 15 Nov. 1998 [IC 49244, Tape 3, 4:20:15–7:36:13].

13. B: Stockholm, 31 Jan. 1996 [IC 8855, Tape 1, 14:52:05–15:43:23].

14. B: Stockholm, 1 Dec. 1997 [IC 37539, Tape 2, 9:36:24–10:47:09].

15. M: Stockholm, 29 June 1997 [IC 31424, Tape 1, 22:20:17–23:25:23].

16. R: Stockholm, 16 Apr. 1997 [IC 28877, Tape 1,2:12:15–2:10:10].

17. Follow-up Interview 38, Kaplan S. (2002a)

18. M: Stockholm, 29 June 1997 [IC 31424, Tape 1, 17:53:10–22:20:17].

19. B:Gothenburg, 6 Jan. 1997 [IC 25458, Tape 1, 20:00:26–20:45:17].

20. Follow-up Interview 16, Kaplan S. (2002a)

21. B: Stockholm, 1 Dec. 1997 [IC 37539, Tape 1, 15:59:02–17:35:15].

22. G: Stockholm, 13 Jan. 1996 [IC 7779, Tape 1, 12:21:02–13:07:19].

23. H: Stockholm, 24 Oct. 1997 [IC 34658, Tape 1, 7:17:15–9:02:07].

24. Follow-up Interview 8, Kaplan S. (2002a)

25. Follow-up Interview 40, Kaplan S. (2002a)

26. S: Stockholm, 17 Apr. 1997 [IC 30578, Tape 1, 15:10:05–21:07:20].

27. Follow-up Interview 27, Kaplan S. (2002a)

28. R: Helsingborg, 19 June 1997 [IC 32714, Tape 1, 10:50:10–13:00:15].

29. W: Stockholm, 17 Jan. 1997 [IC 26154, Tape 3, 1:33:13–9:52:01].

30. Follow-up Interview 36, Kaplan S. (2002a)

31. B: Stockholm, 1 Dec. 1997 [IC 37539, Tape 1, 17:35:15–20:20:25].

32. Z: Stockholm, 23 Mar. 1997 [IC 27838, Tape 1, 13:10:15–13:22:22].

33. Follow-up Interview 11, Kaplan S. (2002a)

34. R: Stockholm, 29 Oct. 1996 [IC 21246, Tape 2, 7:40:06–15:06:22].

35. Follow-up Interview 16, Kaplan S. (2002a)

36. Follow-up Interview 12, Kaplan S. (2002a)

37. Follow-up Interview 12, Kaplan S. (2002a)

38. Follow-up Interview 36, Kaplan S. (2002a)

39. B: Stockholm, 15 Apr. 1996 [IC 13515, Tape 1, 1:7:56:12–12:52:12].

40. R: Stockholm, 29 Oct. 1996 [IC 21246, Tape 2, 7:40:06–15:06:22].

41. B: Stockholm, 31 Jan. 19967 [IC 8855, Tape 1, 19:55:08–21:01:06].

42. F: Stockholm, 16 Nov. 1996 [IC 22948, Tape 1, 6:40:02–10:52:10].

43. W: Stockholm, 17 Jan. 1997 [IC 26154, Tape 2, 2:02:15–14:03:09].

44. B: Stockholm, 5 Mar. 1997 [IC 27632, Tape 4, 0:34:05–5:07:15].

45. B: Stockholm, 5 Mar. 1997 [IC 27632, Tape 2, 3:38:17–4:56:12].

46. G: Stockholm, 13 Jan. 1996 [IC 7779, Tape 1, 15:06:16–17:33:15].

47. S: Stockholm, 2 Dec. 1996 [IC 23505, Tape 1, 13:20:05–15:51:22].

48. A: Stockholm, 5 Dec. 1996 [IC 23226, Tape 1, 11:10:20–14:19:12].

49. H: Ystad, 7 Apr. 1997 [IC 30051, Tape 1, 2, 4:24:15–6:27:05].

50. Follow-up Interview 12, Kaplan S. (2002a)

51. G: Malmö, 27 Oct. 1997 [IC 37470, Tape 5, 15:32:17–20:56:18].

52. Follow-up Interview 16, Kaplan S. (2002a)

53. B: Stockholm, 1 Dec. 1997 [IC 37539, Tape 2, 25:56:11–28:33:05].

54. W: Stockholm, 17 Jan. 1997 [IC 26154, Tape 2, 2:02:15–14:03:09].

55. A: Stockholm, 5 Dec. 1996 [IC 23226, Tape 1, 11:10:20–14:19:12].

56. Z: Stockholm, 23 Mar. 1997 [IC 27838, Tape 1, 20:48:15–22:13:07].
57. Follow-up Interview 30, Kaplan S. (2002a)
58. Follow-up Interview 1, Kaplan S. (2002a)
59. Follow-up Interview 11, Kaplan S. (2002a)
60. B: Stockholm, 15 Apr. 1996 [IC 13515, Tape 1, 12:52:12–16:38:09].
61. Follow-up Interview 17, Kaplan S. (2002a)
62. B: Stockholm, 4 Dec. 1996 [IC 23600, Tape 1, 15:37:05–19:31:21].
63. Follow-up Interview 32, Kaplan S. (2002a)
64. B: Stockholm, 14 Nov. 1997 [IC 34712, Tape 2, 1:25:05–2:40:14].
65. B: Stockholm, 1 Dec. 1997 [IC 37539, Tape 1, 15:59:02–17:35:15].
66. Follow-up Interview 2, Kaplan S. (2002a)
67. L: Malmö, 3 Aug. 1997 [IC 31973, Tape 1, 23:19:07–28:22:22].
68. R: Helsingborg, 19 June 1997 [IC 32714, Tape 1, 10:50:10–13:00:15].
69. M: Stockholm, 29 June 1997 [IC 31424, Tape 1, 15:0406–17:53:10].
70. Follow-up Interview 24, Kaplan S. (2002a)
71. Follow-up Interview 4, Kaplan S. (2002a)
72. Follow-up Interview 9, Kaplan S. (2002a)
73. B: Gothenburg, 6 Jan. 1997 [IC 25458, Tape 1, 12:30:00–13:31:00].

Section B

1. Z: Lund, 16 Apr. 1997 [IC 29958, Tape 2, 2:1:12:00–1:15:14].
2. R: Stockholm, 29 Oct. 1996 [IC 21246, Tape 3, 15:14:23–22:06:02].
3. R: Stockholm, 29 Oct. 1996 [IC 21246, Tape 2, 7:40:06–15:06:22].
4. Follow-up Interview 1, Kaplan S. (2002a)
5. W: Stockholm, 17 Jan. 1997 [IC 26154, Tape 2, 2:02:15–14:03:09].
6. Z: Lund, 16 Apr. 1997 [IC 29958, Tape 5, 1:11:15–3:04:00].
7. R: Stockholm, 29 Oct. 1996 [IC 21246, Tape 2, 17:30:02–18:03:17].
8. B: Stockholm, 1 Dec. 1997 [IC 37539, Tape 2, 13:50:21–15:44:10].
9. Follow-up Interview 20, Kaplan S. (2002a)
10. R: Stockholm, 29 Oct. 1996 [IC 21246, Tape 3, 0:1:22–2:4:25].
11. C: Linköping, 18 Apr. 1997 [IC 30570, Tape 1, 20:43:17–29:25:15].
12. R: Stockholm, 29 Oct. 1996 [IC 21246, Tape 3, 7:37:06–12:40:25].
13. Follow-up Interview 17, Kaplan S. (2002a)
14. B: Stockholm, 4 Dec. 1996 [IC 23600, Tape 4, 13:20:05–23:22:11].
15. S: Stockholm, 2 Dec. 1996 [IC 23505, Tape 1,19:15:06–24:16:05].
16. R: Stockholm, 29 Oct. 1996 [IC 21246, Tape 1, 10:18:20–12:19:05].
17. F: Stockholm, 11 Aug. 1997 [IC 35135, Tape 1 16:19:00–18:04:00].
18. R: Stockholm, 16 Apr. 1997 [IC 28877, Tape 1, 29:10:10–Tape 2, 00:40:10].
19. A: Stockholm, 5 Dec. 1996 [IC 23226, Tape 2, 10:35:14–13:41:19].
20. B: Stockholm, 15 Apr. 1996 [IC 13515, Tape 3, 13:10:15–21:54:03].
21. B: Stockholm, 14 Nov. 1997 [IC 34712, Tape 2, 14:14:06–16:18:17].
22. G: Stockholm, 13 Jan. 1996 [IC 7779, Tape 1, 21:36:16–23:50:08].

23. L: Uppsala, 28 Feb. 1997 [IC 28737, Tape , 26:46:02–27:43:12].
24. Follow-up Interview 29, Kaplan S. (2002a)
25. Follow-up Interview 47, Kaplan S. (2002a)
26. B: Stockholm, 31 Jan. 1996 [IC 8855, Tape 2, 25:52:23–29:43:26].
27. Follow-up Interview 20, Kaplan S. (2002a)
28. Z: Stockholm, 23 Mar. 1997 [IC 27838, Tape 1, 20:48:15–22:13:07].
29. B: Stockholm, 15 Apr. 1996 [IC 13515, Tape 1, 16:38:09—26:30:15].
30. R: Stockholm, 29 Oct. 1996 [IC 21246, Tape 3, 15:14:23–22:06:02].
31. Follow-up Interview 11, Kaplan S. (2002a)
32. R: Helsingborg, 19 June 1997 [IC 32714, Tape 1, 15:25:25–18:18:10].
33. Follow-up Interview 17, Kaplan S. (2002a)
34. L: Malmö, 3 Aug. 1997 [IC 31973, Tape 2, 20:46:1425:55:18].
35. Follow-up Interview 36, Kaplan S. (2002a)
36. Follow-up Interview 21, Kaplan S. (2002a)
37. W: Stockholm, 17 Jan. 1997 [IC 26154, Tape 2, 15:01:05–16:46:22].
38. L: Lund, 15 Nov. 1998 [IC 49244, Tape 1, 22:25:00–25:13:05].
39. B: Stockholm, 5 Mar. 1997 [IC 27632, Tape 2, 15:48:22–18:24:05].
40. Follow-up Interview 31, Kaplan S. (2002a)
41. R: Helsingborg, 19 June 1997 [IC 32714, Tape 1, 23:50:10–25:25:20].
42. Follow-up Interview 32, Kaplan S. (2002a)
43. Follow-up Interview 32, Kaplan S. (2002a)
44. S: Stockholm, 17 Apr. 1997 [IC 30578, Tape 1, 15:10:05–21:07:20].
45. B: Stockholm, 1 Dec. 1997 [IC 37539Tape 3, 25:01:06–26:57:21].
46. S: Stockholm, 17 Apr. 1997 [IC 30578, Tape 1, 24:58:09–27:13:08].
47. B, Stockholm, 31 Jan. 1996 [IC 8855, Tape 2, 25:52:23–29:43:26].
48. S: Stockholm, 2 Dec. 1996 [IC 23505, Tape 1,19:15:06–24:16:05].
49. Follow-up Interview 11, Kaplan S. (2002a)
50. B: Stockholm, 15 Apr. 1996 [IC 13515, Tape 4, 6:36:19–11:33:05].
51. Follow-up Interview 29, Kaplan S. (2002a)
52. Follow-up Interview 1, Kaplan S. (2002a)
53. Follow-up Interview 36, Kaplan S. (2002a)
54. B: Stockholm, 5 Mar. 1997 [IC 27632, Tape 1, 24:43:02–25:12:07].
55. Follow-up Interview 4, Kaplan S. (2002a)
56. R: Stockholm, 16 Apr. 1997 [IC 28877, Tape 1,13:30:05–19:52:00].
57. C: Linköping, 18 Apr. 1997 [IC 30570, Tape 1, 12:26:05–1:43:17].
58. S: Stockholm, 2 Dec. 1996 [IC 23505, Tape 2, 8:31:05–10:55:04].
59. Follow-up Interview 20, Kaplan S. (2002a)
60. R: Helsingborg, 19 June 1997 [IC 32714, Tape 1, 1:15:25–18:18:10].
61. B: Gothenburg, 21 Sept. 1997 [IC 39900, Tape 2, 15:59:09–28:24:0].
62. Follow-up Interview 2, Kaplan S. (2002a)
63. Z: Stockholm, 23 Mar. 1997 [IC 27838, Tape 2, 3:02:07–5:22:15].
64. Z: Stockholm, 23 Mar. 1997 [IC 27838, Tape 2, 5:29:15–7:25:14].
65. P: Lund, 22 Jan. 1997 [IC 27108, Tape 2, 0:32:29–2:05:36:22].

66. Follow-up Interview 2, Kaplan S. (2002a)
67. F: Stockholm, 16 Nov. 1996 [IC 22948, Tape 1, 6:40;02–10:59·10]
68. Follow-up Interview 21, Kaplan S. (2002a)
69. R: Helsingborg, 19 June 1997 [IC 32714, Tape 1, 21:00:07–23:10:15].
70. Follow-up Interview 29, Kaplan S. (2002a)
71. R: Stockholm, 29 Oct. 1996 [IC 21246, Tape 4, 19:37:1623:33:25].
72. Follow-up Interview 14, Kaplan S. (2002a)
73. B: Stockholm, 31 Jan. 1996 [IC 8855, Tape 1, 14:52:05–15:43:23].
74. B: Stockholm, 31 Jan. 1996 [IC 8855, Tape 2, 15:11:18–18:23:05].
75. Follow-up Interview 22, Kaplan S. (2002a)
76. Follow-up Interview 34, Kaplan S. (2002a)
77. Z: Stockholm, 23 Mar. 1997 [IC 27838, Tape 1, 27:40:02–8:18:05].
78. A: Stockholm, 5 Dec. 1996 [IC 23226, Tape 1, 22:33:17–28:04:17].
79. B: Stockholm, 31 Jan. 1996 [IC 8855, Tape 2, 4:08:12–8:00:11].
80. R: Stockholm, 29 Oct. 1997 [IC 21246, Tape 2:2:17:20–5:34:10].

Section C

1. Follow-up Interview 17, Kaplan S. (2002a)
2. S: Stockholm, 2 Dec. 1996 [IC 23505, Tape 5, 8:33:21–12:53:07
3. B: Stockholm, 15 Apr. 1996 [IC 13515, Tape 4, 12:08:13–22:11:16].
4. Follow-up Interview 4, Kaplan S. (2002a)
5. B: Uppsala, 25 June 1998 [IC 45295, Tape 2, 0:57:21–7:14:25].
6. B: Uppsala, 25 June 1998 [IC 45295, Tape 2, 0:57:21–7:14:25].
7. B: Stockholm, 15 Apr. 1996 [IC 13515, Tape 3, 2:18:13–2:20:25].
8. B: Stockholm, 15 Apr. 1996 [IC 13515, Tape 3, 2:18:13–2:20:25].
9. W: Stockholm, 27 Mar. 1996 [IC 12783, Tape 3, 4:00:12–8:34:19].
10. Follow-up Interview 21, Kaplan S. (2002a)
11. B: Stockholm, 15 Apr. 1997 [IC 13515, Tape 3, 2:18:13–21:54:03].
12. Follow-up Interview 21, Kaplan S. (2002a)
13. S: Stockholm, 2 Dec. 1996 [IC 23505, Tape 3, 6:43:07–14:17:15].
14. S: Stockholm, 2 Dec. 1996 [IC 23505, Tape 3, 6:43:07–14:17:15].
15. S: Stockholm, 2 Dec. 1996 [IC 23505, Tape 3, 23:15:02–30:13:25].
16. S: Stockholm, 2 Dec. 1996 [IC 23505, Tape 3, 23:15:02–30:13:25].
17. Z: Lund, 16 Apr. 1997 [IC 29958, Tape 3, 5:3:10–15:32:00].
18. F: Stockholm, 11 Aug. 1997 [IC 35135, Tape 3, 4:10:17–8:54:25].
19. Z: Malmö, 15 Dec. 1996 [IC 23346, Tape 1, 19:49:07–27:33:20].
20. Follow-up Interview 21, Kaplan S. (2002a)
21. S: Stockholm, 2 Dec. 1996 [IC 23505, Tape 2, 4:55:05–16:20:12].
22. B: Stockholm, 15 Apr. 1996 [IC 13515, Tape 2, 5:52:03–13:45:04].
23. S: Stockholm, 2 Dec. 1996 [IC 23505, Tape 3, 6:43:07–14:17:15].
24. Follow-up Interview 6, Kaplan S. (2002a)
25. S: Stockholm, 2 Dec. 1996 [IC 23505, Tape 2, 8:31:05–10:55:04].
26. Z: Malmö, 15 Dec. 1996 [IC 23346, Tape 1, 13:08:09–19:25:00].

27. B: Stockholm, 15 Apr. 1996 [IC 13515, Tape 4, 6:36:19–11:33:05].
28. B: Stockholm, 5 Mar. 1997 [IC 27632, Tape 1, 14:01:05–1:46:05].
29. Z: Stockholm, 23 Mar. 1997 [IC 27838, Tape 2, 18:48:15–19:04:13].
30. S: Stockholm, 2 Dec. 1996 [IC 23505, Tape 4, 0:40:05–5:48:14].
31. Follow-up Interview 17, Kaplan S. (2002a)
32. B: Stockholm, 15 Apr. 1996 [IC 13515, Tape 4, 12:08:13–22:11:16].
33. S: Stockholm, 2 Dec. 1996 [IC 23505, Tape 4, 9:20:24–12:00:21].
34. S: Stockholm, 27 Dec. 1996 [IC 25870, Tape 2, 4:55:05–16:20:12].
35. Follow-up Interview 1, Kaplan S. (2002a)
36. Follow-up Interview 14, Kaplan S. (2002a)
37. B: Gothenburg, 21 Sept. 1997 [IC 39900, Tape 2, 3:58:00–26:35:10].
38. Z: Malmö, 15 Dec. 1996 [IC 23346, Tape 1, 13:08:09–19:25:00].
39. R: Stockholm, 26 Jun. 1997 [IC 3130, Tape 1, 7:20:18–14:10:15].
40. Follow-up Interview 17, Kaplan S. (2002a)
41. Follow-up Interview 28, Kaplan S. (2002a)
42. B: Gothenburg, 21 Sept. 1997 [IC 39900, Tape 2, 3:58:00–26:35:10].
43. P: Stockholm, 22 Jan. 1996 [IC 23505, Tape 2, 24:25:17–30:42:17].
44. Follow-up Interview 32, Kaplan S. (2002a)
45. Z: Malmö, 15 Dec. 1996 [IC 23346, Tape 1, 13:08:09–19:25:00].

Section D

1. B: Stockholm, 15 Apr. 1996 [IC 13515, Tape 5, 4:52:15–13:43:20].
2. Follow-up interview 14, Kaplan S. (2002a)
3. Follow-up Interview 30, Kaplan S. (2002a)
4. Follow-up Interview 15, Kaplan S. (2002a)
5. H: Stockholm, 24 Oct. 1997 [IC 34658, Tape 2, 6:33:0–10:38:15].
6. L: Uppsala, 28 Feb. 1997 [IC 28737, Tape 3, 14:28:00–25:28:00].
7. L: Uppsala, 28 Feb. 1997 [IC 28737, Tape 3, 7:15:26–14:01:02].
8. Follow-up Interview 10, Kaplan S. (2002a)
9. B: Uppsala, 25 June 1998 [IC 45295, Tape 2, 18:05:02–26:15:19].
10. Z: Stockholm, 23 Mar. 1997 [IC 27838, Tape 2, 25:20:01–25:14:17].
11. L: Uppsala, 28 Feb. 1997 [IC 28737, Tape ,3, 26:46:02–27:43:12].
12. B: Stockholm, 15 Apr. 1996 [IC 13515, Tape 4, 22:11:16–30:10:20].
13. Follow-up Interview 9, Kaplan S. (2002a)
14. B: Uppsala, 25 June 1998 [IC 45295, Tape 2, 21:03:14–28:41:05].
15. Follow-up Interview 36, Kaplan S. (2002a)
16. Z: Stockholm, 23 Mar. 1997 [IC 27838, Tape 2, 20:07:02–Tape 3, 10:46:06].
17. Follow-up Interview 20, Kaplan S. (2002a)
18. B: Stockholm, 15 Apr. 1996 [IC 13515, Tape 5, 4:52:15–13:43:20].
19. Z: Stockholm, 23 Mar. 1997 [IC 27838, Tape 1, 23:30:15–24:13:22].
20. L: Malmö, 15 Nov. 1998 [IC 49244, Tape 5, 22:50:17–27:35:08].
21. L: Malmö, 15 Nov. 1998 [IC 49244, Tape 2, 18:13:07–21:50:15].

Section E

1. R: Stockholm, 29 Oct. 1997 [IC 21246, Tape 1, 0:48.00–2.47:16].
2. Follow-up Interview 7, Kaplan S. (2002a)
3. B: Stockholm, 4 Dec. 1996 [IC 23600, Tape 5, 4:1:07–7:57:05].
4. B: Stockholm, 4 Dec. 1996 [IC 23600, Tape 5, 4:1:07–7:57:05].
5. Follow-up Interview 13, Kaplan S. (2002a)
6. Follow-up Interview 13, Kaplan S. (2002a)
7. Follow-up Interview 22, Kaplan S. (2002a)
8. P: Lund, 22 Jan. 1997 [IC 27108, Tape 2, 6:29:02–18:16:18].
9. G: Stockholm, 13 Jan. 1996 [IC 7779, Tape 3, 16:32:05–19:19:22].
10. Follow-up Interview 4, Kaplan S. (2002a)
11. Z: Malmö, 15 Dec. 1996 [IC 23346, Tape 1, 19:49:07–27:33:20].
12. Follow-up Interview 2, Kaplan S. (2002a)
13. Follow-up Interview 1, Kaplan S. (2002a)
14. Z: Malmö, 22 Mar. 1997 [IC 29598, Tape 2, 24:20:00–26:47:10].
15. Follow-up Interview 2, Kaplan S. (2002a)
16. Follow-up Interview 3, Kaplan S. (2002a)
17. P: Lund, 22 Jan. 1997 [IC 27108, Tape 2, 6:29:02–18:16:18].
18. Follow-up Interview 1, Kaplan S. (2002a)
19. G: Stockholm, 13 Jan. 1996 [IC 7779, Tape 2, 17:08:03–22:00:03].
20. C: Linköping, 18 Apr. 1997 [IC 30570, Tape 2, 2:42:04–10:07:22].
21. Follow-up Interview 2, Kaplan S. (2002a)
22. B: Stockholm, 1 Dec. 1997 [IC 37539, Tape 5, 23:32:03–25:00:04].
23. Follow-up Interview 25, Kaplan S. (2002a)
24. B: Stockholm, 1 Dec. 1997 [IC 37539, Tape 5, 25:7:16–28:56:04].
25. G: Malmö, 27 Oct. 1997 [IC 37470, Tape 9, 9:26:19–16:09:21].
26. S: Stockholm, 17 Apr. 1997 [IC 37539, Tape 2, 6:14:25–9:31:07].
27. Follow-up Interview 1, Kaplan S. (2002a)
28. Follow-up Interview 31, Kaplan S. (2002a)
29. B: Stockholm, 1 Dec. 1997 [IC 37539, Tape 4, 5:41:22–7:00:09].
30. B: Stockholm, 4 Dec. 1996 [IC 23600, Tape 5, 9:15:12–18:51:02].
31. Follow-up Interview 2, Kaplan S. (2002a)
32. S: Stockholm, 17 Apr. 1997 [IC 37539, Tape 2, 15:51:15–24:1315].
33. R: Stockholm, 23 Nov. [IC 35338, Tape 4, 18:11:25–19:57:10].
34. Follow-up Interview 25, Kaplan S. (2002a)
35. B: Gothenburg, 21 Sept. 1997 [IC 33900, Tape 4, 0:58:00–31:00].
36. Z: Malmö, 22 Mar. 1997 [IC 29598, Tape 4, 0:58:00–3:11:00].
37. P: Lund, 22 Jan. 1997 [IC 27108, Tape 2, 6:29:02–18:16:18].
38. Follow-up Interview 2, Kaplan S. (2002a)
39. Z: Malmö, 22 Mar. 1997 [IC 29598, Tape 1, 16:16:00–16:56:00].
40. R: Stockholm, 29 Oct. 1996 [IC 21246, Tape 1, 17:57:12–22:46:26].
41. Follow-up Interview 1, Kaplan S. (2002a)
42. Z: Lund, 16 Apr. 1997 [IC 29958, Tape 3, 17:11:20–26:07:00].

43. Follow-up Interview 22, Kaplan S. (2002a)
44. B: Stockholm, 5 Mar. 1997 [IC 27632, Tape 4,10:00:05–18:12:18].
45. B: Stockholm, 4 Dec. 1996 [IC 23600, Tape 5, 9:15:12–18:51:02].
46. B: Stockholm, 5 Mar. 1997 [IC 27632, Tape 4, 22:20:19–23:05:10].
47. Follow-up Interview 24, Kaplan S. (2002a)
48. Follow-up Interview 2, Kaplan S. (2002a)
49. P: Lund, 22 Jan. 1997 [IC 27108, Tape 2, 6:29:02–18:16:18].
50. B: Stockholm, 4 Dec. 1996 [IC 23600, Tape 1, 7:42:07–9:31:26].
51. B: Stockholm, 4 Dec. 1996 [IC 23600, Tape 6, 2:45:15–5:49:05].
52. Follow-up Interview 5, Kaplan S. (2002a)
53. G: Malmö, 27 Oct. 1997 [IC 37470, Tape 9, 2:33:02–3:52:05].
54. B: Stockholm, 31 Jan. 1996 [IC 8855, Tape 3, 10:31:14–13:48:15].
55. Follow-up Interview 25, Kaplan S. (2002a)
56. Z: Malmö, 15 Dec. 1996 [IC 23346, Tape 2, 0:38:00–6:09:17].
57. Follow-up Interview 18, Kaplan S. (2002a)
58. C: Linköping, 18 Apr. 1997 [IC 30570, Tape 2, 3:19:05–28:41:22].
59. F: Stockholm, 16 Nov. 1996 [IC 22948, Tape 3, 24:57:14–25:45:20].

Section F

1. Follow-up Interview 22, Kaplan S. (2002a)
2. R: Stockholm, 29 Oct. 1996 [IC 21246, Tape 5, 3:06:09–13:29:19].
3. C: Linköping, 18 Apr. 1997 [IC 30570, Tape 3, 1:22:13–11:12:26].
4. B: Stockholm, 31 Jan. 1996 [IC 8855, Tape 5, 02:59:02-07:14:12].
5. B: Stockholm, 5 Mar. 1997 [IC 27632, Tape 4, 19:17:06–20:04:00].
6. W: Stockholm, 17 Jan. 1997 [IC 26154, Tape 5, 16:49:06–29:28:20].
7. B: Stockholm, 5 Mar. 1997 [IC 27632, Tape 6, 14:02:08–48:15].
8. Follow-up Interview 24, Kaplan S. (2002a)
9. Follow-up Interview 40, Kaplan S. (2002a)
10. B: Stockholm, 4 Dec. 1996 [IC 23600, Tape 7, 0:16:22–3:52:15].
11. S: Stockholm, 2 Dec. 1996 [IC 23505, Tape 5, 8:33:21–12:53:07].
12. L: Malmö, 3 Aug. 1997 [IC 31973, Tape 3, 20:07:02–21:48:20].
13. R: Stockholm, 16 Apr. 1997 [IC 28877, Tape 2:15:10:05–22:04:10].
14. R: Stockholm, 29 Oct. 1996 [IC 21246, Tape 6, 0:35:12–10:17:24].
15. B: Uppsala, 25 June 1998 [IC 45295, Tape 3:18:08:21–25:33:26].
16. C: Linköping, 18 Apr. 1997 [IC 30570, Tape 3, 12:16:04–15:37:12].
17. P: Lund, 22 Jan. 1997 [IC 27108, Tape 2, 6:29:02–18:16:18].
18. P: Lund, 22 Jan. 1997 [IC 27108, Tape 2, 6:29:02–18:16:18].
19. Z: Lund, 16 Apr. 1997 [IC 29948, Tape 4, 10:47:12–15:04:00].
20. B: Uppsala, 25 June 1998 [IC 45295, Tape 3, 8:50:05–11:20:10].
21. Follow-up Interview 33, Kaplan S. (2002a)
22. C: Linköping, 18 Apr. 1997 [IC 30570, Tape 3, 1:22:13–11:12:26].
23. A: Stockholm, 5 Dec. 1996 [IC 23226, Tape 3, 1:12:22–5:07:05].
24. Follow-up Interview 21, Kaplan S. (2002a)

25. P: Lund, 22 Jan. 1997 [IC 27108, Tape 2, 6:29:02–18:16:18].
26. B: Stockholm, 4 Dec. 1996 [IC 23600, Tape 7, 0:16:22–3:52:15]
27. B: Stockholm, 15 Apr. 1997 [IC 13515, Tape 6, 9:25:13–15:42:06].
28. B: Stockholm, 14 Nov. 1997 [IC 34712, Tape 5, 1:31:23–8:59:22].

Section G

1. R: Stockholm, 29 Oct. 1996 [IC 21246, Tape 1, 28:42:9–30:32:05].
2. C: Linköping, 18 Apr. 1997 [IC 30570, Tape 3, 18:34:15–21:23:12].
3. P: Lund, 22 Jan. 1997 [IC 27108, Tape 2, 24:44:16–29:15:24].
4. B: Stockholm, 4 Dec. 1996 [IC 23600, Tape 7, 11:51:12–18:58:08].
5. Follow-up Interview 2, Kaplan S. (2002a)
6. Follow-up Interview 21, Kaplan S. (2002a)
7. Follow-up Interview 24, Kaplan S. (2002a)
8. H: Stockholm, 24 Oct. 1997 [IC 34658, Tape 2, 27:10:05–29:24:22].
9. H: Stockholm, 24 Oct. 1997 [IC 34658, Tape 2, 21:59:15–27:00:07].
10. P: Lund, 22 Jan. 1997 [IC 27108, Tape 3, 14:42:09–23:35:22].
11. P: Lund, 22 Jan. 1997 [IC 27108, Tape 3, 14:42:09–23:35:22].
12. P: Lund, 22 Jan. 1997 [IC 27108, Tape 2, 29:44:16–29:15:24].
13. Follow-up Interview 5, Kaplan S. (2002a)
14. Follow-up Interview 2, Kaplan S. (2002a)
15. W: Malmö, 7 Jan. 1997 [IC 25537, Tape 1, 2:27:10–2:31:55
16. Follow-up Interview 1, Kaplan S. (2002a)
17. Follow-up Interview 2, Kaplan S. (2002a)
18. Follow-up Interview 4, Kaplan S. (2002a)
19. Follow-up Interview 28, Kaplan S. (2002a)
20. F: Stockholm, 16 Nov. 1996 [IC 22948, Tape 5, 27:32:20–28:55:12].
21. S: Stockholm, 17 Apr. 1997 [IC 37539, Tape 4, 11:23:15–14:27:05].
22. Follow-up Interview 18, Kaplan S. (2002a)
23. Follow-up Interview 3, Kaplan S. (2002a)
24. G: Stockholm, 13 Jan. 1996 [IC 7779, Tape 4, 0:24:23–1:56:18].
25. Follow-up Interview 7, Kaplan S. (2002a)
26. Follow-up Interview 28, Kaplan S. (2002a)
27. Follow-up Interview 21, Kaplan S. (2002a)
28. Follow-up Interview 42, Kaplan S. (2002a)
29. R: Helsingborg, 19 June 1997 [IC 32714, Tape 3, 3:00:00–7:07:10].
30. L: Lund, 15 Nov. 1998 [IC 49244, Tape 5, 19:48:12–20:40:08].
31. B: Gothenburg, 21 Sept. 1997 [IC 39900, Tape 4, 11:09:00–15:42:00].
32. W: Malmö, 7 Jan. 1997 [IC 25537, Tape 1, 19:12:05–21:10:20].
33. B: Stockholm, 31 Jan. 1996 [IC 8855, Tape 6, 5:05:16–12:23:15].
34. S: Stockholm, 2 Dec. 1996 [IC 23505, Tape 5, 15:51:21–20:05:12].
35. Z: Stockholm, 23 Mar. 1997 [IC 27838, Tape 4, 2:10:05–2:21:21].
36. Follow-up Interview 36, Kaplan S. (2002a)
37. L: Lund, 15 Nov. 1998 [IC 49244, Tape 3, 14:50:20–15:55:04].

38. Z: Malmö, 15 Dec. 1996 [IC 23346, Tape 2, 0:38:00–6:09:17].
39. Follow-up Interview 28, Kaplan S. (2002a)

Chapter 6

1. Interview, Kigali, Kaplan & Eckstein (2004)
2. Interview, Kigali, Kaplan & Eckstein (2004)

Chapter 7

1. R: Stockholm, 29 Oct. 1996 [IC 21246, Tape 4, 6:38:10–15:40:03].
2. Follow-up Interview 7, Kaplan S. (2002a)
3. Follow-up Interview 3, Kaplan S. (2002a)
4. Follow-up Interview 24, Kaplan S. (2002a)
5. Follow-up Interview 25, Kaplan S. (2002a)
6. Z: Lund, 16 Apr. 1997 [IC 29958, Tape 2, 13:03:12–25:02:00].
7. Z: Malmö, 15 Dec. 1996 [IC 23346, Tape 1, 19:49:07–27:33:20].
8. Follow-up Interview 14, Kaplan S. (2002a)

Chapter 8

1. R: Stockholm, 23 Nov. 1997 [IC 35338, Tape 5, 25:19:20–29:16:14].
2. R: Stockholm, 23 Nov. 1997 [IC 35338, Tape 3, 0:14:21–12:54:25].
3. Interview, Kigali, Kaplan & Eckstein (2004)
4. R: Stockholm, 29 Oct 1996 [IC 21246, Tape 2, 21:26:14–24:14:13].
5. Interview, Kigali, Kaplan & Eckstein (2004)
6. Follow-up Interview 38, Kaplan S. (2002a)
7. S: Stockholm, 17 April 1997 [IC 37539, Tape 1, 15:10:05–21:07:20].

Chapter 9

1. Interview, Kigali, Kaplan (2005a)

Appendix

1. Z: Stockholm, 23 Mar. 1997 [IC 27838, Tape 3, 15:27:10–15:37:15].

REFERENCES

Anzieu, D. (Ed.) (1985). *The Skin Ego*. New Haven: Yale University Press, 1989.

Bachner, H. (1999). *Återkomsten: Antisemitism i Sverige efter 1945* [The Return: Anti-Semitism in Sweden after 1945]. Stockholm: Natur och Kultur.

Balas, A. (2000). Book review: *Children Surviving Persecution: An International Study of Healing and Trauma*: Judith Kestenberg & Charlotte Kahn. Westport, CT: Praeger. 1998. *International Journal of Psychoanalysis, 81*: 235–238.

Bauer, Y. (2001). *Rethinking the Holocaust*. New Haven & London: Yale University Press.

Bauman, J. (2003). Moral choices at the time of gas chambers. In: P. Wagner & B. Strath (Eds.), *Between Two Wars: Janina and Zygmund Bauman's Analyses of the Contemporary Human Condition*. Florence: European University Institute [available at http://cadmus.iue.it/dspace/bitstream/1814/1864/2/HEC03-04.pdf].

Berg, L. (2001). Rwanda i stort "rättsexperiment" [Rwanda in a large "judicial experiment"]. *Dagens Nyheter* [Daily newspaper], Stockholm, 7 December.

Bergman, M. S., & Jucovy, M. E. (Eds.). (1982). *Generations of the Holocaust*. New York: Basic Books.

Bibring, G. L. (1961). A study of the psychological processes in pregnancy and of the earliest mother–child relationship. *Psychoanalytic Study of the Child*, 16: 9–72.

Bick, E. (1968). The experience of the skin in early object-relations. *International Journal of Psychoanalysis, 49*: 484–486.

Bion, W. R. (1959). Attacks on linking. *International Journal of Psychoanalysis 40*: 5–6. Also in *Second Thoughts: Selected Papers on Psychoanalysis.* London: Heinemann, 1967; reprinted London: Karnac Books, 1984.

Bion, W. R. (1962). *Learning from Experience.* London: Heinemann; reprinted London: Karnac Books, 1984.

Bion, W. R. (1967). *Second Thoughts: Selected Papers on Psychoanalysis.* London: Heinemann; reprinted London: Karnac Books, 1984.

Böhm, T. (1993). *Inte som vi* [Not like us]. Stockholm: Natur och Kultur, 2004.

Böhm, T. (2006). Psychoanalytic aspects on perpetrators in genocide: Experiences from Rwanda. *Scandinavian Psychoanalytic Review, 29*: 22–32.

Böhm, T., & Kaplan, S. (1985). Aktuellt om andragenerationsfenomenet. [About second-generation phenomena]. *Psykisk Hälsa, 3*: 119–122.

Böhm, T., & Kaplan, S. (2006). *Hämnd—och att avstå från att ge igen* [Revenge—and refraining from retaliation]. Stockholm: Natur och Kultur. German edition: *Rache* [Revenge]. Giessen: Psychosocial Verlag, in press.

Bowlby, J. (1988). *A Secure Base: Parent–Child Attachment and Healthy Human Development.* New York: Basic Books.

Bremner, J. D., Staib, L. H., Kaloupek, D., Southwick, S. M., Soufer, R., & Charney, D. S. (1999) Neural correlates of exposure to traumatic pictures and sound in combat veterans with and without posttraumatic stress disorder: A positron emission tomography study. *Biological Psychiatry, 45*: 806–818.

Bruchfeld, S., & Levine, P. A. (1999). *Om detta må ni berätta: En bok om Förintelsen i Europa 1933–1945* [About this you have to tell: A book about the Holocaust in Europe 1933–1945]. Stockholm: Swedish Government.

Cesarani, D., & Levine, P. (Eds.) (2000) "Bystanders" to the Holocaust: A reevaluation. *Journal of Holocaust Education, 9* (2&3: Autumn/Winter).

Christianson, S.-Å. (1994). *Traumatiska minnen* [Traumatic memories]. Stockholm: Natur och Kultur.

Cicchetti, D. (1994). Integrating developmental risk factors: Perspectives from developmental psychopathology. In C. A. Nelson (Ed.), *Minnesota Symposium on Child Psychology, Vol. 27: Threats to Optimal Development* (pp. 285–325). Hillsdale, NJ: Lawrence Erlbaum.

Damasio, A. R. (1994). *Descartes' Error: Emotion, Reason and the Human Brain.* New York: Avon Books.

Davis, J. T. (2001). Revising psychoanalytic interpretations of the past: An examination of declarative and non-declarative memory processes. *International Journal of Psycho-Analysis, 82*: 449–462.

Deri, S. (1978). Vicissitudes of symbolization and creativity In: A. S. Grolnik & L. Barkin (Eds.), *Between Reality and Fantasy: Transitional Objects and Phenomena* (pp. 43–60). New York: Jason Aronson.

Duhl, L. (2000). "Rocking an empty cradle: A psychological study of Yiddish Holocaust lullabies." Paper presented at the 7th World Congress of the World Association for Infant Mental Health.

Dwork, D. (1991). *Children with a Star: Jewish Youth in Nazi Europe.* New Haven: Yale University Press.

Dyregrov, A., Gupta, L., Gjestad, R., & Mukanoheli, E. (2000). Trauma exposure and psychological reactions to genocide among Rwandan children. *Journal of Traumatic Stress, 13:* 3–21.

Edelman, G. M. (1989). *The Remembered Present: A Biological Theory of Consciousness.* New York: Basic Books.

Emde, R. N. (1999). Moving ahead: Integrating influences of affective processes for development and for psychoanalysis. *International Journal of Psychoanalysis, 80:* 317.

Erikson, E. H. (1982). *The Life Cycle Completed.* New York: Norton.

Etchegoyen, R. H. (1991). *The Fundamentals of Psychoanalytic Technique.* London: Karnac.

Faimberg, H. (1988). The telescoping of generations: Genealogy of certain identifications. *Contemporary Psychoanalysis, 24:* 99–118.

Felman, S., & Laub, D. (1992). *Testimony: Crises of Witnessing in Literature, Psychoanalysis and History.* London: Routledge.

Ferrari, A. B. (2004). *From the Eclipse of the Body to the Dawn of the Thought.* London: Free Association Books.

Fonagy, P. (1998). "Attachment, the Holocaust and the Outcome of Child Psychoanalysis: The Third Generation." Paper presented at the 3rd Congress of the European Federation for Psychoanalytic Psychotherapy in the Public Sector, Cologne, Germany, 28 March.

Fonagy, P., Gergely, G., Jurist, E. L., & Target, M. (2002). *Affect Regulation, Mentalization, and the Development of the Self.* New York: Other Press.

Freud, A., & Burlingham, D. (1943). *War and Children.* New York: Medical War Books.

Freud, A., & Burlingham, D. (1973). *Infants without Families: Reports on the Hampstead Nurseries, 1939–1945.* London: Hogarth & The Institute of Psycho-Analysis.

Freud S (1920g). *Beyond the Pleasure Principle. SE, 18.*

Freud, S. (1923b). *The Ego and the Id. SE, 19.*

Friedländer, S. (1997) *Nazi Germany and the Jews, Vol. I: The Years of Persecution 1933–1939.* New York: HarperCollins.

Glaser, B. G. (1978). *Theoretical Sensitivity: Advances in the Methodology of Grounded Theory.* Mill Valley, CA: Sociology Press.

Goldman, E. (1986). Livsvilja—vilja till överlevnad [The will to live—the will to survive]. *Psykisk Hälsa, 22* (monograph).

Gourevitch, P. (1998). *We Wish to Inform You That Tomorrow We Will Be Killed with Our Families: Stories from Rwanda.* London: Picador.

Graml, H. (1992). *Antisemitism in the Third Reich.* Oxford: Blackwell.

Green, E. C., & Honwana, A. (1999). Indigenous healing of war-affected children in Africa. *IK Notes* (World Bank), *10*: 1–4.

Grubrich-Simitis, I. (1984). From concretism to metaphor: Thoughts on some theoretical and technical aspects of the psychoanalytic work with children of Holocaust survivors. *Psychoanalytic Study of the Child*, 39: 301–319.

Gutman, I. (Ed.). (1990). *Encyclopedia of the Holocaust, Vol. 3*. New York: Macmillan.

Heaney, S. (1980). Feeling into words. In: *Preoccupations: Selected Prose, 1968–1978* (pp. 41–60). New York: Noonday.

Helmreich, W. B. (1992) *Against All Odds: Holocaust Survivors and the Successful Lives They Made in America*. New York: Simon & Schuster.

Herman, J. (1992). *Trauma and Recovery: The Aftermath of Violence—From Domestic Abuse to Political Terror*. New York: Basic Books.

Hjern, A. (1997). I skottlinjen. Om barns utveckling och psykiska hälsa under våldsammapolitiska konflikter [In shooting range: On development and psychic health of children during violent political conflicts]. Rapport från Flyktingteamet i samarbete med Centrum för Barn- & Ungdomshälsa, 10 (CBU) offensiv strategi. *Socialmedicinsk tidskrift, 9*.

Igra, L. (2001). *Den tunna hinnan mellan omsorg och grymhet*. [The thin membrande between caring and cruelty]. Stockholm: Natur och Kultur.

Johansson, B. (Ed.). (2000). *Judiska minnen: Berättelser från Förintelsen* [Jewish memories: Narratives from the Holocaust]. Stockholm: The National Museum for Cultural History.

Josselson, R., & Lieblich, A. (Eds.). (1993). *The Narrative Study of Lives*. Newbury Park, CA: Sage.

Jucovy, M. E. (1992). Psychoanalytic contribution to Holocaust studies. *International Journal of Psychoanalysis, 73*: 267–282.

Kaplan, S. (2000). Child survivors and childbearing: Memories from the Holocaust invading the present. *Scandinavian Psychoanalytic Review, 23*: 249–282.

Kaplan, S. (2002a). *Children in the Holocaust: Dealing with Affects and Memory Images in Trauma and Generational Linking*. Doctoral Thesis, Department of Education, Stockholm University.

Kaplan, S. (2002b). Two boys—one event. How memories are recalled in interviews about massive trauma. *Scandinavian Psychoanalytic Review, 25* (1): 108–116

Kaplan, S. (2003). *Barn under Förintelsen—då och nu*. Affekter och minnesbilder efter extrem traumatisering [Children in the Holocaust—then and now: Affects and memory images after extreme traumatization]. Stockholm: Natur och Kultur.

Kaplan, S. (2005a). *Kindheit im Schatten von Völkermord Massives seelisches Trauma in der Kindheit und seine Folgen* [Children in the shadow of genocide: Massive psychic trauma in childhood and its consequences]. Nierstein: Iatros Verlag.

Kaplan, S. (2005b). *Children in Africa with Experiences of Massive Trauma: A Research Review.* Stockholm: Sida Department for Research Cooperation.

Kaplan, S. (2006). Children in genocide: Extreme traumatization and the "affect propeller". *International Journal of Psychoanalysis, 87*: 725–746.

Kaplan, S., & Eckstein, H. (2004). *Kinderchirurg Dr. Alfred Jahn und die Waisenkinder von Kigali* [Pediatric surgeon Dr Alfred Jahn and the Orphans from Kigali]. Nierstein: Iatros Verlag.

Kaplan, S., & Laub, D. (2007). *Dept. of Psychiatry, Yale University School of Medicine: Videotestimony Study of Chronically Hospitalized Holocaust Survivors/ Traumatic Psychosis Research.* Unpublished manuscript, Yale University, New Haven, CT.

Keilson, H. A. (1992). *Sequential Traumatization in Children.* Jerusalem: Magnes Press.

Kestenberg, J. S., & Brenner, I. (1986). Children who survived the Holocaust: The role of rules and routines in the development of the superego. *International Journal of Psychoanalysis, 67*: 309–315.

Kestenberg, J. S., & Brenner, I. (1996). *The Last Witness: The Child Survivor of the Holocaust.* Washington, DC: American Psychiatric Press.

Kestenberg, J. S., & Fogelman, E. (Eds.). (1994). *Children during the Nazi Reign: Psychological Perspective on the Interview Process.* Westport, CT: Praeger.

Klein, M. (1975). *The Writings of Melanie Klein, Vol. 3: Envy and Gratitude and Other Works, 1946–1963.* London: Hogarth Press.

Koblik, S. (1988). *The Stones Cry Out: Sweden's Response to the Persecution of Jews, 1933–1945.* New York: Holocaust Library.

Korczak, J. (1992). *When I Am Little Again and the Child's Right to Respect.* Lanham, MD: University Press.

Krall, H. (2000). *Där ingen flod längre finns* [Where no river exists any more]. Stehag: B. Östlings bokförlag Symposion.

Krystal, H. (Ed.). (1968). *Massive Psychic Trauma.* New York: International Universities Press.

Krystal, H. (1978). Trauma and affects. *Psychoanalytic Study of the Child, 33*: 81–112.

Krystal, H. (1988). *Integration and Self-healing: Affect, Trauma, Alexithymia.* Hillsdale, NJ: Analytic Press.

Künstlicher, R. (2000). *Mänsklig tid och drömmande* [Human time and dreaming]. *Swedish Psychoanalytic society, Skriftserie 4* (4).

Langer, L. L. (1991). *Holocaust Testimonies: Ruins of Memory.* New Haven: Yale University Press.

Langer, L. L. (1995). *Admitting the Holocaust: Collected Essays.* Oxford: Oxford University Press.

Langer, L. L. (1998). *Preempting the Holocaust.* New Haven & London: Yale University Press.

Laplanche, J., & Pontalis, J.-B. (1973). *The Language of Psycho-Analysis.* New York: Norton. Reprinted London, Karnac, 1988.

Laub, D. (2005). From speechlessness to narrative: The cases of Holocaust historians and of psychiatrically hospitalized survivors. *Literature and Medicine, 24* (2): 253–265.

Laub, D., & Auerhahn, N. C. (1993). Knowing and not knowing massive psychic trauma: Forms of traumatic memory. *International Journal of Psychoanalysis, 74*: 287–302.

Lerner, M. (1999). *Psykosomatik: Kroppens och själens dialog* [Psychosomatics: The dialogue of body and soul]. Stockholm: Natur och Kultur.

Levine, H. B. (1982). Toward a psychoanalytic understanding of children of survivors of the Holocaust. *Psychoanalytic Quarterly, 51*: 70–92.

Levine, P. A. (1998). *From Indifference to Activism: Swedish Diplomacy and the Holocaust, 1938–44*. Uppsala: Department of History, Uppsala University.

Lomfors, I. (1996). *Förlorad barndom—återvunnet liv: De judiska flyktingbarnen från Nazityskland* [Lost childhood—regained life: The Jewish refugee children from Nazi Germany]. Göteborg: Department of History, Gotheborg University.

Mamdani, M. (2001). *When Victims Become Killers*. Princeton, NJ: Princeton University Press.

Matthis, I. (2000). Sketch for a metapsychology of affect. *International Journal of Psychoanalysis, 8*: 215–227.

McIntyre, E. (Dir.) (1997). *The Lost Children of Berlin* [documentary film]. Los Angeles: USC Shoah Foundation Institute.

Melvern, L. (2000). *A People Betrayed*. London & New York: Zed Books.

Modell, A. H. (1990). *Other Times, Other Realities: Toward a Theory of Psychoanalytic Treatment*. Cambridge, MA: Harvard University Press.

Modell, A. H. (1993). *The Private Self*. Cambridge, MA: Harvard University Press.

Modell, A. H. (2003). *Imagination and the Meaningful Brain*. Cambridge, MA: MIT Press.

Moll, J. (Dir.) (1998). *The Last Days* [documentary film]. Los Angeles: USC Shoah Foundation Institute.

Moskovitz, S. (1983). *Love Despite Hate: Child Survivors of the Holocaust and Their Adult Lives*. New York: Schocken Books.

Nathanson, D. L. (1992). *Shame and Pride: Affect, Sex and the Birth of the Self*. New York: London: Norton.

Ofer, D., & Weitzman, L. J. (Eds.). (1998). *Woman in the Holocaust*. New Haven: Yale University Press.

Ogden, T. H. (2001). Reading Winnicott. *Psychoanalytic Quarterly, 70* (2): 299–323.

Pagnier, J. (2004). "Gacaca Tribunals: Justice and Reconcilliation in Rwanda?" Master's Thesis, University of Amsterdam.

Pally, R. (1997). Memory: Brain systems that link past, present and future. *International Journal of Psychoanalysis, 78*: 1223–1234.

Pally, R. (2000). *The Mind–Brain Relationship*. New York: Other Press.

Pearlman, L. A., & Saakvitne, K. W. (1995). *Trauma and the Therapist: Counter-transference and Vicarious Traumatization in Psychotherapy with Incest Survivors*. New York & London: Norton.

Rakita, S. (2003). Rwanda Lasting Wounds: Conseqences of Genocide and War for Rwanda's Children, *15* (5) [available at http://hrw.org/reports/2003/rwanda0403].

Reeder, J. (1996). *Tolkandets gränser: Berättelse och avgörande i den psykoanalytiska erfarenheten* [The limits of interpreting: Narrative and decision in the psychoanalytic experience]. Stockholm: Natur och Kultur.

Reynolds, P. (1996). *Traditional Healers and Childhood in Zimbabwe*. Athens, OH: Ohio University Press.

Ringelheim, J., & Department of Oral History Staff (1998). *Oral Interview Guidelines*. Washington, DC: United States Holocaust Memorial Museum.

Rosenberg, G. (2000). *Tankar om journalistik* [Reflections on journalism]. Stockholm: Prisma.

Rubovits-Seitz, P. F. D. (1998). *Depth-Psychological Understanding: The Methodologic Grounding of Clinical Interpretations*. London: Analytic Press.

Sandler, J., & Fonagy, P. (Eds.) (1997). *Recovered Memories of Abuse: True or False?* London: Karnac.

Schacter, D. L. (1996). *Searching for Memory: The Brain, the Mind and the Past*. New York: Basic Books.

Schacter, D. L. (1999). The seven sins of memory: Insights from psychology and cognitive neuroscience. *American Psychologist, 54*: 182–203.

Schore, A. N. (1994). *Affect Regulation and the Origin of the Self: The Neurobiology of Emotional Development*. Hillsdale, NJ: Lawrence Erlbaum.

Schore, A. N. (2003a). *Affect Dysregulation and Disorders of the Self*. New York & London: Norton.

Schore, A. N. (2003b). *Affect Regulation and the Repair of the Self*. New York & London: Norton.

Segal, H. (1957). Notes on symbol formation. *International Journal of Psychoanalysis, 38*: 391–397.

Sgofio, A., Koolhaas, J., De Boer, S., Musso, E., Stilli, D., Buwalda, B., & Meerlo, P. (1999). Social stress, autonomic neural activation, and cardiac activity in rats. *Neuroscience and Biobehavioral Reviews, 23*: 915–923.

Spence, D. P. (1982). *Narrative Truth and Historical Truth: Meaning and Interpretation in Psychoanalysis*. New York: Norton.

Staub, E. (1989). *The Roots of Evil: The Origins of Genocide and Other Group Violence*. Cambridge: Cambridge University Press.

Staub, E. (2000). Genocide and mass killing: Origins, prevention, healing and reconciliation. *Political Psychology, 21* (2).

Suedfeld, P. (1996). Thematic content analyses: Nomothetic methods for using Holocaust survivor narratives in psychological research. *Holocaust and Genocide Studies, 2*: 168–180.

Summerfield, D. (1998). Children affected by war must not be stigmatised as permanently damaged [letter]. *British Medical Journal, 317*: 249.

Toth, S. C., & Cicchetti, D. (1998). Remembering, forgetting, and the effects of trauma on memory: A developmental psychopathologic perspective. *Developmental Psychopathology, 10*: 589–605.

Tulving, E., & Thompson, D. M. (1973). Encoding specificity and retrieval processes in episodic memory. *Psychology Review, 80*: 352–373.

Tutté, J. C. (2004). The concept of psychical trauma: A bridge in interdisciplinary space. *International Journal of Psychoanalysis, 85*: 897–921.

Valent, P. (1994). *Child Survivors: Adults living with Childhood Trauma*. Melbourne: Heinemann.

van der Kolk, B. A., & Fisler, R. E. (1994). Childhood abuse and neglect and loss of self-regulation. *Bulletin of the Menninger Clinic, 58*: 145–168.

van der Kolk, B. A., & Fisler, R. E. (1995). Dissociation and fragmentary nature of traumatic memories: Overview and exploratory study. *Journal of Traumatic Stress, 8*: 505–525

Varvin, S. (2003). *Mental Survival Strategies after Extreme Traumatisation*. Copenhagen: Multivers Academic.

Volkan, V. (2004). *Blind Trust*. Charlottesville, VA: Pitchstone Publishing.

Williams, M. (1997). *Cry for Pain*. London: Penguin.

Winnicott, D. W. (1945). Primitive emotional development. In: *Through Paediatrics to Psycho-Analysis*. London: Hogarth Press, 1978; reprinted London: Karnac, 1984.

Winnicott, D. W. (1953). Transitional objects and transitional phenomena. In: *Playing and Reality*. London: Tavistock Publications, 1971.

Winnicott, D. W. (1956). The antisocial tendency. In: *Through Paediatrics to Psycho-Analysis*. London: Hogarth Press, 1978; reprinted London: Karnac, 1984.

Winnicott, D. W. (1958). The capacity to be alone. In: *The Maturational Processes and the Facilitating Environment*. London: Hogarth Press, 1979; reprinted London: Karnac, 1990.

Winnicott, D. W. (1967). Mirror-role of mother and family in child development. In: *Playing and Reality*. London: Tavistock Publications, 1971.

Winnicott, D. W. (1971). *Playing and Reality*. London: Tavistock Publications.

Winnicott, D. W. (1984). *Deprivation and Delinquency*. London: Tavistock Publications.

Wittling, W., & Schweiger, E. (1993). Alterations of neuroendocrine brain symmetry: A neural risk factor affecting physical health. *Neuropsychobiology, 28*: 26–29.

Wroblewski, R. (Ed.). (1995). *6 tusen av 6 miljoner: Ett requiem* [6 thousand of 6 million: A requiem]. Stockholm: Reproprint.

INDEX

abortion, 26, 39, 41, 45, 201, 213
  see also childbearing
acting out, destructive, 217
affect(s):
  activating, 213–214, 216, 226
  categories, xix, 222
  concept of, 184
  encasement, 213
  evacuating, 212, 214–215, 226
  imploding, 213
  invading, 25, 27, 29, 43, 47–48, 184,
    196, 202, 212–215, 224–225,
    230
  isolating, 212–214, 216, 225, 230
  propeller, 4, 13, 201, 214–217, 225,
    228–231, 234
    as analytic tool for trauma-related
      affects, 201–224
    applications of: trauma linking
      and generational linking,
      225–232
  regulating/regulation, 4, 13, 197,
    201, 210–212, 214–217, 222,
    230, 233, 234

  in cross-scientific light, 222–224
  symbolizing, 213–214, 216, 226,
    227
  unimaginable primitive, 202, 233
age distorting, 63, 95, 108
  in Africa, 178
  anti-Semitism/racial laws, 83–85
  as collective concept, 57
  as concept, and generational
    collapse, 210
  concentration camps/work camps,
    145–147
  depersonalization/emotional
    stunting:
    anti-Semitism/racial laws, 83–84
    concentration camps/work
      camps, 145–146
    deportation, 104–105
    ghetto, 117–118
    hidden/fugitive/partisan,
      127–128
    liberation, 156
    post-war, 165
  deportation, 104–108